ALL FOR NOTHING

D1603814

SHORT CIRCUITS

Slavoj Žižek, editor

ALL FOR NOTHING

HAMLET'S NEGATIVITY

Andrew Cutrofello

THE MIT PRESS   CAMBRIDGE, MASSACHUSETTS   LONDON, ENGLAND

MIT Press books may be purchased at special quantity discounts for business or sales promotional use. For information, please email special_sales@mitpress.mit.edu.

This book was set in Copperplate and Joanna by The MIT Press. Printed and bound in the United States of America.

Library of Congress Cataloging-in-Publication Data is available.
ISBN: 978-0-262-52634-0

10   9   8   7   6   5   4   3   2   1

Knock, knock.

Who's there?

Nay, answer me. Stand and unfold yourself!

"'Who are you?' asked K., and immediately sat halfway up in bed. But the man ignored the question, as if his presence would have to be accepted, and merely said in turn: 'You rang?'"

Franz Kafka, *The Trial*, trans. Breon Mitchell

CONTENTS

A short circuit occurs when there is a faulty connection in the network—
faulty, of course, from the standpoint of the network's smooth functioning.
Is not the shock of short-circuiting, therefore, one of the best metaphors
for a critical reading? Is not one of the most effective critical procedures to
cross wires that do not usually touch: to take a major classic (text, author,
notion) and read it in a short-circuiting way, through the lens of a "minor"
author, text, or conceptual apparatus ("minor" should be understood here
in Deleuze's sense: not "of lesser quality," but marginalized, disavowed by
the hegemonic ideology, or dealing with a "lower," less dignified topic)? If
the minor reference is well chosen, such a procedure can lead to insights
which completely shatter and undermine our common perceptions. This is
what Marx, among others, did with philosophy and religion (short-circuiting
philosophical speculation through the lens of political economy, that is to say,
economic speculation); this is what Freud and Nietzsche did with morality
(short-circuiting the highest ethical notions through the lens of the unconscious libidinal economy). What such a reading achieves is not a simple
"desublimation," a reduction of the higher intellectual content to its lower
economic or libidinal cause; the aim of such an approach is, rather, the inherent decentering of the interpreted text, which brings to light its "unthought,"
its disavowed presuppositions and consequences.

And this is what "Short Circuits" wants to do, again and again. The underlying premise of the series is that Lacanian psychoanalysis is a privileged
instrument of such an approach, whose purpose is to illuminate a standard text or ideological formation, making it readable in a totally new way—
the long history of Lacanian interventions in philosophy, religion, the arts
(from the visual arts to the cinema, music, and literature), ideology, and
politics justifies this premise. This, then, is not a new series of books on
psychoanalysis, but a series of "connections in the Freudian field"—of short

Lacanian interventions in art, philosophy, theology, and ideology. "Short Circuits" intends to revive a practice of reading which confronts a classic text, author, or notion with its own hidden presuppositions, and thus reveals its disavowed truth. The basic criterion for the texts that will be published is that they effectuate such a theoretical short circuit. After reading a book in this series, the reader should not simply have learned something new: the point is, rather, to make him or her aware of another—disturbing—side of something he or she knew all the time.

Slavoj Žižek

ACKNOWLEDGMENTS

Figuring out what exactly I had to say about Hamlet took far more time than I expected, and I wouldn't have figured it out without the assistance of many people. Paul Kottman helped me to recognize two false starts for what they were and eventually gave me extensive feedback on a draft of the entire manuscript. He and Philip Lorenz gave me the opportunity to share a draft of my prologue with the members of a seminar at the 2012 meeting of the Shakespeare Association of America. On top of all this, Paul presented a thoughtful response to a section of "Hamlet's Melancholy" at another conference. In many ways he has been this book's guardian angel. Working with Russell Newstadt on his philosophical reconstruction of the history of the concept of negation enabled me to realize that I too was writing a book whose overarching theme was *Omnis determinatio est negatio*. At one point I looked to Mladen Dolar's *A Voice and Nothing More* for a possible model for organizing my research, so when he offered to include my book in the series he edits with Slavoj Žižek and Alenka Zupančič I immediately felt that this would be a perfect fit. I thank all three of them for their collective imprimatur, Mladen for publishing a Slovenian translation of an earlier version of "Hamlet's Tarrying" in his journal *Problemi*, Maja Lovrenov for translating that article, and Slavoj for giving me the opportunity to present a version of the book's epilogue at a conference on Hegel at Birkbeck in May 2013. Suzanne Gossett offered sage advice early on and was an enthusiastic partner in co-organizing a symposium entitled "Shakespeare and the History of Philosophy" at the Newberry Library in March 2009. For sponsoring this symposium I thank Carla Zecher, the director of the Newberry's Center for Renaissance Studies; Samuel Attoh, the dean of the Graduate School at Loyola University Chicago; Marcela Gallegos, the Graduate School's pinch-hitting coordinator for special events; and Nicole Lassahn, who first encouraged us to propose the symposium. Over the years, Eric Byville and Tripthi Pillai have been absolutely delightful interlocutors and

ACKNOWLEDGMENTS

interdisciplinary tutors. So has Ned Lukacher, whose *Daemonic Figures: Shake-speare and the Question of Conscience* helped to launch my own research project. For invaluable comments on drafts of various chapters I thank Jennifer Bates, Anthony Burton, Angela Capodivacca, Shane Ewegen, Kristin Gjesdal, Joshua Kates, Matthew Kelsey, James Knapp, Katherine Cox Knapp, Leonardo Lisi, Paul Livingston, Edward McGushin, Colin McQuillan, James Rutherford, Paula Schwebel, Anita Sherman, and Scott Trudell. Since undertaking this project I have talked with so many people about Hamlet that I'm afraid I'm unable to remember them all. To anyone I neglect to mention by name I can only offer my apologies, as well as my genuine, if indirect, gratitude. Besides those already mentioned I vividly recall helpful conversations with Thomas Altizer, Chris Anderson, Albert Russell Ascoli, Emiliano Battista, Jeremy Ben-dik-Keymer, Andrew Benjamin, Tina Beyene, Peg Birmingham, James Blacho-wicz, Ian Blecher, Nora Brank, Allan Breedlove, Thomas Bretz, Edward Casey, Cameron Coates, Rosy Colombo, Rebecca Comay, KellyAnn Corcoran, Blake Dutton, Matthias Fritsch, Erik Gardner, Theodore George, Stefano Giacchetti, Avery Goldman, Olga Graham, Craig Greenman, Kristina Grob, Anthony Gud-wien, Michael Gutierrez, Andrew Hass, Laura Hengehold, Dominiek Hoens, David Ingram, Arun Iyer, Hanne Jacobs, Patrick Kain, Chin-Tai Kim, Peggy Knapp, Mira Kraft, Maria Kulp, Maggie Labinski, Len Lawlor, Paul Leisen, Julia Reinhard Lupton, John Lysaker, John McCumber, Elissa Marder, Bill Mar-tin, Hugh Miller, Andrew Mitchell, Paul Moser, Jake Nabasny, Catlyn Origi-tano, Kyoungnam Park, Gail Kern Paster, Adriaan Peperzak, Diane Perpich, Trevor Perri, Sean Petranovich, Iolanda Plescia, Daniel Price, Alexei Procyshyn, Lawrence Rhu, Gabriel Rockhill, Matthew Ross, Brian Schroeder, David Sch-weickart, Jacqueline Scott, Rebecca Scott, Sally Sedgwick, Ezgi Sertler, Virginia Strain, Richard Strier, Kristi Sweet, Blaine Swen (and every other member of the Improvised Shakespeare Company, with whom I've enjoyed many stimu-lating conversations), Annika Thiem, Tzuchien Tho, Daniel Vallaincourt, Pol Vandevelde, Victoria Wike, Heather Wilcox, Cynthia Willett, Shannon Win-nubst, Michael Witmore, and Rachel Zuckert. I thank Simon Critchley, Jamie-son Webster, and their editor Josefine Kals for sending me an advance copy of *Stay, Illusion! The Hamlet Doctrine*. I am extremely grateful to my own acquisi-tions editor, Roger Conover, for his faith in this somewhat unusual project. I thank Justin Kehoe, for his congenial and professional assistance, and Judith Feldmann, for her keen editorial eye and ear. A research leave from Loyola University Chicago in the fall of 2011 enabled me to complete this project. "Hamlet's Nihilism" grew out of an essay that appeared under the same title in *The Movement of Nothingness: Trust in the Emptiness of Time*, edited by Daniel Price and Ryan Johnson. I thank the Davies Group Publishers for permission to reuse this material. For their love and support I once again thank my parents, Paul Cutrofello and Rita Carroll Cutrofello; my siblings, Mary Cushing, Tom

Cutrofello, and Susan Miele; and everyone else in my extended family. Attending multiple performances of "Shakespeare on the Green" productions at Barat College with my wife, Dianne Rothleder, and our children, Megan and Quinn, first sparked my scholarly interest in Shakespeare. Having dedicated an earlier book to Megan, I dedicate this one to Quinn. To Dianne, my partner of thirty-one years, whose own book on Shakespeare has progressed far more smoothly than this one, I am grateful not only (but not least) for astute comments on a penultimate draft and countless conversations: "I do love nothing in the world so well as you—is not that strange?"

As this book was going to press I discovered that Martin Scofield, in *The Ghosts of Hamlet: The Play and Modern Writers*, also juxtaposes the passages from *Hamlet* and *The Trial* that I have used as epigraphs (albeit without, as I have, transforming the former into a joke that, with apologies to Thomas De Quincey, might be called "On the Knocking at the Gate in *Hamlet*").

HOW TO PHILOSOPHIZE WITH A HAMLET

And all for nothing,
For Hecuba!
Hamlet 2.2.557–558[1]

Hamlet did think a great many things; does it follow that he existed?
Jaakko Hintikka, "Cogito, Ergo Sum"

Actors, taught not to let any embarrassment show on their faces, put on a
mask. I will do the same. So far, I have been a spectator in this theatre which
is the world, but I am now about to mount the stage, and I come forward
masked.
René Descartes, *Cogitationes Privatae*

Who is Shakespeare's Hamlet?

In "Who Is Nietzsche's Zarathustra?" Martin Heidegger characterizes Zarathustra as Nietzsche's *Fürsprecher*, his advocate or spokesman, for the twofold
doctrine that the essence of being is will to power, and that the being of
beings is the eternal return of the same.[2] In *What Is Philosophy?* Gilles Deleuze
and Félix Guattari refine this idea, representing Zarathustra as Nietzsche's *per-
sonnage conceptuel*, a conceptual persona, or character.[3] Whereas a spokesman,
even one "prophetically poetized," remains a mere stand-in or representative
for a thinker, a conceptual character is intrinsic to the thought it expresses.[4]

Conceptual characters are played by philosophers rather than by actors,
and they advance arguments rather than plots. Most would cut poor figures
on the stage. No doubt a philosophical dramatist such as Tom Stoppard could
write an absurdist comedy featuring Berkeley's Hylas and Philonous, or the
Property Dualist, the Smooth Reductionist, and the Eliminativist; but such
characters are better suited to the space that philosophers enter when they

argue about the nature of mental phenomena.[5] The space of philosophical positions has its own kind of proscenium, center, thrust, wings, and orientation. Within it, many a dramatic character would seem out of place, occupying static coordinates instead of developing dynamic lines of thought. Others, such as Goethe's Mephistopheles and Beckett's Vladimir, would be right at home, for even within their plays they are better at advancing arguments than plots. Such a one is Hamlet. An actor could be bounded in a nutshell while reciting the "To be or not to be" soliloquy, but Hamlet is pirouetting across a kingdom of infinite space. To follow him is to follow his graceful lines of thought. To pursue those lines of thought to the imaginary places at which they converge outside Shakespeare's play is to locate him in the space of philosophical positions. When philosophers do this they make it possible to "play" Hamlet in a way that is different from the way in which actors play him.

Not every reference to Hamlet automatically counts as a Hamlet performance. When Jaakko Hintikka observes that Descartes's formula "I think, therefore I am" doesn't license us to conclude that the thinking Hamlet exists, we may feel that he doesn't so much play the prince as treat him as an arbitrary example. We feel differently when Nietzsche *articulates* Hamlet's "will-negating mood," when Hegel *approves* Hamlet's questioning of the veracity of the Ghost, and when Schopenhauer *endorses* Hamlet's assessment of oblivion as a "consummation / Devoutly to be wish'd" (3.1.62–63).[6] However fleetingly or surreptitiously, these philosophers activate Hamlet's conceptual character.

Hamlet is a role player himself. Perhaps the only moment in the play when he fully identifies with his role is when he leaps into Ophelia's grave with the cry "This is I, / Hamlet the Dane!" (5.1.257–258).[7] This performative act is akin to the one that a philosopher makes when he or she plunges into the space of philosophical positions ("This is I, the Hard Determinist!"). Margherita Pascucci has recently identified Hamlet's conceptual character with "the Self," or "that first self-affection that Deleuze discovers in Kant."[8] On this interpretation, "This is I, / Hamlet the Dane!" would mean something like "This is I, I!" Taking this idea one step further (from Kant and Deleuze to Hegel and Žižek), I contend that the capacity for self-affection is rooted in a more fundamental power of negativity, and that it is this power that Hamlet personifies.

There are as many ways of playing Hamlet within the space of philosophical positions as there are of playing him on the stage. Just as theatrical performance histories compare Garrick's, Schröder's, Kemble's, Siddons's, Kean's, Bernhard's, Olivier's, Gielgud's, and Branagh's Hamlets, so we may compare those of Kant, Hegel, Schopenhauer, Kierkegaard, Nietzsche, Russell, Heidegger, Arendt, Derrida, and Žižek. Even Hintikka's could be accounted a Hamlet performance insofar as the question Hintikka poses about the fictional Hamlet echoes Hamlet's own question about the fictional Hecuba

("What's Hamlet to Descartes, or Descartes to Hamlet?").[9] To block the inference that since Hamlet thinks he must exist, Hintikka recalls Descartes's
observation that "I think, therefore I am" isn't a syllogistic inference (i.e., it
isn't of the form "Everything that thinks is; I think; therefore I am"). Rather,
it expresses a necessary connection between the act of thinking and the existence of the agent who performs that act. Hintikka concludes that Cogito ("I
think") "refers to the 'performance' (to the act of thinking) through which
the sentence 'I exist' may be said to verify itself."[10] Shakespeare could have
ascribed such a performance to the fictional Hamlet, but doing so wouldn't
have brought him into existence.

Hintikka could have made the same point about any fictional thinker, but
Hamlet's penchant for philosophical reflection makes him an especially apt
example. Coleridge observes that Hamlet is the only character to whom
Shakespeare could convincingly have given the "To be or not to be" soliloquy.[11] Analogously, he is the only character to whom Shakespeare might plausibly have given the line "I think, therefore I am." Philosophers and critics
alike have been struck by a surface similarity between these two early modern memes.[12] "To be or not to be" is the problem-setting first line of Hamlet's
most philosophical soliloquy; "I think, therefore I am" is the first positive
conclusion of Descartes's solitary meditations. Each statement proposes a thesis about the existence of the self-reflecting subject. Descartes's claim is theoretical and apodictic; Hamlet's is practical and problematic. Descartes asserts
that he is certain that he exists, even if he is deceived in everything else by
an evil genius. Hamlet reflects that he is uncertain whether he will eventually cease to exist, and he doesn't yet know whether he has been deceived by
an evil genius ("The spirit that I have seen / May be a dev'l" [2.2.598–599]).
"I think, therefore I am" arms Descartes against a sea of epistemic troubles,
while "To be or not to be" expresses Hamlet's skepticism, or what I prefer
to characterize as his negative faith.[13] Hamlet doesn't go so far as to call into
question the reality of the external world, but his loss of interest in the world
is no less extreme ("How weary, stale, flat, and unprofitable / Seem to me
all the uses of this world!" [1.2.133–134]). His worry that the Ghost may be
a devil taking advantage of his melancholy finds a double echo at the beginning and end of the Meditations. In the first meditation Descartes considers
whether he himself might be suffering from melancholy. In the sixth, having
supposedly resolved all such worries, he considers how he should respond to
a ghostly apparition: "If, while I am awake, anyone were suddenly to appear
to me and then disappear immediately, as happens in sleep, so that I could
not see where he had come from or where he had gone to, it would not be
unreasonable for me to judge that he was a ghost, or a vision created in my brain [un
spectre ou un fantôme formé dans mon cerveau], rather than a real man."[14] The phrase
un spectre ou un fantôme formé dans mon cerveau is ambiguous. Descartes could mean

that he should judge any otherwise inexplicable apparition to be nothing but a creature of his brain (*un-spectre-ou-un-fantôme formé dans mon cerveau*). On the other hand, he could mean that he should judge any such apparition to be *either* a ghost (*un spectre*) or a creature of his brain (*un fantôme dans mon cerveau*).

Phantoms are *phantasms*, ideas of the imagination that play a mediating role between our minds and our bodies. Gilbert Ryle famously characterized Cartesian dualism as the doctrine of the "ghost in the machine," but a ghost in this sense (that of a spiritual substance) is not the same thing as a phantom.[15] Accounting for the mind's mysterious ability to generate phantasms is a problem that goes back to antiquity and continues to haunt not only contemporary dualists but reductive and eliminative materialists who deride belief in "spooky stuff."[16] Mental images alert us to the presence of physical objects.[17] Without them, our capacity for forming intellectual ideas of bodies would remain idle and we would know nothing of the external world. The trouble is that some physiological processes prompt our minds to generate images that don't represent anything real. Such is the case in the experience of phantom limbs.

Since traveling English players are known to have enacted some version of *Hamlet* in Dresden in 1626, it is tempting to imagine Descartes attending a performance of the play when he was stationed in Germany in the winter of 1619–20.[18] During a stay in Ulm he had a series of dreams that he took to foretell his future success in the sciences. In the first he was pursued by ghosts (*fantômes*) and then buffeted about by strong winds.[19] Someone in a school courtyard told him that Monsieur N. "had something to give him" that Descartes "imagined … was a melon from a foreign land."[20] According to Adrien Baillet's second-hand report, Descartes associated this melon with the "charms of solitude, but presented by purely human solicitations."[21] In the second dream he heard a noise that sounded like thunder. In the third he opened up a dictionary and an anthology of poems called *Corpus Poetarum* in which he came upon the question, *Quod vitae sectabor iter?* ("What way in life shall I follow?").[22] Next, a stranger gave him a poem whose first line was "*Est & Non*, which is the Yes and the No of Pythagoras."[23] In his dream Descartes believed that this was one of the "Idylls" of the Latin poet Ausonius and proceeded to seek it in the collection. Meanwhile, another dictionary appeared that he saw wasn't as complete as the first. Unable to find the poem he was looking for, he told the stranger that Ausonius had written another poem that began, "What way in life shall I follow?" The stranger asked him to find it in the collection, but again Descartes couldn't. Then the stranger and the two books vanished.[24] Upon awakening, Descartes took the *Corpus Poetarum* to symbolize "Revelation and Enthusiasm, for the favors of which he did not despair at all."[25]

Three hundred years later, Maxime Leroy—author of *Descartes, the Masked Philosopher* (*Descartes, le philosophe au masque*, 1929)—wrote to Freud to ask him to interpret Descartes's dreams. Curiously, Freud's letter, like Descartes's dream report, exists only in a French translation. In it Freud characterizes Descartes's dreams as "dreams from above"—that is, dreams whose latent contents could be readily deciphered by the dreamer because they derived from his waking preoccupations. It was more difficult to say why his dreams expressed these preoccupations in just the form they did. Freud dismisses Descartes's own interpretation of the melon, conjecturing that it "might stand for a sexual picture which occupied the lonely young man's imagination."[26] Over the years, Descartes's "foreign melon" has been subjected to numerous psychoanalytic interpretations.[27] Whatever its underlying significance might be, my own preferred "wild" conjecture would be that it was a "day's residue" of an encounter with the *foreign* English players' melon-choly prince.[28]

Could the play have been the thing that caught the conscience of the philosopher? Probably not. As far as we know, Descartes never read or saw a Shakespeare play. Nor did his enthusiasm for poetry last very long. In his *Discourse on Method* (published in 1637) he acknowledges the "ravishing delicacy and sweetness" of poetry but immediately goes on to explain why he "abandoned the study of letters … to seek no knowledge other than that which could be found in myself or else in the great book of the world."[29] That book, as Galileo had said, was written in the language of mathematics, not poetry. Yet the superficial similarities between *Hamlet* and the *Meditations* point to a deeper connection. If Pascucci is right to represent the conceptual character of *Hamlet* as the Self, it is because Hamlet performs the same self-reflective act that Hintikka ascribes to Descartes. Both "To be or not to be" and "I think, therefore I am" give voice to a distinctively modern experience of subjectivity. In 1947 Max Horkheimer observed that Hamlet "is often called the first truly modern individual."[30] Two decades later, Adorno, Horkheimer's erstwhile partner in diagnosing the ills of modernity, remarked that what links Hamlet and Descartes is their shared capacity for self-reflection.[31] Following Hegel, Adorno identifies the capacity for self-reflection with negativity, or the ability to draw distinctions.[32] As Hegel himself makes the connection in a celebrated passage from the *Phenomenology of Spirit*:

> The activity of dissolution is the power and work of the *Understanding*, the most astonishing and mightiest of powers, or rather the absolute power. The circle that remains self-enclosed and, like substance, holds its moments together, is an immediate relationship, one therefore which has nothing astonishing about it. But that an accident as such, detached from what circumscribes it, what is bound and is actual only in its context with others, should attain an existence of its own and a separate freedom—this is the tremendous power of the negative; it is the energy of thought, of the pure "I."[33]

In exercising this tremendous power of the negative, Hamlet and Descartes open up a whole series of divisions: between subject and object, mind and body, inner and outer sense, theoretical and practical reason, consciousness and action.[34] They differ in only one fundamental respect, namely, that Hamlet *tarries* with the negative in the manner described by Hegel, whereas Descartes reduces negativity to a power of affirmation.

To illustrate this point, it is helpful to consider the difference that Ivan Turgenev perceived between Hamlet and Don Quixote. Don Quixote isn't a Cartesian, nor is Descartes in any way Quixotic. On the contrary, as Foucault demonstrates in *The Order of Things*, Don Quixote is a comic figure because, on the cusp of scientific modernity, he continues to find truth in books about knights-errant rather than in the book of nature.[35] What nevertheless links Don Quixote to Descartes is a common conception of thought as affirmation. In his essay on the relationship between Don Quixote and Hamlet, Turgenev emphasizes the affirmative character of Don Quixote's faith in his chivalric ideals. The Don may be mad, but he is the ultimate "knight of faith" in Kierkegaard's sense of the term. Hamlet, by contrast, personifies negation:

> In him is embodied the principle of *negation*,—the same principle which, separated from everything human, is presented to us by another great poet in the figure of Mephistopheles. Hamlet is the same Mephistopheles enclosed in the living circle of human nature; therefore his negation is not evil, and it is directed against evil. The negation of Hamlet does not doubt the good; but it suspects its truth and genuineness, and fights it, not as a good, but as a false good, under whose mark evil and falsehood, its old foes, are hidden. … The scepticism of Hamlet, rejecting the possibility of realizing truth, is an implacable foe of falsehood; and thus he becomes one of the chief defenders of the same truth in which he cannot believe. But in negation, as in fire, there is a destructive power; and how are you going to keep that power within bounds, to show it where it should stop, when that which is to be destroyed and that which is to be saved are often joined and mixed together?[36]

This observation highlights the underlying connection that Turgenev perceived between Hamlet and the nihilist Bazarov in his novel *Fathers and Sons*.

Hamlet's negativity resembles not just that of Bazarov and Mephistopheles, but that of the ancient figure of the Sophist as well. In Plato's *Sophist*, the Eleatic Stranger offers six definitions of this essentially elusive figure of negation. The Sophist is defined as (1) a hunter of young men, (2) a merchant of knowledge of the soul, (3) a retailer of such knowledge, (4) a seller of his own knowledge, (5) an eristic (or quibbler), and (6) a purifier of souls (or critic).[37] He is also depicted as a fabricator of illusions. At the end of the dialogue, it is unclear whether any of these definitions has captured its quarry, or how exactly they are to be collectively unified. One thing has become clear, namely, that *the Sophist says what is not*. The Stranger had been taught by

Parmenides that only that which *is* can be said. If that which *is not* cannot be said, there is a sense in which the Sophist himself is not. Yet his nonbeing cannot be absolute. As the Stranger points out, being and nonbeing are as essentially interwoven as affirmation and negation. If, in contrast to the Sophist, the Philosopher is to be capable of saying what is—if the Philosopher is allowed to *be*—he must drag his shadow along with him and say what Parmenides prohibited his followers from saying.[39] Like Mephistopheles to Faust, the clinging Sophist could well whisper in the Philosopher's ear: *Ich bin der Geist, der stets verneint!* ("I am the spirit that ever negates!").[39]

To avoid the implication that the Philosopher is indistinguishable from the Sophist, the Stranger distinguishes the kind of negation that is involved in differentiation (saying that something is not something else) from the kind that is involved in false utterance (affirming what is not *simpliciter*). The capacity to say that which is requires differentiation, but differentiation per se involves neither error nor deception. The Philosopher's true negation of falsehoods is different in kind from the Sophist's false affirmation of simulacra. Thus the Philosopher can be distinguished from the Sophist. Both remain elusive figures, but for different reasons. The Philosopher eludes the capture of those whose intellects are used to grasping images of things rather than things themselves. This may explain why Socrates remains in the background during the Stranger's dialogue with Theaetetus, and why Plato never actually wrote his "missing" dialogue *The Philosopher*. The elusiveness of the Sophist, by contrast, is due to the fact that he is a purveyor of phantasmatic simulacra who is himself a kind of phantasm or self-negating being. The problem that Plato never fully resolves is that to allow for differentiation is to open the metaphysical door to phantasms and thus to let the Sophist get a foothold in being. Only by perpetually scapegoating the Sophist can Plato appropriate negation while keeping it at bay.

For Aristotle phantasms are images abstracted from the forms of objects of perception. As such they are derivative phenomena rather than manifestations of nonbeing. Unlike Plato, Aristotle famously claims that the soul never thinks without images.[40] Aristotle also has a different way of thinking about negation. By anchoring his subject-predicate logic in his substance-property metaphysics he is able to assert the primacy of affirmation (the *S is P* form of categorical judgment) and to demote negation (*S is not P*) to a privative status. To say of some logical subject *S* that it *is not P* is not to posit the *nonbeing* of P but to posit *S* itself with whatever positive property it possesses by virtue of which the property of *being* P is excluded from its being. Intrinsically negative predicates of the form *not-P* are treated as defective forms of positive predicates.

For centuries after Aristotle, negation was represented as the shadow of affirmation. Augustine associated it with evil conceived both as "a privation

of good" and as the "perversion of the will."[41] There was, however, a coun-
tertradition. Plato's representation of the Good as beyond being and nonbeing encouraged mystics such as Pseudo-Dionysius and John Scottus Eriugena
to reinterpret negation as the very path to the divine (the famous *via negativa*).
For Eriugena, "God is the source of being but is Himself not a being."[42] Such
statements transposed the paradoxes of the Sophist into theological paradoxes. At one extreme, the infinite being could be represented as nothing; at
the other, nothing could be regarded as the source of being (in keeping with
the doctrine of *creatio ex nihilo*). Rosalie Colie observes that

> there was speculation into "nothing" during the Renaissance, usually under-
> taken in conjunction with notions of infinity. Nicholas of Cusa, as concerned
> with infinitesimals as with infinity, was never questioned on grounds of
> heresy, though his works are full of the metaphysics of "nothing." … Within
> orthodoxy, the negative theology capitalized upon the attribution of transcen-
> dence to divinity—but the negative theology had to be carefully expressed,
> too, so as not to verge upon blasphemy.[43]

In Elizabethan and Jacobean England there was a profusion of popular "enco-
mia" to nothing that toyed with such semiblasphemous ideas.[44] Many poets,
including Shakespeare and John Donne, followed suit. From *Much Ado* to
the "crooked figure" of the "wooden O" (*Henry V*, Prologue, 13, 15) to Lear's
"Nothing will come of nothing" (1.1.90), Shakespeare frequently questions
the nature of nothing.[45] Such questions were aided and abetted by the redis-
covery of Lucretius's *De rerum natura*, which encouraged natural philosophers
to think of empty space as an all-encompassing "nothing."

Descartes resisted this way of thinking. Identifying extension with mate-
riality, he represents the physical world as a plenum. While his methodological skepticism deploys the negativity of thought, it does so not for the sake
of persisting in paradox but to demonstrate the absolute reality of the infinite and the absolute unreality of nothing (the absence of the void). Maire
Jaanus Kurrik notes that this philosophical agenda marks a return to Parmenides's fundamental idea that being is and nonbeing is not: "Descartes was
determined, as most of the men of the Renaissance, except for Shakespeare,
to take the advice of Parmenides and 'never let this thought prevail … that
not-being is.'"[46] Descartes further adheres to Parmenides's dictum that thinking and being are one.[47] Hence his suppression of the ontological negativity
that Hamlet and the Sophist personify. As Hegel puts the point: "Descartes
accepts Being in the entirely positive sense, and has not the conception of its
being the negative of self-consciousness."[48] At the same time, his deontologization of negation accompanies a revolutionary shift by which the *logical* subject of predication—the posited substance in which properties inhere—is

epistemologically subordinated to the *thinking* subject, the one who *represents* an object *as* having this or that property. The power to affirm and negate becomes the prerogative of the thinking subject, not only insofar as logical thinking requires discrimination (*pace* Plato), but also insofar as the subject is free to affirm or deny the reality of the objects of its ideas. Negation's world-encompassing potential is unleashed in the hyperbolic skepticism that prompts Descartes to relocate the ground of predication in the *predicating* subject rather than in the subject/object of predication. But he is not yet prepared to conclude, as Hegel will, that the power of predication is nothing but the power of negativity. Privileging affirmation over negation, Descartes represents both himself and the objects of his predicating acts as fully real substances. Despite the extravagance of the hypothesis of the evil genius, he reduces the inherent negativity of subjectivity to the mysterious power of imagination to conjure phantasms.

Hume went one step further. When he turned his gaze inward, he could find no substantial thinking thing but only a congeries of impressions and ideas. Colin McGinn has argued that this experience is akin to that of Hamlet.[49] His lack of a sense of self leads him to think of all potential identities as so many optional roles he can play. In his conception of role-playing Hamlet anticipates not only Hume but Sartre, who argues that there is no substantial self *because* subjectivity is pure negativity.[50] Sartre's conception of negativity (like that of Adorno) ultimately derives from Hegel's, while Hegel's derives, in turn, from Kant's anti-Cartesian representation of the thinking subject as a pure power of synthesis. Kant's crucial step consists in blocking Descartes's illegitimate inference that the predicating subject must be a substance to which positive predicates can be assigned. According to Kant, the self-affecting subject never coincides with itself but can only appear to itself in time, the form of inner sense.[51] It is this experience of self-affection that Pascucci takes Hamlet to personify. Following Hegel, I identify it with Hamlet's negativity. As Hecuba brings tears to the eyes of the First Player *despite* being nothing to him, Hamlet brings thoughts to the minds of philosophers *insofar as* he personifies negation.

Hamlet first appeared on philosophers' radar in the middle of the eighteenth century—at roughly the same time that critics began to offer psychological explanations about why it takes him so long to kill Claudius. Goethe's Wilhelm Meister represents Hamlet as a delicate vase or pot that cracks when a huge oak is planted in it.[52] For Coleridge, who was influenced by Kant, Hamlet's mind is dissociated from the world around him; the division between his sensibility and his thought makes him incapable of worldly action.[53] This division is equivalent to that between being and thought. It can also be related to Coleridge's conception of the "willing suspension of disbelief" or "*negative* faith" that is required when we enter a work of fiction.[54] Keats was probably thinking of Hamlet when he described Shakespeare's "Negative Capability," or his capacity to linger, or tarry, in uncertainty or mystery. Keats's only criticism of Coleridge (like Hegel's only criticism of Descartes) is that he is unable to *tarry* in negativity.[55] Under the influence of Keats, T. S. Eliot rejects Goethe's and Coleridge's psychological interpretations of Hamlet's tarrying.[56] He attributes to Hamlet another type of negativity, his famous lack of an objective correlative.[57] For Eliot, Hamlet's soul is, as it were, an *empty* vase that gives place to *nothing*.[58]

James Calderwood observes that 39 percent of Hamlet's first forty-six lines contain negatives, compared to 9.5 percent of Claudius's first ninety-three lines.[59] By itself this tells us little, as Calderwood concedes, but it is significant that throughout the play Hamlet's speech has a characteristically negative form.[60] One passage that Calderwood singles out for special attention is Hamlet's advice to Gertrude about what she *shouldn't* do:

> Not this, by no means, that I bid you do:
> Let the bloat king tempt you again to bed,
> Pinch wanton on your cheek, call you his mouse,
> And let him, for a pair of reechy kisses,
> Or paddling in your neck with his damn'd fingers,
> Make you to ravel all this matter out,
> That I essentially am not in madness,
> But mad in craft.
>
> (3.4.181–188)

As Calderwood observes, these lines have the paradoxical effect of presenting the very thing they would negate. For Freud one of the psychological benefits of negation is that it enables the negating subject to undo a repression, to admit something into consciousness without having to embrace it.[61] Calderwood implicitly highlights the flip side of this logic: Hamlet's negation expresses something in *order to* erase it. "Not this, by no means" lets something *be* so that it will *not be*. Calderwood concludes that "To be *and* not to be" is the basic logical form of Hamlet's assertions.[62]

Graham Priest reaches a similar conclusion by somewhat different means. Priest is a proponent of dialetheism, the doctrine that some (but not all) contradictions are true. The final section of his book *Doubt Truth to Be a Liar* is entitled "To Be *and* Not to Be—That Is the Answer."[63] The title of the book is borrowed from Hamlet's love letter to Ophelia:

> Doubt thou the stars are fire,
> Doubt that the sun doth move,
> Doubt truth to be a liar,
> But never doubt I love.
>
> (2.2.116–119)

Priest detects a "double irony" in these lines—one "external" to the text, and one "internal." The external irony is that we know today that stars are not made of fire and that the sun doesn't move in the way that Hamlet's letter implies. The internal irony is that as the play progresses it becomes clear that Hamlet's "claim to love … is false."[64] Priest concludes that this double irony undermines the apparently nondialetheic thrust of "Doubt truth to be a liar": at face value, Hamlet appears to be saying that something that is true cannot be false, but Shakespeare implies otherwise. I take Priest's point to be that when Hamlet says "I lov'd Ophelia" (5.1.269), his statement is not false *rather than* true, but both true *and* false.[65] Hence the dialetheic moral of the play: "To be *and* not to be."

Dialetheism aside, the disjunctive "To be *or* not to be" is Hamlet's philosophical signature. It is not, however, the only line that has caught the conscience of philosophers. Others include: "Seems, madam? nay, it is" (1.2.76; Wollstonecraft, Russell); "Give it an understanding but no tongue" (1.2.249; Kierkegaard); "It is an honest ghost" (1.5.138; Ayer); "Well said, old mole" (1.5.162; Hegel, Marx); "There are more things in heaven and earth, Horatio" (1.5.166; Schopenhauer, Kierkegaard); "The time is out of joint" (1.5.188; Derrida, Arendt, Agnes Heller); "There is nothing either good or bad, but thinking makes it so" (2.2.249–250; Wittgenstein); "The King is a thing … Of nothing" (4.2.28, 30; Lacan); "What is a man, / If his chief good and market of his time / Be but to sleep and feed? a beast, no more" (4.4.33–35; Benjamin); "The readiness is all" (5.2.222; Heidegger); and "The rest is silence" (5.2.358; Bataille). Many of these lines involve implicit or explicit negations. To Ophelia's remark "I think nothing, my lord" (3.2.117), Hamlet replies, "That's a fair thought to lie between maids' legs" (3.2.119–121). This line not only alludes to the vulgar term for vagina, but in so doing hints at an unexpressed desire to return to the womb in the specific sense of never having been born ("O cursed spite" [1.5.188]). Over the course of the play Hamlet berates himself for *saying* nothing (2.2.569) and *doing* nothing (4.4.32–33). When the Ghost reappears in the closet scene, he marvels that Gertrude did "*see* nothing" nor "nothing *hear*" (3.4.131, 133, italics added). His last words to Horatio ("the rest is silence") represent a final act of self-negation, albeit one problematized by his earlier reflection that death's character as absolute negation is not guaranteed. Like Melville's Bartleby, Hamlet *would prefer not to*.[66]

Like Bartleby and the Sophist, Hamlet is an essentially elusive character who reproves those who would pluck out the heart of his mystery. His elusiveness can, in part, be attributed to the simple fact that he doesn't exist outside Shakespeare's play (or the texts of Saxo Grammaticus, Belleforest, etc.). Eliot argued against critics who treated the character of Hamlet as the play's "primary problem" rather than the play itself.[67] More recently, Margreta de Grazia has argued that to focus on the character of the prince is to lose sight of the play's central theme, namely, the variety of human relationships to plots of land.[68] Such critical reminders are well-taken, but like materialist critiques of spooky stuff they have the curious effect of underscoring the peculiar manner in which the immaterial or virtual Hamlet leaps off the page or stage. Some fictional characters arouse our curiosity more than others. No one has written about the childhood of Marcellus—not even A. C. Bradley, notorious for speculating about the lives of Shakespeare's characters.[69] Intriguing characters arouse our curiosity because something important about them seems to be concealed. Lady Macbeth's "I have given suck" (1.7.54) gives point to the question "How many children had she?" despite the fact that it lacks a determinable answer.[70] Likewise, Iago's true motivation for tormenting Othello may lie outside the picture-frame of the play, but the several explanations he gives us all converge at this imaginary focal point.[71] Ophelia is another character whose inner life intrigues us, as it does those in the court who "botch the words up fit to their own thoughts" (4.5.10). Her "winks and nods and gestures" (4.5.11) are not just *intriguing*; they hint that she has inherited something of the *intriguer* from Polonius.

Intriguing characters tend to divide critics into "hunters" and "Parmenideans"—that is, into those who would pluck out the heart of their mysteries and those who deny that there are any mysteries to pluck. Characters who conceal themselves from other characters pose a special problem. Iago's pointed refusal to disclose his inner being ("Demand me nothing" [5.2.303]) makes him, like Hamlet, resemble the Sophist in a way that goes beyond the generic elusiveness that all fictional characters possess. The difference between Hamlet and Iago is that Hamlet dissembles for the sake of distinguishing true appearances from false appearances ("What, frighted with false fire?" [3.2.266]), whereas Iago dissembles for the sake of making the weaker argument seem stronger ("I told him what I thought, and told no more / Than what he found himself was apt and true" [5.2.176–177]). It is tempting to conclude that Iago *is* a sophist, whereas Hamlet merely *resembles* one in much the same way that Socrates does. Yet this formulation overlooks a number of complications. . For one thing, as G. Wilson Knight points out, when Hamlet casts aspersions on Ophelia's virtue he effectively plays Iago to his own Othello.[72] Others have felt that Hamlet's misogyny is no less malignant than Iago's generic misanthropy.[73] If we didn't know which of the two says "O gentle lady, do not put me to 't, / For I am nothing if not critical" (*Othello* 2.1.118–119), would we guess it wasn't Hamlet? As Turgenev perceived, there is a dark side to Hamlet's negativity that links him, no less than Iago, to both the devil and the Sophist. Kierkegaard draws a similar connection when he writes, "What a Sophist once said, that he could carry the whole world in a nutshell, now appears to be being realized in the modern overview of world history."[74] Turgenev notes that Hamlet's negativity "is directed against evil," and this certainly cannot be said of Iago's.[75] The problem is that "in negation, as in fire, there is a destructive power; and how are you going to keep that power within bounds, to show it where it should stop, when that which is to be destroyed and that which is to be saved are often joined and mixed together?" A similar problem arises for Descartes when he lights the fuse of his skepticism. Stanley Cavell has argued that Cartesian skepticism is less an exercise in epistemic prudence than it is a way of annihilating the world in thought, as if to avenge a psychic injury.[76] In unleashing his negativity, Descartes effectively plays Iago to his Othello. If we accept Michael Gillespie's assessment that Descartes's identification of thought with self-assertion is an incipient form of nihilism, then distinguishing the modern philosopher from the nihilist may be no less difficult than distinguishing Socrates from the Sophist.[77]

Hamlet's negativity has many forms. Psychologically, it manifests itself in his *melancholy*, a frame of mind intensified by the death of his father and remarriage of his mother. Epistemically, it takes the form of his skepticism or *negative faith*—a mental attitude that Coleridge associates with imagination and distinguishes from absolute or dogmatic faith. Existentially, it arises in the *nihilism* of the "To be or not to be" soliloquy. Practically, it informs the negative action that critics have traditionally called Hamlet's "delay" but which I prefer to characterize as his lingering or *tarrying*. Metaphysically, it bears on his *nonexistence*: not only his death at the end of the play but his sheer fictionality. In singling out just these five forms of Hamlet's negativity—his melancholy, negative faith, nihilism, tarrying, and nonexistence—I do not mean to suggest that they are the only ones or that they are mutually exclusive categories. Like the Sophist, Hamlet's negativity can be defined in many ways. The five rubrics I have selected roughly correspond to five successive stages of the play (although not quite to the five-act division). They also provide a narrative frame for a history of the development of modern philosophical conceptions of negation from Descartes to the present. My reconstruction of this history is not strictly chronological and certainly not exhaustive. It is structured around a series of questions that have arisen in connection with Hamlet. First, what is the *psychological* nature of Hamlet's melancholy? Is the negativity of melancholy something that ought to be embraced or overcome? Second, what is the *epistemological* character of Hamlet's negative faith—his attitude toward the undiscovered country from whose bourn no traveler returns? Third, what is the *existential* significance of Hamlet's alleged nihilism? Is annihilation a consummation devoutly to be wished or shunned? The fourth question concerns Hamlet's tarrying. In the eighteenth century, critics began to question the *moral* character of Hamlet's decision to wait to kill Claudius until the king's soul was likely to be damned for all eternity. This decision was judged to be a cover story for Hamlet's indecisiveness, which in the nineteenth century came to be regarded as a symbol of *revolutionary* inde-cision. My fourth question, then, is about the *political* significance of Hamlet's tarrying: should we take it to symbolize revolutionary failure or revolutionary potential? Finally, what is the *metaphysical* status of the fictional Hamlet? In what sense, if any, does Hamlet have being? In engaging with this question, Bertrand Russell will be my principal interlocutor (as Kant will be in my discussion of negative faith). As a logician, Russell was puzzled by Hamlet's ontological status; or rather, as he preferred to put it, he was interested in the logical character of nonreferring pseudo-names, of which he takes "Ham-let" to be an exemplary example. Hamlet the fictional character also plays an important role in what it is tempting to call the existentialist side of Russell's thought.[78] How the strictly *logical* conception of negation that Russell (in tan-dem with Frege) bequeathed to analytic philosophy stands with respect to the *metapsychological* conception that Freud bequeathed to psychoanalysis is a topic that I will indirectly broach in my epilogue, where I briefly compare Robert Brandom's and Slavoj Žižek's respective interpretations of Hegel's conception of *determinate* negation. For the past four hundred years, Hamlet has been lurk-ing (or "miching" [3.2.137]) in the space of philosophical positions, much as Socrates does during the Stranger's conversation with Theaetetus. It is time to bring him to center stage. Perhaps he has something to teach us about the nature of negation—and about what it means to say "I think, therefore I am."

> I know of no more heart-rending reading matter than Shakespeare: what
> must a person have suffered if he needs to be a clown that badly!—Is *Hamlet*
> understood? It is not doubt but *certainty* that drives you mad. ... But you
> need to be profound, abyss, philosopher to feel that way. ... We are all *afraid*
> of the truth.
>
> Friedrich Nietzsche, *Ecce Homo*

In the first edition of *The Birth of Tragedy* (1872), Nietzsche compares Hamlet
to "Dionysian man": "both have gazed into the true essence of things, they
have *acquired knowledge*, and they find action repulsive, for their actions can
do nothing to change the eternal essence of things; they regard it as laugh-
able or shameful that they should be expected to set to rights a world so out
of joint."[1]

To gaze into the true essence of things is to discover that it is better not to
be than to be. Such is the verdict of the Chorus in Sophocles's *Oedipus at Colonus*: "Not to be born surpasses thought and speech. / The second best is to
have seen the light / and then to go back quickly whence we came."[2] Referring to an older Greek myth, Nietzsche calls this "the wisdom of Silenus."[3]
A companion of the god Dionysus, Silenus was a satyr or daemon whom
King Midas forced to reveal what would be best for human beings. According
to Nietzsche, the arrival of the cult of Dionysus disturbed what had been a
serene Apollonian culture. Apollonian art covered up the truth with attractive
images. For "Homeric man," "the very worst thing ... was to die soon, the second worst ever to die at all."[4] By tearing away the Apollonian veil of illusion,
Silenus revealed the naked Dionysian truth—a truth that music alone could
adequately express. Greek tragedy arose out of a synthesis of these two fundamental artistic impulses. Socrates destroyed this synthesis. Under his influence, Euripides composed an entirely new kind of tragic drama that changed
the purpose of playing. Instead of enabling spectators to lose themselves in

the ritual destruction and rebirth of the god Dionysus, Euripides taught them to maintain their self-control. The proper response to a tragic performance was not to swoon but to judge. Corresponding to this shift in the attitude of the spectator was a change in the form of the spectacle itself. Until then, it had been a shimmering dream image; now it became a mirror of nature. In the dialogues of Plato, Socratic dialectics supplants music as the primary vehicle for the disclosure of truth. In the *Phaedo*, Plato reports that while awaiting execution Socrates began to compose hymns to Apollo. A recurring dream had long admonished him to "make music." He had always taken this imperative to mean that he should continue to philosophize, but now he wondered if he should have taken it more literally.[5] Unfortunately, Socrates's swan song failed to ignite a "rebirth of tragedy."[6] Instead of celebrating the "*music-making Socrates*," Plato promoted the spiritual ideal of the "dying Socrates."[7] Thereafter the dream of a music-making Socrates lay dormant within a ring of magic fire until it was revived some two thousand years later—not by Wagner, the artist we would expect Nietzsche to name in this context, but by Shakespeare, whom Nietzsche dubs *der musiktreibender Sokrates* in a passage he eventually deleted.[8] Echoes of this honorific appear in the published text's comparisons of Hamlet to Dionysian man.

According to Nietzsche, the "lesson of *Hamlet*" cannot be grasped by exclusively attending to "the words of the play" ("Words, words, words" [2.2.192]) but only "from intense contemplation of, and reflection on, the whole."[9] As a whole the play conveys the same metaphysical insights that Nietzsche identifies with the wisdom of Silenus. Hamlet's "revulsion" for existence "outweighs every motive for action" and fills him with a "longing for a world beyond death."[10] In keeping with Nietzsche's expectations, the play is, in fact, a "musically driven" work of art. There are flourishes and cannon booms. A fanfare announces the dumb show. Polonius advises Reynaldo to let Laertes "ply his music" (2.1.70). After the performance of "The Mousetrap" Hamlet cries, "Come, some music! Come, the recorders!" (3.2.291), and he chides Rosencrantz and Guildenstern for thinking they can play him like a pipe (3.2.364–372). He assures Gertrude that his "pulse as yours doth temperately keep time, / And makes as healthful music" (3.4.140–141). In the graveyard he wistfully recalls the songs of Yorick (5.1.190). Ophelia contrasts the "honey" of Hamlet's "music vows" with his "sweet bells jangled out of time [or tune], and harsh" (3.1.156, 158). She herself sings mangled ballads and dirges, encouraging Laertes to join in a refrain (4.5.171–172). The Queen describes Ophelia's swan song, her chanting of "snatches of old lauds" just before she drowns (4.7.177). The lusty warbling of the Gravedigger compensates in some measure for the unsung requiem that the "churlish priest" refuses to perform at her funeral (5.1.240). Conversely, Hamlet's death is registered not by the "flights of angels" Horatio bids to sing him to his rest but by the "drum" of Fortinbras's army (5.2.260–261). The substitution of this "warlike noise" (5.2.349) for the unheard heavenly choir recalls the opening scene's contrast between "the crowing of the cock" (1.1.157) that Horatio says is "trumpet to the morn" (1.1.150) and the "bird of dawning" that "singeth all night long" on Christmas Eve (1.1.160). The play ends with Hamlet's body being raised upon a stage to the firing of "soldiers' music" (5.2.399). The rest is silence.

Nietzsche doesn't mention any of these motifs, but he clearly thinks of *Hamlet*, as he does all genuine tragedy, as fundamentally musical. According to Aristotle, tragic drama developed out of the dithyrambs sung by the Chorus in praise of Dionysus.[11] Nietzsche took this historical observation one step further by representing the Apollonian components of Greek tragedy—its words and images—as comforting illusions that compensated for the harsh truths that the singing of the Chorus conveyed.[12] Like Wagner, the young Nietzsche accepted Schopenhauer's belief that music had a unique capacity to express the eternal striving of the will, the pulsating metaphysical ground of everything that exists in nature. For Schopenhauer, nature is nothing more than a projection of the will. Since all willing is ultimately purposeless and painful—sometimes excruciatingly so—the best thing would have been for the will never to have manifested itself at all; given that it has, the second best thing would be for it to annihilate both nature and itself. Until then, the (third) best thing for a human being is to suspend the will's activity, something that can be temporarily accomplished through disinterested contemplation of the plastic arts.

In *The Birth of Tragedy*, Nietzsche projected this pessimistic doctrine back into antiquity, identifying the plastic arts with Apollo and the suffering will with Dionysus. But he gave the doctrine an extra turn of the screw by arguing that tragic performances stimulated rather than stilled the will of the spectators, seducing them to affirm rather than to negate their individuated lives. The difference between Schopenhauer's will-negating sensibility and Nietzsche's life-affirming inversion of it can be likened to that between Hamlet's melancholy and his antic (or manic) disposition. Hamlet is always more cheerful when "the tragedians of the city" (2.2.328) are about. Unfortunately, Nietzsche blunts his critique of Schopenhauer by highlighting Hamlet's darker moods and by associating Shakespeare's play with *Tristan und Isolde*, whose aesthetic effect on Wagner's transfixed audiences was more drowsing than rousing. Eventually he would profess to prefer Rossini and Bizet, but in *The Birth of Tragedy* he followed Wagner's lead in condemning the Italian and French operatic traditions for their alleged superficiality. Instead of directly expressing the tortured striving of the suffering will and then providing compensatory imagistic consolation (as Wagner had in *Tristan*), opera took refuge from suffering in distracting words and images to which it then supplied a merely programmatic form of musical entertainment. Paradoxically, this made opera an *optimistic* art designed for those who couldn't bear to face reality, whereas tragedy and music drama were *pessimistic* art forms that in principle affirmed life.[13] The birth of Wagnerian music drama out of the spiritless operatic tradition represented an inversion of the decline of Aeschylean–Sophoclean tragedy into Euripidean melodrama and Hellenistic New Comedy.

Shakespeare began writing for the Elizabethan theater at roughly the same time that the Florentine Camerata invented opera with the intention of reviving Greek tragedy. Henry Purcell's *Fairy Queen* (1692), an adaptation of *A Midsummer Night's Dream*, is the first extant opera based directly on a Shakespearean play. The first full-scale operatic version of *Hamlet* was composed by Scarlatti in 1715. In the late seventeenth century, Samuel Pepys commissioned the composer Cesare Morelli to set the "To be or not to be" soliloquy as an operatic recitative with guitar accompaniment.[14] Other operas based on *Hamlet* were composed by Francesco Gasparini, Ambroise Thomas, Aristide Hignard, Saverio Mercadante, Franco Faccio, Humphrey Searle, and others.[15] Berlioz, Liszt, Tchaikovsky, Prokofiev, and Shostakovich all composed *Hamlet*-inspired pieces.[16] Given Nietzsche's representation of Shakespeare as a music-making Socrates, it is particularly noteworthy that in the eighteenth century Heinrich Wilhelm von Gerstenberg wrote two different vocal lines for a fantasy by C. P. E. Bach—the first a German paraphrase of the "To be or not to be" soliloquy, the second a free translation of Socrates's last words in the *Phaedo* just before he drinks the hemlock.[17] In a letter from Nice dated October 27, 1887, Nietzsche told his friend Peter Gast (the composer Heinrich Köselitz) that he was looking forward to a performance of Thomas's *Hamlet*, along with other "pieces for connoisseurs."[18] Thomas's opera had premiered in Paris in 1868, three years after *Tristan*. It is not the kind of composition that Nietzsche would have extolled at the time he wrote *The Birth of Tragedy*. Its "operatic" character is reflected in its optimistic ending (the prince survives and is crowned) and its *faux*-Dionysian "Drinking Song" ("O vin, dissipe la tristesse").[19]

Vincenzo Galilei, a member of the Camerata, believed that operatic music should serve the libretto rather than vice versa. Wagner thought so too at the time that he composed *Das Liebesverbot*, his 1834 opera based on *Measure for Measure*. As a teenager he had written a drama called *Leubald und Adelaïde* whose plot was loosely based on that of *Hamlet*.[20] In "The Art-Work of the Future" (1849), he envisioned a rebirth of tragedy through the synthesis of Shakespeare and Beethoven.[21] In likening Hamlet to Dionysian man, the young Nietzsche was following his master's lead. Despite the fact that Hamlet appeared on the Renaissance stage at roughly the same time as Monteverdi's *Orpheus*, he is characterized in *The Birth of Tragedy* as closer in spirit to Siegfried and Tristan. Several months after the publication of *The Birth of Tragedy*, Nietzsche attended a ceremony in Bayreuth to celebrate the laying of the cornerstone of Wagner's new theater. In his adulatory report he heralded the "*mighty future of that event*," but in notes from the same period he was already registering doubts.[22] By the time he appended his "Attempt at a Self-Criticism" to the second edition of *The Birth of Tragedy* in 1886, his enthusiasm not only for Wagner, but for Schopenhauer and *Hamlet*, had considerably waned.

In a note from 1883, he characterizes *Hamlet* as "above all a failed work."[23] In a section of the 1882 edition of *The Gay Science* entitled "In Praise of Shakespeare," he exclaims, "What is all of Hamlet's melancholy [*Hamletmelancholie*] compared to that of Brutus!"[24] Hamlet's melancholy expresses a "longing for a world beyond death," but Brutus's expresses a more profound longing for personal freedom. He betrays "his dearest friend" not for the sake of Rome (as he supposes) but for his own "independence of soul."[25] By 1882, Nietzsche had reason to identify with Brutus, having "betrayed" Wagner for a similar reason. Summing up his new attitude toward Shakespeare, he writes in *Ecce Homo* (1888): "If I seek my highest formula for *Shakespeare*, then I only ever find this: that he conceived the type of Caesar."[26] His *lowest* formula was that Shakespeare brought the rabble onto the stage; thus in *Beyond Good and Evil* (1886), he sneers at "that astonishing Spanish-Moorish-Saxon synthesis of tastes over which an ancient Athenian of the circle of Aeschylus would have half-killed himself with laughter or annoyance."[27] Turning specifically against the figure of Hamlet he adds: "There are free insolent spirits who would like to conceal and deny that they are broken, proud, incurable hearts (the cynicism of Hamlet—the case of Galiani); and sometimes folly itself is the mask for an unhappy, all too certain knowledge."[28] This passage, like the one from *The Gay Science*, suggests that Nietzsche was trying to undo his earlier identification with Hamlet.[29] In his "Attempt at a Self-Criticism" he dismissed his "questionable book" as a product of "youthful melancholy."[30] But his earlier identification with Hamlet reappears in *Ecce Homo: How to Become What You Are*, particularly in the slide from "Is Hamlet *understood?*" to "Have I been understood?" and in his remark that "Richard Wagner was the man who was by far the most closely related to me … The rest is silence … ."[31]

In *The Gay Science*, Nietzsche asked what Brutus's melancholy revealed about Shakespeare's psyche: "Could it be that we confront some unknown dark event and adventure from the poet's own soul about which he wanted to speak only in signs?"[32] Analogously we may wonder what unknown dark event and adventure from Nietzsche's soul led him to speak of Hamlet in signs. One such sign is his interest in the authorship controversy. Immediately after asking "Is Hamlet *understood?*" he adds, "And let me confess it [*Und, dass ich es bekenne*]: I feel instinctively sure and certain that Lord Bacon was the originator, the self-tormentor of this uncanniest kind of literature. … We are very far from knowing enough about Lord Bacon, the first realist in every great sense of that word, to know everything he did, wanted, and experienced in himself."[33] Duncan Large suggests that by claiming authorship for Bacon,

Nietzsche was better able to mask himself.[34] Having originally identified with Hamlet, he first tried to switch Shakespearean masks, substituting Brutus's for Hamlet's. He then changed tack, representing all of Shakespeare's masks (Hamlet, Brutus, Caesar, etc.) as masks of a mask worn by a disinterested scientist who (like the masked Descartes) kept himself safely hidden.

Freud underwent a similar adventure: first identifying with Hamlet, then diagnosing his melancholy, and eventually denying Shakespeare's authorship of the play. In his correspondence Freud frequently quotes the prince.[35] Two letters to Wilhelm Fliess from 1897 are particularly important. In the first, he reluctantly concludes that he had been mistaken in supposing that childhood seduction was the universal cause of hysteria. Trying to remain optimistic despite this theoretical setback he remarks: "I vary Hamlet's saying, 'To be in readiness': to be cheerful is everything!"[36] Less than a month later, he announces his breakthrough discovery of the Oedipus complex by offering an analysis of "Hamlet the hysteric." Why is it, he asks Fliess, that the only thing Hamlet is incapable of doing resolutely is killing the man who murdered his father and married his mother? Is it not because Hamlet unconsciously knows himself to be guilty of having once wanted to kill his father and marry his mother himself? Perhaps something happened when Shakespeare was writing the play to revive his own repressed Oedipus complex and make him project it onto the character of Hamlet. When Hamlet says "conscience does make cowards of us all" (3.1.82) and "use every man after his desert, and who shall scape whipping?" (2.2.529–530), he reveals that "his conscience is his unconscious sense of guilt."[37]

Freud develops this argument further in *The Interpretation of Dreams*. The event that triggered the revival of Shakespeare's Oedipus complex must have been the recent death of his father.[38] Freud's own father died shortly before he wrote *The Interpretation of Dreams*. His self-analysis had uncovered an Oedipus complex similar to the one that he ascribes to Shakespeare on the basis of his interpretation of *Hamlet*. His own identification with Hamlet was therefore built into the very theory of the Oedipus complex. This identification is made explicit in a 1936 letter in which Freud urges Arnold Zweig not to write a biography about him since "the truth is not practicable, humans don't deserve it, and besides, isn't our Prince Hamlet right to ask if anyone could 'scape whipping if he were treated according to his merit?"[39]

In "Mourning and Melancholia" (1917), Freud represents Hamlet not as an hysteric (as he did in his letter to Fliess) but as a melancholic. Since Hamlet is represented by Shakespeare both as constitutionally melancholy and as in mourning, his ambiguous predicament may have encouraged Freud to represent melancholia as a pathological form of mourning. Just as nonpathological mourning involves coming to terms with a loss, so does melancholia. One important difference is that someone suffering from melancholia doesn't necessarily know what he or she has lost. Another is that melancholia is accompanied by "self-criticism" of the sort that Hamlet expresses in his soliloquy "O, what a rogue and peasant slave am I!" (2.2.550).⁴⁰ Once again Freud takes Hamlet's remark to Polonius—"use every man after his desert, and who shall 'scape whipping?"—to be the sign of an underlying pathology: "For there can be no doubt that whoever holds and expresses to others such an opinion of himself—one that Hamlet harbored of himself and all men—that man is ill, whether he speaks the truth or is more or less unfair to himself."⁴¹ To explain this illness Freud conjectures that someone suffering from melancholia has identified part of his or her ego with the lost object. This partial identification provides the subject both with a substitute love-object and with an outlet for hitherto repressed hatred that resurfaces under the guise of self-criticism. The division of the ego into narcissistic and self-critical components soon became the basis for Freud's account of the developmental split between the ego and its ego ideal or superego. A subject acquires a superego by identifying part of itself with a figure of paternal authority. Feelings of guilt express the superego's punishment of the ego. The sexualization of this process can result in moral masochism, which might be characterized as a "dialect" of the language of melancholia.⁴² During the Oedipal phase of development, children harbor a desire to be punished by their fathers. When a repressed Oedipus complex is revived in later life, this latent structure is reactivated under the guise of a desire to be punished by one's superego. Alternatively, the motive for self-punishment can arise on the side of a sadistic superego. Whether Hamlet's (or Shakespeare's) unconscious guilt should be regarded as more masochistic or sadistic Freud doesn't venture to say. What primarily matters to him in "Mourning and Melancholia" is to apply his original insight—that Hamlet suffers from the revival of a repressed Oedipus complex—to the illness Hamlet calls "my melancholy" (2.2.601).

Like the triumphant Polonius, Freud believed that he had "found / The very cause of Hamlet's lunacy" (2.2.48–49). He frequently represents his interpretation of the play as a cornerstone of psychoanalysis.⁴³ At the same time, he doesn't hesitate to appeal to Hamlet's authority when he wishes to castigate incompetent analysts for their interpretive overconfidence. In "On Psychotherapy" he provides a lengthy citation of Hamlet's admonition to the prying Guildenstern ("Why, look you now, how unworthy a thing you make of me!" [3.2.363–364]) before pedantically concluding: "it is not so easy to play upon the instrument of the mind."⁴⁴ More defensively, in *The Question of Lay Analysis*, he forestalls the objections of an "Impartial Person" whom he imagines skeptically dismissing psychoanalysis with the thought: "Nothing more than that? Words, words, words, as Prince Hamlet says."⁴⁵ In these passages Freud not only appropriates Hamlet's resistance to analysis but uses it to confirm his own analysis of the prince. Hamlet may have been on his mind when he wrote in "Negation" that a patient's denial that his dream was about his mother proves that the dream *was* about his mother.[46]

Like Nietzsche, Freud eventually came to believe that "the man from Stratford" wasn't the author of the works written under his name.[47] Instead of subscribing to the Baconian hypothesis he opted for the more fashionable Oxfordian theory that Edward de Vere was the man behind "Shakespeare." It followed that *Hamlet* wasn't written by someone whose father had just died, for De Vere was only twelve years old when his father died. J. Thomas Looney, the first proponent of the Oxfordian hypothesis, speculated that de Vere's mother may have remarried as o'erhastily as Gertrude.[48] It was therefore possible to "save the phenomena" as Freud understood them, although he doesn't make this point himself. It is natural to wonder if his authorial speculations, like those of Nietzsche, were motivated by a desire to undo, or refashion, his earlier identification with Hamlet. To Fliess he had admitted that, like Hamlet, he had been in love with his mother and jealous of his father.[49] Did the Oxfordian theory strengthen or weaken this identification?[50] Whatever the answer to this question might be, we might say of the Oedipus complex what Nietzsche says of *Julius Caesar*: "It is still called by the wrong name."[51]

According to Freud, every repression has three stages. The first is that of primary repression, or "fixation"—the tarrying of something that lags behind an overall developmental trend. Next is "repression proper," or the active effort to prevent the represented object of a fixation from resurfacing. Finally, there is the "return of the repressed," when an actively repressed representation begins to show through in the very forces repressing it.[52] Slavoj Žižek observes that to speak of the return of the repressed is not to say that the past acts on the present but rather to say that the present acts on the past. To illustrate this point Žižek refers to the renewal of interest in Shakespeare in the eighteenth century: "When Shakespeare was suddenly 'rediscovered,' it is not appropriate to say that he 'began to exert renewed influence'—the crucial event is the inner shift in the then 'spirit of the age' so that suddenly it became susceptible to Shakespeare."[53] This example is particularly apt given the role that the supposed return of Shakespeare's Oedipus complex plays in Freud's elaboration of the very theory of repression. Just as something must have happened in the eighteenth century to make the "spirit of the age" susceptible to Shakespeare, something must have happened in Freud to make him interpret *Hamlet* as he did. That the theory of repression can accommodate its own inscription within the return of something repressed may be regarded as a paradoxical confirmation of the principle that the repressed returns in the very forces that repress it.[54] Harold Bloom is perfectly justified in saying that psychoanalysis suffers from a Shakespeare complex; the remarkable thing is the ability of psychoanalysis to account for this very fact.[55]

So, what exactly happened in the eighteenth century? What "inner shift" in the "spirit of the age" made modernity "susceptible" to Shakespeare? Karl Löwith observes that the very concept of a "spirit of the age" was first developed in the eighteenth century with Shakespeare in mind.[56] In response to Christian Adolf Klotz's 1760 satire *Genius seculi* ("Genius [or Spirit] of the Age"), Johann Gottfried Herder coined the German word *Zeitgeist*.[57] In an essay on Shakespeare he argued that every culture had a distinctive historical spirit. By understanding how Shakespeare expressed the spirit of his age, German writers could learn how to express theirs. The English Romantics adapted this idea to their cultural context. Hazlitt's *Spirit of the Age* (1825) bore as an epigraph Hamlet's remark to Osric: "To know a man well were to know himself" (5.2.139–140).[58] By then Hamlet had come to be regarded as a proto-Romantic genius. Psychological interpretations of his melancholy had begun to flourish in the late eighteenth century. Over the next hundred years so many more would appear that by 1908 the Shakespeare scholar Horace Howard Furness could quip that "were I told that my closest friend was lying at the point of death, and that his life could be saved by permitting him to divulge his theory of Hamlet, I would instantly say, 'Let him die! Let him die! Let him die!'"[59] Freud had propounded one such theory to his closest friend a decade earlier. He was clearly disappointed when Fliess's next letter made no mention of his theory.[60] Perhaps Fliess and Furness were of one mind. In any case, it is important to remember that Freud's interpretation of Hamlet's melancholy belongs to a series of effects of the "return" of Hamlet's melancholy in the eighteenth century.

Even if every repression is retroactively constituted, the strange attractor that it finds in the past must exhibit special features that make it capable of playing the role of a thing repressed. We may therefore wonder what it is about Hamlet's melancholy that has made it seem so special. Bridget Gellert Lyons observes that Hamlet mimics the melancholy of several stock dramatic types that were familiar on the Elizabethan stage.[61] In *As You Like It*, Jaques alludes to such types when he boasts that his melancholy is

> neither the scholar's melancholy, which is emulation; nor the musician's, which is fantastical; nor the courtier's, which is proud; nor the soldier's, which is ambitious; nor the lawyer's, which is politic; nor the lady's, which is nice; nor the lover's, which is all these: but it is a melancholy of mine own, compounded of many simples, extracted from many objects, and indeed the sundry contemplation of my travels, in which my often rumination wraps me in a most humorous sadness. (4.1.10–20)

In response to this self-analysis Rosalind scoffs at the idea that a melancholy acquired through traveling could be something truly Jaques's own.[62]

In truth, she says, he has "nothing" (4.1.24). She herself would "rather have a fool to make me merry than experience to make me sad—and to travel for it too!" (4.1.28–29). This brief exchange encapsulates a recurring theme in Shakespeare, that of a "humoral" contest between a melancholy character and a character who exudes the good humor of sanguinity. In *As You Like It* the contest between Jaques and Rosalind is relatively mild since Jaques is more akin to the clown Touchstone than to an intriguer like Don John the Bastard in *Much Ado About Nothing*. Indeed, the implicit stake of the contest between Jaques and Rosalind is the allegiance of Touchstone, in whom they both delight but in opposite ways. Jaques's melancholy makes him suspicious of love. He is disappointed to learn that Touchstone wants to marry Audrey. He makes a token effort to undermine Orlando's love for Rosalind ("I do not like her name. ... Will you sit down with me? and we two will rail against our mistress the world, and all our misery" [3.2.265, 277–279]), but the love-besotted Orlando is completely ague-proof. Ultimately less of a cynic than an ascetic priest, Jaques is merely being honest when he predicts at the end of the play that Touchstone's marriage to Audrey "is but for two months victuall'd" (5.4.192). He blesses all four marriages before quietly excluding himself from the festivities.[63]

More sinister melancholy characters appear in *Much Ado About Nothing*, *Othello*, and *Cymbeline*. In each of these plays, a malcontent intriguer—Don John, Iago, and Iachimo—seeks to destroy a marriage by inducing jealousy in the husband or fiancé. An interesting variation on this theme is the scene in *Troilus and Cressida* in which Ulysses enables Troilus to observe Cressida giving his sleeve to Diomedes. Ulysses doesn't deceive Troilus as Iago deceives Othello. On the contrary, he provides "ocular proof" of a sort that Iago couldn't have given Othello. Despite this difference, Ulysses is no less *cynical* than Iago, his motive being, as it were, to "set down the pegs" (*Othello* 2.1.200) of the "Troilus music."[64] Thersites's running commentary ("A proof of strength she could not publish more, / Unless she said, 'My mind is now turn'd whore'" [5.2.24]) is nothing more than the obscene flip side of Ulysses's own sexual cynicism. Troilus's initial response to Cressida's flirtation with Diomedes is to deny that she was even there—a negation that he insists "hath no taste of madness" (5.2.127). For the rest of the play he exhibits a bitter melancholy that is different in kind from the cynical type that Ulysses has in common with Iago.

Bitter melancholy also suffuses *Shakespeare's Sonnets*, a collection that bears comparison with Plato's *Symposium*. The sequence as a whole effectively traces a declining arc from the topmost rung of Diotima's ladder ("From fairest creatures we desire increase" [1.1]) to the most degraded form of bestial lust ("Love's fire heats water, water cools not love" [154.14]). The transformation of the speaker's attitude recalls Troilus's disillusionment with Cressida. It also resonates with Hamlet's hostility toward Ophelia and Gertrude, whom he accuses of leaving a "heaven-kissing hill" (3.4.59) for "the rank sweat of an unseamed bed" (3.4.92). In each of these texts, a disappointed lover comes to experience the world as nothing but "a foul and pestilent congregation of vapors" (2.2.302–303)—what Nietzsche called Hamlet's "sense of revulsion." If Hamlet's melancholy is privileged it is insofar as it condenses not only the bitter melancholy of the disappointed lover but the metaphysical melancholy of the scholar.

Ever since antiquity, melancholy had been divided into benign and pathological types. The author of the pseudo-Aristotelian *Problems* wondered why men of "genius" were disproportionately melancholy.[65] Marsilio Ficino surmised that the earthly properties of "natural" melancholy predisposed the soul to turn inward toward its center, while its Mercurial and Saturnine properties made it susceptible to celestial, angelic, and divine influences.[66] Scholars were susceptible to unnatural forms of melancholy. Excessive "study of philosophy" "dries up the brain," leaving overly zealous philosophers with bodies "half-alive and often melancholic."[67] Any of the bodily humors could be transformed through excessive heat and dryness into "burnt" melancholy (the process of adustion).[68] People who suffered from any kind of melancholy were susceptible to the influence of evil spirits. Knowing this fact, Hamlet prudently seeks grounds more "relative" than the word of the Ghost to determine his uncle's guilt.

Genially melancholy scholars could summon both good and evil spirits. Shakespearean practitioners of "black" magic include the Duchess of Gloucester in 2 *Henry VI* and the Weird Sisters in *Macbeth*. "Lawful" magic is practiced by Paulina in *The Winter's Tale*, Cerimon in *Pericles*, and Prospero in *The Tempest*. Frances Yates speculates that Prospero, like Marlowe's Doctor Faustus, was modeled on the Renaissance magus John Dee.[69] Enthusiasm for genial or "inspired" melancholy led some writers to speculate that Christ had a melancholy temperament, but such enthusiasm, verging on blasphemy, was not universal. There was growing suspicion in the seventeenth century that melancholy people had no special powers, but suffered from clinically identifiable forms of mental illness.[70] Milton could still celebrate "divinest Melancholy" in *Il Penseroso* while natural philosophers such as Descartes were reducing it to its pathological variety.

In his first Meditation, Descartes distinguishes his methodological skepticism from the ravings of "madmen, whose brains are so damaged by the persistent vapours of melancholia that they firmly maintain they are kings when they are paupers, or say they are dressed in purple when they are naked, or that their heads are made of earthenware, or that they are pumpkins, or made of glass. But such people are insane, and I would be thought equally mad if I took anything from them as a model for myself."[71] Michel

Foucault takes this passage to mark the end of a dialogue that reason carried on with madness throughout the Renaissance.[72] Erasmus conversed with Folly, and Montaigne was disturbed by the thought that he himself might be mad.[73] Descartes breaks with this tradition by distinguishing reason from madness.[74] There is a clear and distinct difference between the scruples of a philosopher and the delusions of someone suffering from pathological melancholy. Having reassured himself on this point, Descartes calmly takes up, and eventually dispels, both the hypothesis that he is dreaming and the even more extravagant hypothesis that he is being deceived by an evil genius.

Foucault's interpretation, while certainly powerful, obscures the fact that the topic of the passage in the *Meditations* isn't madness per se but melancholy. Descartes's primary gesture isn't to exclude madness but rather to exclude genial melancholy, which he doesn't even mention. Instead of distinguishing genial from pathological melancholy, as most Renaissance scholars would have done, he implicitly reduces the former to the latter. The philosopher's access to truth will no longer be due to his being an inspired genius but solely to his possession of reason. Foucault overlooks this exclusion. In his description of the Renaissance episteme, he himself remains silent on the topic of genial melancholy. On his account, knowledge in the Renaissance was solely a function of the interpretation of resemblances. He does not mention the melancholy scholar's magical abilities. Instead of supernatural visitations, he focuses on the visionary artist's metaphysical monsters. The paintings of Hieronymus Bosch are said to attest to a "tragic experience of madness" that came to the fore in the literary works of Shakespeare and Cervantes.[75] In the madness of Ophelia, King Lear, and Lady Macbeth, Foucault discerns a point of no return, a loss of reason so pervasive it can culminate only in death. Madness opens up a "tear in the fabric of the world," a conduit not for Ariels but for Calibans, as it is in Bosch and will be again in Goya.[76] The effect of this interpretation is to repeat Descartes's implicit reduction of genial melancholy to its pathological variety. What Foucault objects to in the *Meditations* is only a *secondary* reduction of madness (in the sense of melancholy *tout court*) to reason's other.

Another problem with Foucault's account has to do with where he places Shakespeare in the early modern divide. As Winfried Schleiner has noted, in several of Shakespeare's plays, pathological melancholy is subjected to medical treatments that Foucault assigns to a later period. Lady Macbeth's madness may be beyond the Doctor's practice, as Foucault reminds us, but the melancholy of the Jailer's Daughter in *The Two Noble Kinsmen* is not ("'Tis not an engraff'd madness, but a most thick and profound melancholy" [4.3.48–50]).[77] Other treatments of melancholy range from straightforward attempts to cheer someone up (Antonio in *The Merchant of Venice* [1.1], Olivia in *Twelfth Night* [1.5]) to full-scale theatrical stagings of the sort that were part of a

Renaissance physician's repertoire (Sly in the Induction to *The Taming of the Shrew*, Gloucester in *King Lear* [4.6]). While the madness of Ophelia and Lady Macbeth lead them inexorably toward death, Hamlet and Macbeth pointedly reject suicide as a solution to the melancholy from which they suffer. Lear's melancholy culminates in madness, but his situation is counterpointed with that of Gloucester, who regrets being incapable of both obliviousness ("Better I were distract" [4.6.281]) and oblivion ("Is wretchedness depriv'd that benefit, / To end itself by death?" [4.6.61–62]). His melancholy resists Edgar's theatrical cure, and is perhaps even strengthened by it. Hamlet, who is at most mad north–northwest, puts his melancholy to the test by staging "The Mousetrap," demonstrating to his and Horatio's satisfaction that the Ghost's testimony is trustworthy.

As for Descartes, far from ruling out the possibility that he is pathologically melancholy, he goes on to assume a worst-case scenario, namely, that, like Hamlet, he is being abused by a devil. Only once he has assured himself that he has access to truth is he able, like Hamlet, to affirm the reality of a divinity that shapes our epistemic ends, rough-hew them how we will.

Why was Foucault so convinced that there was a definitive break between Shakespeare and Descartes? Perhaps the answer has to do with the special place that he assigns to *The Birth of Tragedy* in his *History of Madness*. His account of Descartes's break with the tragic experience of madness parallels Nietzsche's account of Plato's suppression of the Greeks' tragic worldview. *The Birth of Tragedy* is as much about the birth of Platonism as it is about the decline of tragedy. Likewise, *History of Madness* is as much about the birth of modern philosophy as it is about the silencing of the mad. Descartes is Foucault's Socrates—the logical, not the musical Socrates—while Shakespeare and Cervantes are his Aeschylus and Sophocles. Nietzsche's account of the passage from the Greeks' tragic view of the world to Socrates's unconditional will to truth has simply been shifted from antiquity to modernity. By making this shift, Foucault implicitly makes good on Nietzsche's association of Hamlet with Dionysian man. Nietzsche had been unable to explain how Shakespeare revived the tragic worldview during a cultural moment better suited to the faux-tragic experience of Italian opera. No doubt this had something to do with his decision to omit a fuller discussion of Shakespeare from *The Birth of Tragedy*. Foucault fills this lacuna by developing the link between tragedy and madness. Dionysian intoxication was a form of madness. Foucault implicitly acknowledges as much when he says that "The Greeks had a relation to a thing they called ὕβρις (hubris). ... But the Greek Logos had no opposite."[78] The madness of Sophocles's Ajax may be temporary rather than final, but like that of Ophelia, Lear, and Lady Macbeth it too leads him inexorably toward death. Although Foucault does not emphasize the musical roots of Shakespearean tragedy, his reference to its Boschian origins performs a similar function (*The Temptation of Saint Anthony* and *Ship of Fools* being decidedly more Dionysian than Apollonian works of art). Just as the young Nietzsche took Wagner to have heralded a rebirth of tragedy, so the young Foucault took Nietzsche himself (along with Hölderlin, Nerval, Van Gogh, and Artaud) to have revived the tragic experience of madness. Indeed, Foucault goes so far as to suggest that the onset of Nietzsche's madness exploded the prosaic "time of the world," the seeds of his madness being already present in *The Birth of Tragedy*.[79] Finally, just as Nietzsche came to regret the Romanticism of *The Birth of Tragedy*, so Foucault regretted the Romanticism implicit in his representation of the silencing of the mad. Moreover, just as Nietzsche accused his erstwhile mentor, Wagner, of succumbing to pessimism, so Foucault criticized his former student, Jacques Derrida, for challenging his reading of Descartes.

Foucault's debate with Derrida bears not only on Descartes but on Hamlet. According to Derrida, when Descartes says "But such people are insane," he is not peremptorily ruling out the possibility that he himself is mad. He is simply entertaining the objection of a "naive interlocutor" unable or unwilling to call into question the trustworthiness of the evidence of the senses.[80] To placate this interlocutor, Descartes pretends to concede that he cannot accept any hypothesis that would make his views of himself and the world indistinguishable from those of people properly labeled insane. The apparently reassuring remark—"But such people are insane"—turns out, however, to be a pedagogical ruse, for when Descartes turns first to the dream hypothesis and then to the still more troubling hypothesis of the evil genius, he shows that he cannot rule out the possibility that he himself is deluded. When he proceeds in the Second Meditation to reason that even if he is deceived in everything else he knows that he exists as a thinking thing, the implication is not, "I know that I exist as a thinking thing, therefore I am not melancholy," but rather, "I know that I exist as a thinking thing *even if I am melancholy*." Only later will he purport to rule out the possibility that he is being deceived by an evil genius. Even then, as we have seen, he remains troubled or haunted by phantasms, every moment being the narrow gate through which an apparition might enter ("What, has this thing appear'd again to-night?" [1.1.21]). Descartes deals with this threat by reducing genial melancholy to pathological melancholy. Hence his reasoning in the Sixth Meditation that if an otherwise inexplicable apparition of a man were to appear out of nowhere and vanish without a trace, he would have to conclude that it was "a specter or a phantom formed in my brain."[81] *Pace* Foucault, it is not the effective exclusion of madness that is at stake at this moment in Descartes's text but rather the ineffective repression of (genial) melancholy. Foucault takes Descartes to confidently sever all relations with those who are truly mad when he is in fact struggling to cure himself of his own melancholy.

Just as Foucault conflates melancholy with madness in his reading of Descartes, so he remains silent about Freud's theorization of melancholia. In *History of Madness* he focuses on those aspects of Freud's case studies that show reason's interrupted dialogue with madness being resumed as techniques of social exclusion give way to techniques of regulated inclusion. By ignoring Freud's treatment of melancholia he misses an opportunity to pick up on another way in which Freud responds to Descartes. By representing melancholia as a pathological form of mourning Freud opens the way to a more general conception of human subjectivity as constitutively "haunted." It is this dimension of Freud's thought that Derrida highlights in his own theorization of "hauntology." By highlighting the moment in the *Meditations* when Descartes verges on recognizing the extravagant and "mad" character of the cogito, Derrida intended to alert Foucault to a different way of thinking about melancholy. He also hinted that by *demonizing* Descartes and Freud, Foucault ran the risk of repeating Descartes's attempt to exorcize his demon.

In his response to Derrida, Foucault stuck to his guns. He accused Derrida of failing to appreciate that when Descartes says "But such people are insane [*amentes*], and I would be thought no less mad [*demens*]," he was using legal terminology to imply that his own status as a sane subject at liberty was different in kind from that of someone rightfully confined to a madhouse.[82] Instead of conceding that the dream hypothesis and the hypothesis of an evil deceiver exacerbate the threat of madness, he argued that these didactic examples reassure the philosopher of his sanity.[83] Derrida, he charged, was so much of a philosopher himself that he could not perceive the constitutive exclusions upon which philosophical discourse rests.[84] Thus it was Derrida himself rather than Foucault who had performed the same exclusionary gesture as Descartes.

The perpetual exchange of accusations that this retort invited—"No *you* are the Cartesian," "No *you* are the Cartesian," and so on—must have been on Derrida's mind when in *Specters of Marx* he analyzed the filial logic of Marx's rivalry with Max Stirner. In this case it was a question not of who was still in the grip of Cartesian rationalism but who was unable to escape the clutches of Hegelian idealism. In *The Ego and Its Own*, Stirner argued that Hegel's speculative account of absolute spirit was unable to resolve the antithesis between things and thoughts. The distinctive feature of modernity was that thought had become unmoored from physical reality. Modern institutions—what Hegel calls the realm of objective spirit—were so many phantoms or ghosts. Instead of exorcizing these ghosts by overcoming the opposition between spirit and nature, Hegel treated them as fully real. Modern men, Stirner concluded, were "haunted" like "fools in a madhouse."[85] The Cartesian cogito and the Lutheran conception of justification through faith were two sides of the same metaphysical coin.[86]

Derrida, recognizing the affinity between Stirner's description of Cartesian subjects haunted like fools in a madhouse and his own reading of the *Meditations*, agrees with Stirner that "'I am' would mean 'I am haunted.'"[87] When Marx railed against Stirner in *The German Ideology*, accusing him of being both insufficiently Hegelian and too Hegelian, he anticipated Foucault's double response to Derrida. In an essay written after Foucault's death, Derrida sought not only to propitiate but to honor his mentor's spirit by calling attention to a passage in *History of Madness* that he had previously overlooked. In this passage Foucault implicitly acknowledges that Descartes's purported exclusion of madness isn't definitive, that the "threat" of an evil genius of one sort or another remains "perpetual."[88] While noting that this passage should have obviated all cause for debate between them, Derrida raises a new question about Foucault's reading of Freud.[89] When Foucault writes in *History of Madness*, "We must do justice to Freud," he implies that there is a "good" Freud—the one who does justice to the tragic experience of madness by revealing the silent work of the death drive—and a "bad" Freud, the Freud of the clinic, who repeats the Cartesian gesture of silencing madness.[90] For Derrida, who in *Specters of Marx* acknowledges that it is always necessary to "filter" a legacy, the good Freud is the one who is alert to the experience of being haunted, while the bad Freud is the one who reduces melancholia to pathological mourning and so fails to do justice to Shakespeare's representation of the uncanny.[91]

According to Freud, what strikes us as uncanny are things that reappear after having been repressed or otherwise apparently annihilated. The appearance of an actual ghost would certainly strike us as uncanny. But literary ghosts are another matter. In fantastic settings, we are prepared to accept their reality. Such is the case, Freud argues, in Shakespeare.[92] Hamlet may find the ghost of his father uncanny, but we don't. Accordingly, Freud excludes uncanniness from his account of what it is we identify with in Hamlet. What unconsciously binds the author of *Hamlet* and us is a shared investment in the revival of Hamlet's repressed Oedipus complex. But that revival is (at least for us) no more uncanny than the Ghost itself. There is a fundamental difference between our fascination for works of art that simultaneously reveal and conceal underlying psychic conflicts and the specific aesthetic feeling of uncanniness that certain works generate by blurring the boundaries between reality and fantasy. An exemplary case is E. T. A. Hoffmann's short story, "The Sandman." By subtly introducing supernatural elements into his apparently natural world, Hoffmann induces us to share the terror of his hero Nathaniel. Surprisingly, Freud doesn't detect anything uncanny in the animated doll Olympia—the thing that, like the Ghost in *Hamlet*, straddles the border between the living and the dead—but only in Nathaniel's terror of having his eyes plucked out. According to Freud, the revival of this childhood terror represents the return of an aspect of his repressed Oedipus complex, namely, castration anxiety. If Nathaniel's fear of the Sandman produces in us a sense of the uncanny that Hamlet's encounter with the Ghost does not, it is because of the way in which Hoffmann undermines our sense of the difference between what is real and what is not in his fictional world. A similar uncertainty can give rise to a sense of the uncanny in everyday life. Freud mentions several instances in which he himself was temporarily uncertain whether something was real or not, including one that involved the apparent return of someone dead. But in eminently Cartesian fashion he maintains that his scientific temperament made him less susceptible to a feeling of the uncanny than people with a weaker sense of reality.[93]

Whatever the cause, Freud's refusal to acknowledge the uncanniness of Shakespeare's ghosts belies the plays' reception history. Eighteenth-century audiences were struck by Garrick's ability to communicate Hamlet's dread at the appearance of the Ghost. Derrida takes Freud to task for failing to do justice to this type of experience. According to the psychoanalyst Nicolas Abraham, Hamlet makes us feel as if we ourselves are haunted by a ghost or phantom, a feeling that persists at the end of a performance or reading of the play. This feeling is fundamentally different from the sense of relief that we feel at the end of *Oedipus Tyrannus*. Freud could explain how Sophocles's play "'purified' the soul," but he was unable to account for the psychological discomfort with which *Hamlet* leaves us.[94] Surmising that we are haunted by an element of the dramatic story that the play hints at but leaves ultimately unexplained—something other than the revival of a repressed Oedipus complex—Abraham sets out "to 'cure' the *public* of a covert neurosis the *Tragedy of Hamlet* has, for centuries, inflicted upon it."[95]

The key to Abraham's endeavor is to rethink the relationship between the living and the dead. With Maria Torok, he had already reformulated Freud's account of the relationship between mourning and melancholia. While agreeing with Freud that melancholia represents a pathological response to loss, Abraham and Torok deny that it involves a straightforward identification with the lost object. Instead, they develop Sándor Ferenczi's distinction between introjection and incorporation. On their account, introjection is the process by which an originally narcissistic subject includes others within its field of concern. Despite the connotation of internalization, introjection involves an outward extension of the boundaries of the ego. As such, it can accommodate loss. Incorporation, by contrast, is the process by which a subject who is unable or unwilling to introject a loss *imagines* or *fantasizes* (typically, unconsciously) that it has internalized the lost object. This fantasy substitutes for the difficult work of mourning. Mourning requires a subject to introject not the lost object itself but the *loss* of that object. By contrast, the fantasy of incorporation consists in the pretense that the object hasn't really been lost but has instead been secretly internalized. Abraham and Torok call the secret psychic "place" where the lost object is located a "crypt." Melancholia, they hypothesize, results when something threatens to reveal the location of a previously encrypted object. It expresses the subject's fear of "losing" the object whose *real* loss it has hitherto denied. Far from being ambivalent toward the encrypted object—and thus from sadomasochistically punishing it and itself—the melancholy subject's relationship to it is one of unmitigated love. The psychoanalyst must reassure the subject that this love will be respected as he or she is coaxed into "letting go" and beginning the work of properly mourning the lost object—that is, of introjecting its loss.

Given this picture, it might be expected that Abraham would take Hamlet's melancholy to be due to encryption. Instead, he takes the appearance of the Ghost to represent another psychological structure. A ghost—or phantom (*fântome*)—stands for a secret that someone else has taken with him or her to the grave. To be haunted by a phantom is to be unconsciously aware of the existence, but not the meaning, of such a secret. Abraham hypothesizes that the discomfort that we feel after a performance of *Hamlet* is a sign that the Ghost is a phantom in this precise sense. We are haunted by the play because Hamlet is haunted by a secret to which the Ghost alludes when it refers to "foul crimes done in my days of nature" (1.5.12). Since the exact nature of these crimes remains hidden, Hamlet—and we—are haunted by them. To "cure" us—by curing Hamlet—Abraham composes a "Sixth Act" in which the play's secrets are revealed. In the presence of the Ghost, Horatio and Fortinbras surmise that, on the day that Hamlet was born, King Hamlet slew King Fortinbras not in fair play, as Horatio has previously led us to believe, but through the use of a poisoned foil supplied by Polonius. They disclose this secret in such a way that the Ghost may depart in peace rather than in shame. This satisfying ending enables a suddenly revived Hamlet—and us—to live without being haunted.

Evidently responding to Abraham, Derrida remarks in *Specters of Marx* that "Hamlet could never know the peace of a 'good ending.'"[96] What it means for time to be out of joint, he argues, is for the condition of being haunted to be irreducible. We are all haunted by phantoms, just as we are all caught between mourning and melancholia. Our Hamlet complexes are irremediable because they are constitutive of our identities. We must learn to live with ghosts. The only alternative would be what Derrida, following Freud, characterizes as mania, a psychological attitude that pretends not to be haunted even as it ruthlessly seeks to annihilate the dead that do in fact haunt it. Derrida associates this frame of mind with Marx's virulent attacks on Stirner.[97] In accusing Stirner of being haunted by the ghost of Hegel, Marx implies that his rival suffers from a Hamlet complex of which Marx himself would be entirely free. In so doing he acts out an essential feature of that very complex, showing himself to be no less haunted than Stirner.

A similar dialectic can be found in Henry Miller's "Hamlet" correspondence with Michael Fraenkel. Between November 1935 and October 1938, the two writers exchanged a series of letters whose original purpose was to exorcize Hamlet's ghost. As Miller explained in his first letter: "If there is to be any success in our endeavor it will be in laying the ghost. For Hamlet still stalks the streets. The fault is not Shakespeare's—the fault is ours. None of us have become naturally modern enough to waylay this ghost and strangle it. For the ghost is not the father which was murdered, nor the conscience which was uneasy, but the time-spirit which has been creaking like a rusty pendulum."[98] Because he cannot set time right, Miller argues, Hamlet cannot tell that he is alive and not dead. To free themselves from this "arch-symbol of death-in-life," Miller tells Fraenkel, "it should be our purpose to set the pendulum swinging smoothly again so that we synchronize with past and future. Are the times out of joint? Then look to the clock! Not the clock on the mantelpiece, but the chronometer inside which tells when you are living and when you are not."[99] To be "naturally modern" is to rely on this living, internal clock. Miller acknowledges that he himself is not yet "naturally modern enough," that "Hamlet is in our bowels."[100] To overcome this malady, the two writers must separately turn inward. The aim of the correspondence was thus to facilitate not so much a joint analysis as two joint *self*-analyses (as Freud conducted his self-analysis in his correspondence with Fliess). In subsequent letters, however, Miller began to write as though he were conducting a unidirectional analysis of Fraenkel, with he himself playing the role of a fully modern ego psychologist. While Fraenkel (anticipating Derrida) maintained that "the Hamlet problem" might be insurmountable for "modern man," Miller insisted that he himself had completely resolved it: "What do I really know … ?" he asks at one point. "Only that I am alive. Does everybody know that he is alive? No! Some only imagine it: they are looking for proofs all the time."[101] Despite his apparent self-confidence, Miller protests too much when he manically insists: "There's no question in my mind of whether I am dead-alive or alive-dead."[102] He urges Fraenkel to do what he himself has done, namely, "kill Hamlet off": "We want to get rid of the ghosts that stalk us." "If you are for the death of an outlived tradition, as you say, you have to be passionate about that and prove to us that it really is dead for you by living deeds."[103]

Miller's diagnosis of the weight of an outlived tradition recalls Marx's formulations in *The Eighteenth Brumaire of Louis Bonaparte*: "Tradition from all the dead generations weighs like a nightmare [*ein Alp*] on the brain of the living." "The revolution of the nineteenth century must let the dead bury the dead in order to realise its own content."[104] Unlike Miller, however, Marx happily identifies with Hamlet when he anticipates "the whole of Europe" celebrating the coming revolution with the cry, "Well grubbed up, old mole! [*Brav gewühlt, alter Maulwurf!*]"[105] Besides Hamlet, Marx loved to "play" Timon of Athens—another of Shakespeare's melancholy characters—at the moment when he unearths—and rails against—gold. Walter Benjamin associates Timon's misanthropy with a melancholy sense of the passage of time: his "rage explodes in time to the ticking of the seconds that enslaves the melancholy man."[106] Just as gold reduces everything to the homogeneous medium of exchange value, so clocks reduce time to the uniform ticking of seconds. On this reading, Timon would be melancholy not because time is out of joint but because it is perfectly linear. Jaques expresses a similar view when he represents the Seven Ages of Man (2.7.139–166) as a relentless passage from birth to death, and when he commends the moralizing of Touchstone: "From hour to hour, we ripe and ripe, / And then from hour to hour, we rot and rot" (2.7.26–27). Benjamin suggests that Hamlet is unique in "striking Christian sparks from the baroque rigidity of the melancholic."[107] Yet a similar sense of the messianic informs all of Shakespeare's melancholy characters. Both Jaques ("Get you to church" [3.3.84–85]) and Timon ("no idle votarist" [4.3.27]) share Hamlet's sense of the difference between "messianic time" and "tragic time."[108] So, arguably, do Antonio in *The Merchant of Venice* and Prospero in *The Tempest*. It is even negatively present in those for whom being born under Saturn marks them as evil (such as Aaron the Moor, Richard III, Don John, Iago, and Edmund), for the diabolical, no less than the angelic, opens up a "tear in the fabric of the world."

In his first response to Foucault, Derrida contested the idea that Descartes's *Meditations* marked a definitive boundary between the Renaissance and modernity. Not only is every historical moment haunted by the past and pregnant with the future, but the very text in which Foucault detected a historical break is one that implicitly discloses the out-of-joint character of time (insofar as the Cartesian "I am" implies "I am haunted"). If Hamlet anticipates Descartes, it is, for Derrida, by showing that a certain kind of melancholy is inescapable. But how should we understand this predicament? Is it simply a matter of knowing that one could never know the peace of a good ending? Or is it, *pace* Miller, the state of not knowing whether one is dead or alive?[109] Does it involve waiting, like Hegel's unhappy consciousness, for a messiah one knows will never arrive?

In his lectures on aesthetics, Hegel represents Hamlet as a "beautiful soul" who is unable to pass from mere aesthetic contemplation of the world—and condemnation of those who play their roles within it—to the performance of a world-transforming act. In effect, Hegel's Hamlet only interprets the world; the point is to change it.[110] Contra Hegel, Jennifer Bates argues that Hamlet is better understood in terms of Hegel's conception of the unhappy consciousness.[111] Hegel's unhappy (or melancholy) consciousness seeks within itself something stable that isn't subject to the evanescent vanities of the world. This fundamentally stoic attitude toward the external world is conjoined to a skeptical attitude that finds nothing within the subject itself that is truly stable. This second attitude accounts for the self-castigating feature of melancholia that Freud traces to unconscious aggression toward a lost object, but that Abraham and Torok take to be a way of protecting an encrypted object from recriminations by others. For Bates, the Ghost's call for revenge opens up the possibility of a definitive act by which Hamlet could in principle overcome his alienation. Over the course of the play, she argues, Hamlet passes from vague intuitions to aesthetic representations to inferential decisions. After several missteps, including his mistaking of Polonius for Claudius, he performs an act that accomplishes the aim of killing Claudius, but without transforming the underlying social conditions that make him an unhappy consciousness. Bates concludes that "Hamlet is … a *successful* Unhappy Consciousness (rather than a cured one)."[112] Like Abraham, she suggests that the play leaves us haunted because Hamlet remains haunted at the moment of his death. Horatio is charged to *narrate* Hamlet's story, but he is not in a position to *analyze* it (in a sense of analysis that for Bates is more Hegelian than Freudian).[113] This interpretation recalls that of Abraham, who assigns Horatio the role of Hamlet's analyst in his Sixth Act, and who revives the prince so that his story can continue up to and including a genuine cure. Implicitly calling into question Derrida's suggestion that Hamlet could never know the peace of a good ending, Bates defends the Hegelian view that it is possible for an unhappy consciousness to know a certain kind of good ending.

Like all of Shakespeare's melancholy characters, Hegel's unhappy consciousness feels cut off from the divine. It overcomes its alienation by confessing its misery to a ministering priest who stands in for the absent God. Bates argues that Horatio plays such a ministering role for Hamlet, even though his counsel isn't sufficient to cure Hamlet of his melancholy.[114] A genuinely cured unhappy consciousness becomes capable of playing the role of a rational agent who must endure further contradictions before being reconciled with the absolute. Under the initial guise of observing reason, this somewhat happier consciousness is forced to take seriously the kind of reductive materialism that in Hegel's day appeared under the guise of phrenology. The infinite judgment that "the *being of Spirit is a bone*" replicates the moment in *Hamlet* when the presence of skulls and corpses makes the Ghost (like the hobbyhorse of 3.2.135) a "great thing of us forgot" (*King Lear* 5.3.237).[115] By "looking the negative in the face, and tarrying with it," spirit recognizes itself to be the power of negativity that it first attributes to death.[116] Hamlet's "success" as an unhappy consciousness would then consist in his ability to use the skull of Yorick to lay the ghost of his dead father to rest. Bates's interpretation implies that there is a kind of uneven development in Hamlet's phenomenological journey, for he resolves a more "advanced" contradiction while remaining stuck at an earlier stage. If he is still haunted at the end of the play, it is not because the Ghost hovers over the strewn corpses, but because his available courses of action are constrained by his Zeitgeist's limited conception of justice.

Bates distinguishes the "upward" dialectical "spiral" of *Aufhebung* from the "downward" dialectical "spiral" of "anti-*Aufhebung*."[117] *Aufhebung*, or sublation, is the process of resolving contradictions, while anti-*Aufhebung* is that of falling back into them. By resolving contradictions, we actualize new shapes of spirit. By falling back into them, or failing to resolve them in the first place, we generate "ghosts" instead of *Geist*. At first blush, generating ghosts might seem to be a way of keeping faith with the past, but because they are "inwardizations" or memory traces they have a phantasmatic dimension of the sort associated by Abraham and Torok with incorporation.[118] Learning to let go of the dead frightens us, in part because we worry about subjecting them to a second, symbolic, death. But introjecting loss can also be a way of vicariously alleviating the suffering of the dead ("Rest, rest, perturbed spirit!" [1.5.182]).

Bates argues that *Hamlet* resolves some contradictions while generating others. Insofar as it resolves contradictions, it has the structure of a comedy; insofar as it generates them, it has the structure of a tragedy. Its tragic, downward spiral is epitomized in the madness and death of Ophelia—the aspect of the play that Foucault emphasized in representing it as a premodern tragedy.[119] Its comic, upward spiral is evidenced in the insights and justice that Hamlet achieves. Each of these achievements remains limited because neither Hamlet nor Denmark (nor Shakespeare's England) had reached an adequate stage of spiritual development. For Hamlet to achieve justice in the "objective" sense in which Hegel conceives it, Denmark would have required legal institutions through which Hamlet could seek redress instead of exacting revenge on a dramatic stage.[120] To achieve true insight, Bates concludes, Hamlet would require not only "inferential cognition" (the capacity to perform practical syllogisms whose conclusions are actions) but "absolute knowing" of the sort that Horatio himself would need were he to be capable of analyzing rather than simply relating Hamlet's story.[121] Absolute knowing involves understanding how contradictions are generated and resolved, namely, through negation. Spirit for Hegel is "*simple negativity*," which comes to know itself by "looking the negative in the face."[122] Hamlet reaches this stage of development when he contemplates the skull of Yorick, but he "only takes negation so far," partly because he is unable to resolve contradictions inherent to his historical situation and partly because he dies immediately after killing the king.[123] As post-Hegelians who understand these limitations, "we can lower the final curtain."[124]

Although Bates concludes that Hamlet *could* know the peace of a good ending, she accepts Derrida's point that time is always out of joint. Her response to Derrida turns on the difference between "objective" and "absolute" spirit—between social institutions and what she calls "universal wit." Within the order of objective spirit time is "always out of joint and thus always already tragic."[125] Prince Hal's promise to "redeem" time when he becomes king (*1 Henry IV* 1.2.217) is belied by his first official act, namely, banishing Falstaff. Far from representing a messianic intervention in world history, Hal's assumption of "the port of Mars" presages more of the same historical nightmare, namely, "famine, sword and fire" (Prologue 6–7). Falstaff opens up a truer conception of redeemed time, one to be achieved not in a theater of war but in a "theater of identity" in which spirit's negativity manifests itself as wit (*ésprit*).[126] Within the comic space of the Boar's Head Tavern, clock time is suspended, as the not-yet-kinged and therefore still witty Hal observes when he chides Falstaff for being "so superfluous to demand the time of the day" (1.2.11–12). There is no room in Eastcheap for melancholy or unhappy consciousnesses, as Falstaff implies when he describes his passing melancholy as that of "a gib cat or a lugg'd bear" (1.2.73–74). Like stray and baited animals, melancholy characters are internal outcasts who either exclude themselves from, or are excluded by, their communities. In Shakespeare's comedies, the negativity of such melancholy characters as Don John, Malvolio, and Shylock is restrained before it culminates in irreversible tragedy. Nevertheless, the potential for tragedy lingers. For Bates, this is a sign that the realms of objective and absolute spirit are essentially intertwined—that universal wit has as its antithesis the social contradictions and egocentricity that Hegel associates with civil society. Hamlet could know the peace of a good ending in those possible worlds (or plays) in which his abundant wit is allowed to flourish as it does at "theatrical" moments in Shakespeare's actual play. In a spirit as welcoming to Derrida's shade as Derrida was to Foucault's, Bates concludes that the theater of identity "does not consign us or Derrida to the role of an Unhappy Consciousness."[127] To the extent that it is possible to actualize absolute spirit—that is, to create cultural institutions, such as theaters, in which *universal* wit can be exercised—we must cultivate forgiveness. For Hegel, forgiveness marks the sublation of tragedy into comedy. In her discussion of the unique kind of comedy that Shakespeare achieves in his late romances, Bates shows the remarkable extent to which Shakespeare's development as a dramatist—passing, roughly, from the writing of histories and relatively light comedies to tragedies to romances—parallels Hegel's *Phenomenology of Spirit*. With Northrop Frye, she agrees "that there is a logical evolution toward romance in Shakespeare's work."[128] Wilson Knight calls this "the Shakespeare Progress."[129]

The telos of the Shakespeare Progress is, as in Hegel, the reconciliation of contradictions, up to and including those resolutely negative stances that actively resist such reconciliation. Because Antonio's negativity in *The Tempest* persists even after Prospero's (grudging) forgiveness, nothing guarantees that the return to Milan will be a happy one. In comedies such as *Twelfth Night*, *Much Ado About Nothing*, and *As You Like It*, the good humor of sanguinity vies with melancholy for predominance. These plays are comedies insofar as the good humor of a Maria, Beatrice, and Rosalind defeats the bad humor of a Malvolio, Don John, and Jaques. These humoral victories remain fragile, however, because melancholy is not sublated but simply repressed. In the romances something different happens. What we might characterize as Antonio's "excluded inclusion" at the end of *The Tempest* leaves just as much room for future tragedy as does Malvolio's "included exclusion" at the end of *Twelfth Night*.[130] If there is a cure for melancholy in *The Tempest*, it is one that works its magic on Prospero. He is cured when he learns from Ariel how to forgive Antonio and the rest of his enemies. The manner of this cure is important. In the sanguine comedies, wit is the prerogative of fools and characters so merry they can be thought of as antimelancholics.[131] Their wit expresses itself in clever wordplay that frequently contributes to the resolution of potentially tragic conflicts but which is condemned as frivolity in *Love's Labor's Lost*. A condition for the possibility of a "good ending," Berowne learns, is that insubstantial wit must give way ("sans 'sans,' I pray you" [5.2.416]) to "honest plain words" (5.2.753). Instead of culminating in four weddings, as so many of Shakespeare's comedies do, *Love's Labor's Lost* ends with an impending funeral and four deferred marriages. In the interim Berowne must learn a new kind of wit, not one that will "move wild laughter in the throat of death" ("that's the way to choke a gibing spirit"), but one that will "enforce the pained impotent to smile" (5.2.854–855, 858). This is similar to the "universal wit" that Shakespeare deploys in the romances. However, in these plays, the power to force the pained impotent to smile is not the possession of any particular character but is rather the prerogative of Providence. However clever Autolycus may be, he does not possess the wit of a Touchstone or Feste. His contribution to *The Winter's Tale*'s happy ending is entirely *unwitting*, though not unwitty. Following Bates, we may say that the *universal* wit of the romances is truly universal in the sense of being wielded by absolute rather than subjective spirit. Conversely, the melancholy that such wit must sublate is the possession of individual characters, a mark of their individuation and separation from the divinity that shapes their ends. Forgiveness releases the *forgiving* subject from its claim to self-possession. For this reason, forgiveness is not a power or capacity possessed by the forgiving subject. Prospero can only purport to forgive his enemies, and his purported act is tinged with resentment.[132] To be released from his bands, he himself must be forgiven by the hands of others—forgiven even his purporting to possess the power of forgiveness.[133]

In Shakespeare's tragedies, melancholy defeats sanguinity and even occludes it altogether. In *Much Ado About Nothing*, the unwittingly witty Dogberry helps to foil the nefarious plot of Don John, but in *Othello* the Clown's few feeble lines do absolutely nothing to prevent Iago from destroying Othello and Desdemona. Don John and Iago are conventionally melancholy machinators, but Iago is far more intelligent and therefore far more dangerous. Stanley Cavell suggests that Othello's tragic flaw is his lack of wit. He is witless not in the sense of being stupid, but rather in the sense of lacking the conversational skills possessed so abundantly by Beatrice and Benedick. In his study of "the Hollywood comedy of remarriage," Cavell highlights the role that conversational wit plays in the repair of broken marriages. As he points out, the genre derives from that of "Shakespeare's romantic comedies," a term that Cavell uses to refer to both the early comedies and the late romances—as well he might, given that *Much Ado* and *The Winter's Tale* both deal with interrupted marriages.[134] There are, however, important differences between these two plays. In *Much Ado*, there are two divided couples who get married only at the end, though there is a sense in which both marriages count as remarriages.[135] In *The Winter's Tale*, a sixteen-year hiatus interrupts one longstanding marriage and leads to another. A more important difference is that in *The Winter's Tale*, there is nothing to match the conversational wit of Beatrice unless it is the fearless speech of Paulina, which serves another purpose. Wit is simply not the prerogative of individuals in the romances. Berowne had to learn from Rosaline to suit the action to the word and the word to the action, but what Shakespeare's later works reveal is a diminishing ability of even genuine conversational wit to prevent tragic endings. Though more effective than the feeble puns of *Othello*'s Clown, the conceits of the Fool in *King Lear* are less therapeutically effective than the timely interventions of Touchstone and Feste. Nothing can prevent the melancholy Lear from descending into madness. No wonder the Fool disappears after 3.6—an exit justified retrospectively by Albany's remark at the end of the play that "vain is it / That we present us to him" (5.3.293–294).

Only a miracle could provide Lear with the peace of a good ending. The problem with the notorious happy ending that Nahum Tate supplied (in which Cordelia lives and marries Edgar) is that it is *not* miraculous but merely sentimental, a good example of what Nietzsche objected to in opera. Miraculous endings are what Shakespeare provides in the romances, in which seemingly incurable melancholy is cured through the exercise of universal—or, as we might also call it, providential—wit. Pericles's spirits are restored not so much by Marina as by the tempestuous seas that have separated them only to reunite them. Likewise, the marriage of Leontes and Hermione is repaired not through conversation but rather through the agency of "pow'rs divine" (3.2.28). If the Shakespeare Progress culminates in something like absolute knowing, it is by tarrying with the negative to the point of discovering that negativity is both the source of the tragic and the very means of its overcoming. This is what Edgar realizes when he leads his blind father to "th' extreme verge" (4.6.26), "trifl[ing] thus with his despair" in order "to cure it" (4.6.33–34). Cavell, thinking that only self-revelation through words could be useful in such a situation, finds Edgar's device to be "grotesque," but the suggestion in the play is that Gloucester's despair could only be cured by having him leap into—rather than shrink back from—the extreme verge.[136] When Iago toys with Othello's melancholy, it is through a truly grotesque deception that functions as an anticure or anti-*Aufhebung*. To be cured, Othello would have to follow his induced jealousy to the extreme verge of its own self-overcoming, as Ford does in *The Merry Wives of Windsor* (although the form of this play is far more comic than romantic). Only such a cure could restore the verbal eloquence that he possesses at the beginning of the play ("Keep up your bright swords, for the dew will rust them" [1.2.59]).[137] If *Othello*, like *Lear*, ends in tragedy, it is because sanguine cures of the sort administered by the merry wives are no longer effective, while romantic cures are not yet available.

How, then, do such cures become available? Is it simply a matter of passing from a pagan world in which men believe that the gods kill them for their sport to a Christian world in which trust in special Providence has replaced mistrust of fickle Fortune? Žižek suggests that by pursuing tragedy to its extreme verge, Shakespeare was led to "the domain of pure fantasy."[138] His point, I take it, is not that the romances are escapist fantasies, but rather that they are works of art in which the poetic imagination has been liberated from a tragic fantasy according to which nature is at best indifferent to us and at worst malevolent. Like Žižek, Bates highlights the role that imagination plays in spirit's progress.[139] The romances *would* be escapist fantasies if they failed to traverse the "way of despair," but the paths traveled by Pericles, Leontes, Posthumus Leonatus, and even Prospero are no less dark than those taken by Lear and Othello.[140] If the Shakespeare Progress culminates in *romantic* rather than *sanguine* "good endings," they are endings in which absolute spirit reconciles all finite spirits (as, paradigmatically, in the final scene of *Cymbeline*). There is no reconciliation without loss: as Lawrence Rhu emphasizes, the cost of finding Perdita (and reviving Hermione) is the death of Mamillius.[141] That the threat of renewed tragedy also cannot be eliminated is evident at the end of *The Tempest* when Antonio offers no reciprocal gesture of reconciliation to Prospero. Auden captures Antonio's implied frame of mind: "As I exist so you shall be denied, / Forced to remain our melancholy mentor."[142]

In keeping with Nietzsche's representation of Shakespeare as a music-making Socrates, romantic cures are fundamentally musical. As Lorenzo explains to Jessica in *The Merchant of Venice*, people who are (genially) melancholy are receptive to "the sweet power of music" (5.1.79), while those who take no pleasure in music show themselves to have souls "fit for treasons, stratagems, and spoils" (5.1.85).[143] Jaques, who "can suck melancholy out of a song, as a weasel sucks eggs" (2.5.12–13) and yet is "for other than for dancing measures"

(5.4.193), may be somewhere in between these extremes. Nietzsche heard Dionysian dithyrambs in *Hamlet*. But if the purpose of playing is to catch consciences, Shakespeare may have built a better "Mousetrap" in romances like *Pericles*, in which the eponymous prince's restoration from despair is accompanied by the music of the spheres (5.1.229). Like Sly in the Induction to the *Taming of the Shrew*, we are subjected by Shakespeare to the same humoral treatment. Whether our cure is successful or not is as uncertain as it is in the case of Sly (the Induction, like an enthymeme, inviting us to make our own deduction). To be capable of the cure of romance, one must be susceptible to inner shifts of the spirit. As Paulina says: "It is requir'd / You do awake your faith" (*The Winter's Tale* 5.3.94–95).

Leontes responds to this requirement: "If this be magic, let it be an art / Lawful as eating" (5.3.110–111). Hamlet personifies a different kind of faith. In contrast to Leontes's positive faith in the revival of Hermione, his is a negative faith in the Ghost's representation of his dead father ("I'll call thee Hamlet, / King, father, royal Dane" [1.4.44–45]). It is negative in Coleridge's sense of a faith that permits images to work on the mind. It is negative, *pace* Keats, because it lingers or tarries in uncertainty. Stuck at the stage of Hegel's melancholy consciousness, Hamlet personifies the negativity of a faith this side of revelation—a faith that is fundamentally Kantian.

CHAPTER 2

> Hume himself could not but have faith in this Ghost dramatically, let his
> anti-ghostism be as strong as Samson against ghosts less powerfully raised.
> Samuel Taylor Coleridge, Notes for a commentary on *Hamlet*

> I therefore had to suspend *knowledge* in order to make room for *faith*.
> Immanuel Kant, *Critique of Pure Reason*

To recognize the affinity between Hamlet and Kant, it is helpful to know
something about the cultural context in which the *Critique of Pure Reason*
appeared in 1781.

In *The Making of the National Poet*, Michael Dobson notes that during the Seven
Years' War (1756–1763) there was an "Anti-Gallican campaign to redefine the
British, in the name of Shakespeare."[1] By the end of the war, a similar campaign was well underway to redefine the Germans in the name, or spirit,
of Shakespeare. Between 1762 and 1766, Christoph Martin Wieland translated twenty-two of Shakespeare's plays. Adaptations had been performed
in Germany since the early seventeenth century, but by the middle of the
eighteenth century what little was known about the originals was filtered
through the British and French critical reception.[2] Shakespeare was celebrated for his portrayal of character and passion but criticized for his frequent offenses against good taste. Alexander Pope, who didn't hesitate to
correct his infelicities, called him a poet of "great excellencies" but "almost
as great defects."[3] Voltaire went further, maintaining that only a "few pearls"
could be found within Shakespeare's "enormous dungheap."[4] There was an
international critical consensus that Shakespeare was an unschooled "genius"
who fell short of neoclassical standards, but as Voltaire became more critical
the English became more defensive. Initially siding with the French, German critics would eventually come to rival, and even surpass, the British

in Bardolatry. By 1901, Ludwig Fulda could characterize the poet as "*unser Shakespeare.*"[5]

The first complete translation of a Shakespeare play into German was Caspar Wilhelm von Borck's of *Julius Caesar*. It appeared in 1741. In his review of it, the Leipzig literary critic Johann Christoph Gottsched repeated stock criticisms that he had voiced before: Shakespeare violated the Aristotelian unities of time, place, and action; he allowed commoners to mingle with nobles; he mixed dramatic genres; and he indulged a popular, superstitious taste for ghosts.[6] Gottsched's student, Johann Elias Schlegel—uncle of the brothers who would do so much to Germanize Shakespeare—was more enthusiastic, noting several affinities between Shakespeare and the seventeenth-century German dramatist Andreas Gryphius. Gotthold Ephraim Lessing went one step further. In 1759, in the seventeenth of his "Letters surveying contemporary literature" (*Briefe, die neueste Literatur betreffend*), he came to Shakespeare's defense by accusing Gottsched of literary parochialism:

> "Nobody," say the authors of the *Bibliothek* [*der schönen Wissenschaften*], "will deny that the German stage owes a large part of its initial improvement to Professor Gottsched."
> I am this Nobody [*Niemand*]; I deny it straightaway.[7]

According to Lessing, Gottsched, like Voltaire, overrated the neoclassical rules that had long been *de rigueur* in France. This critical blind spot prevented him from appreciating the "masterpieces of Shakespeare."[8] Like J. E. Schlegel, Lessing highlighted similarities between Shakespearean and German drama, but he went further than Schlegel by maintaining that Shakespeare expressed the spirit of classical Greek tragedy better than Corneille, Racine, and Voltaire: "Next to Sophocles's *Oedipus*, there can be no work that has more power over our passions than *Othello*, or *King Lear*, or *Hamlet*, etc. Does Corneille have a single tragedy that could have moved you even half as much as Voltaire's *Zaire*? And Voltaire's *Zaire*, how inferior is that work to the *Moor of Venice*, of which it is a weak copy ... ?"[9]

Lessing's intervention came to be regarded as a turning point in the burgeoning Shakespeare wars.[10] His salvo against the French must have looked to his contemporaries like a cultural extension of the military campaign that Prussia and other German states were waging in alliance with the British against France (in alliance with Austria, Russia, Sweden, and Saxony).[11] After the war, Goethe celebrated "Shakespeare's Day" in 1771.[12] The encomium he delivered was inspired by a draft of an essay by Johann Gottfried Herder, the third version of which was published in 1773. Much as Nietzsche would later take Shakespeare to be the missing link between Sophocles and Wagner, so Herder represented Shakespeare as the bridge between Sophocles and Goethe.

He criticized the French for treating Aristotle's *Poetics* as if it had been intended to prescribe transcultural aesthetic norms rather than simply to explicate the specific nature of *Greek* tragedy. Every culture required a different form of poetic expression. Given the nature of the Greek polis, it was appropriate for Sophocles to produce tragedies that presented a unified action in a single place at a single time. It was likewise just as appropriate for Shakespeare, in a sprawling nation with a world-historical sensibility, to portray a wide array of people and events. In their own ways, Sophocles and Shakespeare were both true to nature. By contrast, Corneille, Racine, and Voltaire had failed to create anything distinctively French.[13] To avoid making the same mistake, German dramatists had to throw off the neoclassical yoke and cultivate their own national genius. Herder flattered Goethe by placing him at the forefront of such a literary movement. Instead of *imitating* Sophocles and Shakespeare, he was being *inspired* by their examples to create a distinctively German culture.[14]

Herder's enthusiasm for Shakespeare originated during his time as a student in Königsberg. From 1762 to 1764, he studied with both Kant and Kant's anti-Enlightenment rival, Johann Georg Hamann, the "Magus of the North." Kant was deeply suspicious about Hamann's influence on the impressionable young philosopher.[15] Instead of teaching Herder to exercise his reason, Hamann encouraged his flights of fancy. Hamann also introduced Herder to Shakespeare; in fact, he taught Herder English by reading *Hamlet* together with him.[16] The fruits of these lessons appeared in Herder's essay on Shakespeare, in which Hamlet is characterized as a "touching good fellow [*rührende* good fellow]" whose "youthful toying with action [*Jugendspiel der Handlung*] ... runs throughout the play and does not become full action until almost the end [*und fast bis zu Ende keine Handlung wird*]."[17]

In his correspondence with Herder, Kant doesn't refer to either Shakespeare in general or Hamlet in particular. As Sanford Budick has shown, Kant did engage in a longstanding debate with Herder about how philosophers should respond to Milton's "genius of the sublime."[18] Budick plausibly concludes that Kant was much more interested in Milton than in Shakespeare.[19] Yet Kant's lectures on anthropology show that he was familiar with Shakespeare's plays, and that he had a keen interest in the ongoing Shakespeare wars. Beyond repeating the obligatory platitude that Shakespeare was a genius, he refers with admiration to Falstaff's story about being attacked by rogues in buckram suits, and to Rosalind's observations about "who Time ambles withal, who Time trots withal, who Time gallops withal, and who he stands still withal" (*As You Like It* 3.2.309–311).[20] Against a charge of impropriety, he defends Shakespeare's depiction of the Fool in *King Lear*, although the way he characterizes this depiction suggests that he may have known the play only by hearsay.[21] While warning his students not to rely on either Shakespeare or Milton for lessons about human nature, he maintains Shakespeare's genial right not to be fenced in by the Aristotelian unities. On the other side of the critical fence, he echoes the older complaint that Shakespeare's plays exhibit more spirit (*Geist*) than taste (*Geschmack*).[22]

Spirit, as Kant defines it in the *Critique of Judgment* (1790), is "the animating principle" of a mind or work of art. It is the source of aesthetic ideas, poetic images to which no concept of understanding can be fully adequate. A work of art may be academically correct as far as taste is concerned, but if it is lacking in aesthetic ideas it will strike us as insipid or spiritless.[23] Conversely, if it exhibits too much spirit, taste will be offended. Taste must clip, but not pluck, the wings of genius.[24] Kant defines an aesthetic idea as the "counterpart (pendant) of an *idea of reason*, which is, conversely, a concept to which no *intuition* (representation of the imagination) can be adequate."[25] Philosophy trades in ideas of reason, while poetry deals with aesthetic ideas. Aesthetic ideas should stimulate, but not substitute for, rational ideas. Kant repeatedly criticized Herder, as he did Hamann, for conflating the two. In his published reviews of Herder's *Ideas on the Philosophy of the History of Mankind*, he chided Herder for philosophizing in an essentially *rhapsodic* manner, a charge that bears comparison with Socrates's critique of rhapsody in Plato's *Ion*.[26]

Ion of Ephesus was a professional rhapsode who specialized in the recitation and exegesis of Homer. In Plato's dialogue, Socrates accuses him of not being in a position to tell whether Homer's purported knowledge claims were true or false. He admits that Homer was an inspired (i.e., genial) poet who could write beautifully about many technical arts, and that Ion, in turn, could speak beautifully about these passages. He denies, however, that either Homer or Ion could lay claim to genuine knowledge.[27] To admire Homer's poetry for its aesthetic qualities was one thing, but to look to Homer for philosophical insights (even about the nature of beauty) was another. Kant said much the same thing to Herder about the aesthetic ideas that he relied upon. But Herder knew exactly what he was doing. In his essay on Shakespeare, he had pointedly claimed: "genius is more than philosophy and a creator wholly distinct from an analyzer."[28] John Zammito has called this "Herder's not very gracious public declaration of independence from Kant."[29] Beyond defining the literary program of *Sturm und Drang*, Herder was playing Shakespeare's rhapsode against Kant's critical Socrates. What he could have said in response to Kant's critical reviews is what Ion should have said to Socrates, namely, that philosophy is born and bred in poetry—so much so that it may be difficult, if not impossible, to separate rational ideas from aesthetic ideas. He could also have observed that the *Critique of Pure Reason* is thoroughly imbued with aesthetic ideas. The reason Kant wrote in fetters when he wrote about spirit, and at liberty when of the bounds of possible experience, is because he was a true Poet and of Hamlet's party without knowing it.

In his essay "On Four Poetic Formulas That Might Summarize the Kantian Philosophy," Gilles Deleuze writes: "The *Critique of Pure Reason* is the book of Hamlet, the prince of the north."[30] For both Kant and Hamlet, time is out of joint (or "off its hinges [*hors de ses gonds*]," in Yves Bonnefoy's French translation).[31] In the *Critique of Pure Reason*, Kant replaces the traditional conception of time as the measure of the circular movement of the cosmos with a distinctively modern conception according to which time is a pure line to which movement itself is subordinated.[32] Hamlet enacts the same "reversal" by subordinating *his* movements to the passage of time: "Hamlet is the first hero who truly needed time in order to act, whereas earlier heroes were subject to time as the consequence of an original movement (Aeschylus) or an aberrant action (Sophocles)."[33]

Kant's only explicit reference to Hamlet is a note that alludes to the prince's promise to "delve one yard below" the "mines" of Rosencrantz and Guildenstern (3.4.209):

> Dem A̶t̶t̶ Lauscher der Minen kan man einen Unverschämten entgegen setzen, der ihn durch Blik deconcertire, als wolte er jenes seine Ausspäherey beschämen. Hamlet. [The eavesdropper of the mines would be ashamed of his espionage if he were caught in the act by somebody who boldly reprimanded him with a look. Hamlet.][34]

This note may have been written in response to Moses Mendelssohn's 1758 essay "On the Sublime and Naive in the Fine Sciences." In this essay, Mendelssohn characterizes Hamlet's soliloquies as "sublime," praising "the genius of Shakespeare whenever he had to portray melancholy." He goes on to offer a brief comment on Hamlet's rebuke of Guildenstern ("'Sblood, do you think I am easier to be play'd on than a pipe?" [3.2.369–370]): "Must not the audience be as taken aback as Guildenstern who senses the Prince's superior sagacity and leaves the scene full of shame?"[35] Whether or not Kant was responding to Mendelssohn, his portrait of an eavesdropper caught in the act of spying nicely anticipates a fuller description in Sartre:

> Let us imagine that moved by jealousy, curiosity, or vice I have just glued my ear to the door and looked through a keyhole. I am alone and on the level of a non-thetic self-consciousness. This means first of all that there is no self to inhabit my consciousness, nothing therefore to which I can refer my acts in order to qualify them. They are in no way *known*; I *am my acts* and hence they carry in themselves their whole justification. …
>
> But all of a sudden I hear footsteps in the hall. Someone is looking at me! What does this mean? It means that I am suddenly affected in my being and that essential modifications appear in my structure—modifications which I can apprehend and fix conceptually by means of the reflective *cogito*.[36]

In this passage, Sartre is developing a Kantian thesis, namely, that there is a difference between the empty representation "I think" that "must *be able* to accompany all my representations" and the empirical ego that I am as an object of inner sense.[37] Unlike Sartre, Kant doesn't base the capacity for inner sense on intersubjective recognition (at least not explicitly), but his remark about Hamlet could be taken to suggest that the ability to apprehend oneself as an object of reflection presupposes the ability to see oneself as others see one. Sartre remarks that in order to understand what it is like to be a waiter I must pretend to *be* the waiter in the same way that an actor pretends to be Hamlet.[38] Since the essence of consciousness is negativity for Sartre, Hamlet's own negativity would personify Kantian subjectivity.

Once again, Deleuze makes this link explicit, noting that the Kantian subject, like Hamlet, is divided into a "passive" self that appears in time and an atemporal "active" self that relates to the passive self as an "other": "Hamlet displays his eminently Kantian character whenever he appears as a passive existence, who, like an actor or sleeper, receives the activity of his own thought as an Other, which is nonetheless capable of giving him a dangerous power that defies pure reason. ... Hamlet is not a man of skepticism or doubt, but the man of the Critique."[39] If the Other who thinks in me has the character of a spirit or ghost, it can only be an object of negative faith.

On August 10, 1763—six months after Russian troops withdrew from Königsberg at the close of the Seven Years' War—Kant wrote to a Prussian general's daughter named Charlotte von Knobloch about the "amazing gifts" of the visionary scholar Emanuel Swedenborg.[40] He warned his correspondent to season her admiration for a while as the tale he was about to relate might "activate a shudder, the sort ... evoked by a repetition of one's childhood experiences [*Erziehungseindrücke*]"—a description that anticipates Freud's account of the cause of a sense of the uncanny. Kant further anticipates Freud in professing not to be easily moved by things that make other people shudder: "Regardless of the many tales of apparitions and actions in the realm of spirits that I have heard, I have always submitted these stories to the test of sound reason and have been inclined to regard such tales with skepticism. ... I am therefore not inclined to be afraid of graveyards or the dark." Such was Kant's disposition when he first "became acquainted with the stories about Herr Swedenborg." According to one of these stories, while dining in Gothenburg on the night of July 19, 1759, Swedenborg suddenly announced that a fire had broken out 250 miles away in Stockholm. His detailed description of the event was later confirmed by eyewitnesses. On another occasion he was said to have prevented a goldsmith from cheating the widow of a Dutch envoy by finding out from her dead husband where he had hidden the receipt for a silver tea-service.[41]

At first Kant was as skeptical about these tales of the supernatural as Horatio is about the reports of the Ghost at the beginning of *Hamlet*. As Marcellus tells

Barnardo: "Horatio says 'tis but our fantasy, / And will not let belief take hold of him / Touching this dreaded sight twice seen of us" (1.1.23–25). Horatio confirms his skepticism with the condescending words, "Tush, tush, 'twill not appear" (1.1.30). When the dreaded sight does reappear, he shudders with a sense of uncanniness: "It harrows me with fear and wonder" (1.1.44). Like Horatio, Kant could not at first let belief take hold of him touching the stories about Swedenborg. Yet in his letter to Charlotte von Knobloch he emphasizes the credibility of the witnesses. He knew "a fine gentleman, an Englishman," who testified in a letter that "the most respectable people in Stockholm" had assured him of the veracity of the contents of yet another letter touching on the visions of Swedenborg. The epistemic force of this epistolary chain might seem to be attenuated by its sheer metonymy, but Kant confesses to being "stunned" (stußig) by the "credibility of such a report."[42] In the same way that Hamlet's remembrance of his father ("methinks I see my father" [1.2.184]) predisposes him to accept Horatio and Marcellus's testimony before he himself sees the Ghost, Kant's faith in the reality of immaterial spiritual substances predisposed him to think that under special conditions it might be possible for disembodied spirits to communicate with the living. Yet despite or perhaps because of his eagerness to believe the reports about Swedenborg, he suspended his "own judgments about this slippery business," predicting that "people who possess far greater talents than mine will be unable to draw any reliable conclusions from it."[43]

By 1766, he had ceased to take the stories about Swedenborg seriously. In "Dreams of a Spirit-Seer Elucidated by Dreams of Metaphysics" he chides himself for his earlier credulity. He had never believed that disembodied spirits could be perceived with our bodily sense organs, but he had speculated about the possibility that our imaginations might register their nonbodily interactions with our souls. In such a case, one's imagination would project an external image of the encountered spirit.[44] The projected image would seem to appear to the senses. Unfortunately, there was no way to distinguish such an occasioned projection from a mere hallucination: Is this a spirit which I see before me?

When Macbeth encounters the "air-drawn dagger" (3.4.61) that leads him to Duncan, he cannot say whether it is a real dagger or "a dagger of the mind, a false creation / Proceeding from the heat-oppressed brain" (2.1.38–39). He is equally uncertain about the ghost of Banquo, which he ambiguously calls "horrible shadow! / Unreal mock'ry" (3.4.105–106). Either of these two phantasms could be nothing more than "the very painting of [his] fear" (3.4.60), but he cannot know for sure. Brutus is just as uncertain about the ghost of Caesar, paradoxically addressing it with the question "Art thou any thing?" (4.3.278).[45] In response to his further entreaty—"Speak to me what thou art"—the apparition replies, "Thy evil spirit, Brutus" (4.3.281–282). After it vanishes, Brutus rouses Lucius, Varro, and Claudius in the hope that they will confirm his vision: "Saw you any thing?" (4.3.304). Their negative responses settle nothing—just as nothing is settled by the fact that Gertrude sees nothing in the closet scene in Hamlet.[46] Well before Shakespeare, there was a long-standing belief that spirits could selectively manifest themselves to particular individuals—especially, as we have seen, to those prone to melancholy. Kant was aware of this tradition. In "Observations on the Feeling of the Beautiful and Sublime" (1764), he distinguishes benign melancholy (Melancholie)—the most "noble" of the four temperaments—from pathological melancholy (Schwermut).[47] The latter made one susceptible to fantastic visions like those of Swedenborg. In principle, Ficino was justified in allowing that a genial melancholic might be able to communicate with disembodied spirits, but there was no way to distinguish a genuine visitation from sheer fantasy. Imaginary projections were essentially no different from ghost stories, providing indirect evidence at best. The visions of someone suffering from pathological melancholy were particularly unreliable. Hamlet, knowing himself to be melancholy, has good reason to consult the more balanced Horatio.[48] Perhaps Kant, who regarded himself as temperamentally melancholy, felt the same way about the fine Englishman he mentioned to Charlotte von Knobloch.

Kant never repudiated the theoretical possibility of interaction with disembodied spirits. In both "Dreams of a Spirit-Seer" and the Critique of Pure Reason, he merely stresses the impossibility of verifying such an event. He continued to believe that human souls were immortal and would eventually exist in another state. Indeed, he regarded this belief as essential to morality. The hypothesis of a realm of spirits to which we ourselves belong was justified not as a positive doctrine but as a defensive weapon against reductive materialism.[49] Reductive materialism was no less overreaching than dogmatic spiritualism. Nevertheless, visions like those of Swedenborg had to be explained mechanistically rather than spiritualistically—that is, from the standpoint of empirical rather than rational psychology. In "Dreams," Kant set out to provide such an explanation by speculating about what might be wrong with Swedenborg's brain.

Kant's speculative neuroscience begins with the phenomenological observation that when we perceive an external object, our brains represent it as existing not in our heads but in the place where it is actually located. Kant conjectures that this is a result of the fact that the "direction-lines" of our stimulated nerves converge at the imaginary focal point where the object exists in space. What ordinarily prevents us from confusing the objects we imagine with genuine objects of perception is not the greater vivacity of the latter but the fact that the direction-lines of our nerve-imaginings typically converge inside rather than outside our heads. During sleep we lose our sense of our bodily boundaries and so also our sense of the difference between imagination and perception. This explains both the apparent reality of dreams while we are sleeping and why dreams lose their sense of reality when we awaken. It also explains what happens when we daydream. Swedenborg's hallucinations could be explained in a similar manner. Since they were more vivid than mere daydreams, he naturally affirmed their reality. In principle, however, he could be cured of his delusional beliefs by coming to understand that the spirits he seemed to see before him were nothing but the fictions of his "heat-oppressed brain" (*Macbeth* 2.1.39).[50]

Turning his clinical gaze upon himself, Kant goes on to diagnose the illusions to which metaphysicians are prone. These illusions arise when two parallel lines of reasoning seem to converge at imaginary focal points outside the brains of philosophers. One line of reasoning is regressive and *a posteriori*. It seeks to identify the mechanical causes of empirically given objects and events. This is the path of reasoning pursued in the natural sciences. Its work is interminable, for we know *a priori* that every empirical discovery conceals a further mystery; chains of scientific explanation never reach absolute grounds. Knowing this, yet desirous of grounds that are both absolute and immaterial (i.e., spiritual), rationalist metaphysicians reason in the opposite direction. Instead of regressively seeking absolute grounds for empirically given phenomena, they posit such grounds *a priori* and then seek to progress from them toward the empirical phenomena from which the regressive line of reasoning begins. Unfortunately, this path proves to be no less interminable than the first. Just as natural science can never reach absolute metaphysical grounds, so rationalist metaphysics can never reach empirically given phenomena. In brief, the two lines of reasoning never converge. To the rationalist metaphysician this is dispiriting—literally—for it divests the natural world of any demonstrable spiritual dimension. Instead of acknowledging the gap between the two lines of reasoning, the metaphysicians disavow it by *squinting*. Squinting imparts a slight bend, or clinamen, to each of the two lines, enabling the metaphysicians to believe—or to *pretend* to believe—that they really converge: "Rather than follow the straight line of reasoning, they would rather impart to their arguments an imperceptible clinamen by stealthily squinting [*verstohlen hinschielten*] at the target of certain experiences or testimonies."[51]

"Looking awry" at the stories about Swedenborg, Kant had let himself dream a dream not unlike Bottom's—that is, one that had "no bottom" (4.1.216), no absolute ground. He knew that the regressive path of empirical psychology could never disclose genuine Puckish spirits, just as he knew that the progressive path of rational psychology could never return to Athens. Nevertheless, he had let himself imagine that it was possible for the two worlds to converge.

The sophistical ruse of the dogmatic metaphysician can be likened to what Freud calls "fetishistic disavowal." According to Freud, a fetish is a substitute for something that was once fervently "believed in" by a young boy, namely, his mother's penis.[52] The fetishist disavows his later discovery that this belief was just an illusion. Disavowal takes the form of a compromise. According to the inferentially blocked logic of this compromise (a kind of speculative *akrasia*), I know very well that there is a gap where previously I believed there was an object. I do not close my eyes to this negative fact—the fact that something is "missing." But instead of accepting the consequences of this fact, I squint. With crossed or half-closed eyes I act *as* if there really were something there. Squinting is thus a way of giving airy nothing a local habitation and a name. It is a way of pinning the phallus on the mother—not by groping in the dark, but by bending rays of light. Kant likens this procedure to that of "the romantic author" who "makes his heroine flee to distant countries so that, by means of an [sic] happy adventure, she may accidentally meet her admirer."[53] Such pleasant diversions might be "allowed to penetrate the chambers of lovely women" like Charlotte von Knobloch—or Hippolyta—but they are not for men governed by cool reason.[54] It was Kant's "fate," he says, to have "fallen in love" with metaphysics, a mistress from whom he could "boast of only a few favours." He had hoped to meet his mistress in the distant land where his own imagination had placed her. Now he admits that this was just a fantasy. Instead of continuing to indulge in fairy toys, he proposes to wed metaphysics in another key, namely, as "a science of the *limits of human reason*."[55] He will not be able to satisfy all of his original desires, but he will accept the gap between human understanding and the absolute grounds that reason wishes to embrace.

Similar to the gap between understanding and reason is that between aesthetic and rational ideas. To forsake the extravagant dreams of metaphysics is, in part, to sustain the gap between poetry and philosophy. Kant did not disapprove of fairy toys like *A Midsummer Night's Dream* (the first of the plays that Wieland translated and the only one he versified), but his attitude toward them was similar to that of Shakespeare's Theseus—to whom Hamann had implicitly compared the young Kant in a letter from 1759.[56] Theseus represents plays as pleasant distractions, ways of passing a "torturing hour" or "lazy time." Kant had a slightly higher estimation. The aesthetic ideas that poetry presented were necessary supplements to rational ideas. Nevertheless, he agreed with Theseus that aesthetic experience was essentially a form of leisure and that poetic imagination should be kept subordinate to reason. "Ghost stories," he observes, are welcomed late at night" since night is an appropriate time for "*play*," but they are "found to be distasteful … and entirely inappropriate for conversation as soon as we get up the following morning," morning being a time for serious "*business*."[57] Night should not be made joint-laborer with the day: there is a time for play(s) and a time for work.

"Dreams of a Spirit-Seer" was published in the same year as Wieland's translation of *Hamlet* (1766). Gothic literature had just come into vogue:

Henry Walpole's *Hamlet*-infused (and Voltaire-baiting) *The Castle of Otranto* was published in 1765 (though not translated into German until 1794).[58] In *Die Hamburgische Dramaturgie* on June 5, 1767, Lessing returned to the Shakespeare wars. In the preface to his 1748 play *Sémiramis*, Voltaire had compared his depiction of the specter (*spectre*) of the Assyrian King Ninus to Shakespeare's depiction of the ghost (*ombre*) of King Hamlet. Although *Hamlet* as a whole was a "gross and barbarous piece" that "would never be borne by the lowest of the rabble [*la plus vile populace*] in France or Italy," Shakespeare's ghost was worthy of emulation. What made a ghost dramatically effective was not the audience's or reader's actual belief in ghosts (Voltaire observes that ancient Roman philosophers no more believed in ghosts than did modern Englishmen and Frenchmen) but rather their sense of poetic justice:

> It must be acknowledged, that, among the beauties that shine forth in the midst of all these horrid extravagancies, the ghost of Hamlet's father is one of the most striking: it has always a strong effect on the English. … This ghost inspires more terror, even in the reading, than the apparition of Darius in the "Persians" of Æschylus: and why does it? because Darius … only appears to foretell the misfortunes of his family; whereas, in Shakespeare, the ghost of Hamlet appears to demand vengeance and to reveal secret crimes. It is neither useless, nor brought in by force, but serves to convince mankind, that there is an invisible power, the master of nature. All men have a sense of justice imprinted on their hearts, and naturally wish that heaven would interest itself in the cause of innocence: in every age, therefore, and in every nation, they will behold with pleasure, the Supreme Being engaged in the punishment of crimes which could not come within the reach of human laws.[59]

In his response to Voltaire, Lessing argued that there was in fact a difference between ancient and modern attitudes toward ghosts: "All antiquity believed in ghosts," so "the dramatic poets of antiquity were right in availing themselves of this belief." Modern dramatists didn't have "the same right."[60] This didn't mean that ghosts should be banished from the stage. New poetic techniques were needed to represent them in a psychologically effective manner. Knowing that we "laugh at ghosts by day, and shudder at ghost-stories at night," Shakespeare has his ghost appear only after midnight.[61] Less effectively, Voltaire portrays the ghost of Ninus in broad daylight; instead of making us shudder, the effect is slightly ridiculous. Another effective technique of Shakespeare's is to restrict his ghost's appearance to a small number of characters, and to have it speak only to Hamlet. During the closet scene: "Our whole attention is fixed upon Hamlet, and the more signs we observe in him of a mind excited by horror, so much the more ready are we to hold the apparition that has this effect upon him for what it really is."[62] This effect is far more psychologically riveting than the scene in which Voltaire's ghost addresses a large crowd of people. In Coleridgean terms, while reading or watching *Ninus* we have to suspend our disbelief in an entirely voluntary manner, but while reading or watching *Hamlet* we find our disbelief suspended for us by Shakespeare. His ability to work on our imaginary forces is the mark of his poetic genius.[63] Anticipating Herder's "declaration of independence," Lessing proclaims that "genius defies all our philosophy, and knows how to make things, which cold reason ridicules, fearful to the imagination."[64] The philosopher's shudder may vanish with the night, but during the night we are kept in a state of suspense or *epoché*.

As we have seen, Freud associates the technique of eliciting an involuntary shudder not with Shakespeare, but with Hoffmann. Shakespeare alerts us from the beginning of his supernatural plays that to enter their fictional worlds we must voluntarily suspend our disbelief.[65] From this point of view, there is no essential difference between the specters of Ninus and King Hamlet.[66] It is difficult to say whether Kant would have agreed with Freud or Lessing, but given his views about aesthetic ideas he might have praised Shakespeare for effectively symbolizing the metaphysical wavering to which human reason is naturally subject. Kant wavered between natural and supernatural explanations of the visions of Swedenborg. Even after writing "Dreams of a Spirit-Seer" he continued to be tempted by the dreams of metaphysics. In his *Inaugural Dissertation* (1770), he introduced the idea that space and time were nothing more than forms of human sensibility. It was necessary to distinguish the sensible world of appearances from an intelligible world of things in themselves. The latter was a realm of spirits that couldn't be perceived but could be known through the use of pure concepts of understanding. This neat metaphysical division enabled Kant to revive his earlier belief that spirits were more than just objects of faith. They could be known to exist not through imaginary projections—these would only be further appearances—but through intellectual intuitions. Sensibility and understanding ran on separate tracks that didn't have to converge in the distance. To apprehend the spiritual world, it was sufficient to recognize reason's warrant to posit, and indeed cognize, supersensible substances.

By 1781, Kant had changed his mind again. In the *Critique of Pure Reason* he continued to maintain that spatiotemporal objects were mere appearances, but he now denied that it was possible for us to cognize purely intelligible entities (noumena). Only now did he fully make good on his promise in "Dreams" to establish metaphysics as a science of the bounds of human reason. In the *Inaugural Dissertation* he had resisted the charm of ghost stories by separating sensibility from understanding, but he had allowed spirits to be intellectually intuited. In the *Critique* he restricts the use of the categories of human understanding to the determination of spatiotemporal appearances. Reason is entitled to *posit* the objects of the metaphysical ideas it derives from the categories, but in doing so it subjects us to an inevitable illusion. In its structure, this illusion is akin to that of Swedenborg. Just as Swedenborg's hallucinations arose from the convergence of neural vectors at *foci imaginarii* outside his brain, so metaphysical illusions arise through the convergence of principles of understanding in a *focus imaginarius* beyond the bounds of possible experience. Restricted to possible experience, these principles tell us that everything conditioned has a condition. Through a series of dialectical inferences, reason extends them until they converge in metaphysical ideas of unconditioned conditions. We cannot intuit the objects of these ideas, but it seems as though we can—for just as Swedenborg naturally mistook the projections of his own imagination for objects of perception, so we naturally mistake the projections of our own reason for objects of understanding. Kant identifies three sets of rational illusions: *paralogisms* that represent our souls as simple spiritual substances, *antinomies* that represent the empirical world either as a closed totality or as an infinite whole, and an *ideal* that represents the ultimate source of reality as a perfect being. Each of these illusions plays a regulative role in experience, bidding us to strive to attain maximal comprehension of ourselves and the world. Nevertheless, they remain illusions, "dreams of metaphysics." To see through them, it is necessary to rouse reason from its "dogmatic slumber."[67] Seeing through them is not the same thing as making them disappear. Just as Swedenborg couldn't stop hallucinating but could stop himself from being taken in by his hallucinations, so we can't stop projecting metaphysical illusions but can stop being taken in by them. The difference is that Swedenborg's hallucinations arose from a defective brain, while the dreams of metaphysics arise from healthy reason. Ordinary dreams have a vital purpose: they prevent us from dying in our sleep.[68] Analogously, metaphysical dreams prevent us from succumbing to two forms of spiritual death—one cognitive (that of a "lifeless" understanding that would settle for piecemeal knowledge of the world) and one practical (that of a morally "dead" will unable to sustain its effort to achieve the highest good).

In "Dreams," Kant traced the source of metaphysical illusions to culpable squinting that made parallel lines converge. In the *Critique*, he develops a new optical metaphor based on Newton's explanation of how rays of light converge at imaginary focal points beyond the surface of a mirror. When we look "into" a mirror, we seem to see behind its surface objects that are in fact located behind us. This illusion enables us to extend the scope of our vision. The projections of reason work in precisely the same manner except that they don't show us any actual objects. Implicitly turning Plato's allegory of the cave against Plato's theory of forms, Kant's metaphor suggests that we are like prisoners who project our own ideas onto a concave surface that functions exactly like a mirror. Within the imaginary depth of this mirror, we seem to see objects that we ourselves have projected. This gives rise to the Platonic illusion that if only we could turn around—if only we could free our understanding from the spatiotemporal constraints imposed by our sensibility—we would directly apprehend the *objects* of our ideas.

In "Dreams," Kant hadn't fully distinguished the self-deceptions of metaphysicians from involuntary metaphysical illusions. If only the metaphysicians looked at things aright, their dreams would have "melted into air, into thin air" (*The Tempest* 4.1.150). In the *Critique*, he completes the analogy between Swedenborg's hallucinations and the dreams of metaphysicians by arguing that human reason is hardwired to posit transcendent metaphysical objects. Metaphysical illusion is not a matter of self-deception. We succumb to self-deception only when we disavow the lessons of critique. Such a disavowal would involve another type of squinting—the kind that would enable us to convince ourselves that we actually do possess a faculty of intellectual intuition. Kant believed that Fichte succumbed to this temptation in his 1794 *Wissenschaftslehre*. According to Fichte, Kant had failed to see that the very possibility of critical philosophy rested on the philosopher's intellectual intuition of himself.[69] Through an act of self-positing, the subject distinguished itself from its other, but this in no way left it cut off from any thing in itself. In an open letter to Fichte, Kant rejected this line of argument, accusing Fichte of trying to demonstrate metaphysical truths on the basis of pure logic.[70] The supposition that we could intellectually intuit ourselves was the basis of reason's paralogisms. It arose from a confusion of the *logical* subject of thought (expressed in the representation "I think") with the *real* (but unknown) subject in which our thinking inheres.[71] Self-positing amounted to nothing more than apperception (self-consciousness) and not to an intellectual intuition of the metaphysical *thing* underlying our thoughts. Fichte's mistake was either not to grasp the import of Kant's critique of the paralogisms or else *to grasp but disavow it*—a lapse into culpable squinting.

Kant's critique of the optical illusions of reason is foreshadowed by Sir John Bushy in Shakespeare's *Richard II*. Queen Isabel, grieving at the departure of her "sweet Richard" (2.2.9), is filled with "nameless woe" (2.2.40):

> Some unborn sorrow, ripe in fortune's womb,
> Is coming towards me, and my inward soul
> With nothing trembles; at some thing it grieves,
> More than with parting from my lord the King.
> (2.2.10–13)

Seeking to comfort the Queen, Bushy explains that

> sorrow's eyes, glazed with blinding tears,
> Divides one thing entire to many objects,

Like perspectives, which rightly gaz'd upon,
Show nothing but confusion; ey'd awry
Distinguish form; so your sweet Majesty,
Looking awry upon your lord's departure,
Finds shapes of grief, more than himself, to wail,
Which, look'd on as it is, is nought but shadows
Of what it is not.
(2.2.16–24)

Looking awry is like metaphysical squinting. Both involve the imagination, which represents something where in fact there is nothing. But the Queen (like Fichte) is not convinced by this line of argument. She does not profess to see something where in fact there is nothing; her point is that she *sees nothing*; and it is the sight of nothing itself that makes her tremble in anticipation at the *pending* appearance of something other than the return of the king.[72] Her rejoinder to Bushy recalls Hippolyta's resistance to Theseus's dismissal of the metaphysical dreams of "the lunatic, the lover, and the poet" (5.1.7) in *A Midsummer Night's Dream*. In the guise of a critical philosopher, Theseus patiently explains how "imagination bodies forth / The forms of things unknown" (5.1.14–15), turning a bushy nothing into a bearish something. Unpersuaded, Hippolyta persists in regarding the confluence of the lovers' reported dreams as "strange and admirable" (*A Midsummer Night's Dream* 5.1.27). In a similar manner, Queen Isabel dismisses Bushy's effort to brush aside her sense of foreboding. She does not deny that her premonition of an impending something is caused by brooding on nothing—"I cannot but be sad; so heavy sad, / As, though on thinking on no thought I think, / Makes me with heavy nothing faint and shrink" (2.2.30–32)—but she regards her melancholy as prophetic (i.e., genial) rather than fanatical. Her presentiment of nothing she can *sensibly* intuit is quickly confirmed by Green's report that the banished Bolingbroke has taken advantage of the king's absence to return to England. At this disheartening news she renounces the false comfort that Bushy has just offered her:

I will despair, and be at enmity
With cozening hope. He is a flatterer,
A parasite, a keeper-back of death,
Who gently would dissolve the bands of life,
Which false hope lingers in extremity.
(2.2.68–72)

Despite this denunciation of hope, just a few lines later she bids the Duke of York to "speak comfortable words" (2.2.76). Her oscillation between hope and despair is repeated by Richard when he returns to England. He too eventually settles on despair, rebuking his cousin Aumerle: "By heaven, I'll hate him everlastingly / That bids me be of comfort any more" (3.2.207–208).[73] Like the unkinged Lear, Richard must learn that kings are not ague-proof. Hope prevents nominal kings and commoners alike from coming to terms with the impending nothingness of death: "What e'er I be, / Nor I, nor any man that but man is, / With nothing shall be pleas'd, till he be eas'd / With being nothing" (5.5.38–41). In the passage cited above the Queen seems to go one step further, expressing an actual longing for nothingness. Her repudiation of wide-eyed, Bushy-hailed optimism suggests that the "thing of nothing" on which melancholy subjects dwell is not absolute nothingness but an uncanny Thing or *Unding* that comes into view precisely when one looks at it awry. The king is not yet dead, but already the queen is haunted by his ghost—a distinctive feature of melancholia.[74]

In the preface to the first edition of the *Critique of Pure Reason*, Kant represents metaphysics as the "queen of the sciences." The queen was once honored, but now "the matron, outcast and forsaken, mourns like Hecuba: *Modo maxima rerum, tot generis natisque potens—nunc trahor exul, inops* [Greatest of all things by birth and power, now I am exiled and destitute]." Prior to her dethronement, the queen had been a dogmatic despot, so it is not surprising that her skeptical subjects rebelled (as do Richard's). The subsequent history of metaphysics has been a seemingly interminable conflict not unlike the Trojan War (as Kant's reference to Hecuba implies) or Shakespeare's depiction of the Wars of the Roses. Like Bushy, Kant promises to comfort his queen. The king may be absent, but there is consolation in faith. The queen should not despair and be at enmity with hope, for when hope is guided by a sense of moral duty it is a wise counselor, not a cozening flatterer.

If Kant's aim is to comfort the queen, we may wonder why he chooses Ovid's Hecuba—the classical figure of an *inconsolable* queen—to personify metaphysics. When Hecuba utters the lament that Kant quotes, Priam is not merely absent but dead, and Hecuba will never reign again. Kant's prosopopoeia seems to work against his philosophical intention. Perhaps its purpose is to represent the critical philosopher as a modern Aeneas, the founder of a new Troy. The *translatio imperii* would serve as an apt metaphor for Kant's ambition to found a philosophical republic in which rational disputes could be adjudicated by law. The negative task of the *Critique* would be to explain why the dogmatically metaphysical Trojans were defeated by the skeptical Greeks. Its positive task would be to show how a new Troy could be founded on republican principles.

In *Troilus and Cressida*, Shakespeare represents the Trojan War as a contest between idealizing Trojans and skeptical Greeks.[75] Troilus personifies the downfall of the Trojan cause. While acknowledging that it would be more reasonable to give Helen back to the Greeks than to keep her, he dogmatically defends the worthiness of the Trojan cause. Paradoxically, the same blinkered idealism makes him acquiesce into giving Cressida to the Greeks in exchange for Antenor. When Ulysses provides him with an opportunity to see Cressida give his sleeve to Diomedes, he becomes, like Othello, "perplexed in the extreme" (*Othello* 5.2.346). His description of his state of shock is akin to Kant's description of reason's discovery of its antinomies—the apparently contradictory metaphysical doctrines whose clashes Kant likens to the Trojan War:

> O madness of discourse,
> That cause sets up with and against itself!
> Bi-fold authority, where reason can revolt
> Without perdition, and loss assume all reason
> Without revolt.
>
> (5.2.142–146)

Troilus's initial response is to deny that Cressida was ever really there. When Ulysses replies "Most sure she was" (5.2.126), he refuses to admit it: "Let it not be believ'd for womanhood! Think we had *mothers*" (5.2.129–130, my italics). To save the honor of Hecuba (as well as that of Priam), Troilus distinguishes the *empirical* Cressida ("Diomed's Cressida" [5.2.137]) from the *transcendent* Cressida (his Cressida). But he cannot sustain this conceit. Instead of dividing Cressida in two, he becomes disillusioned. While pledging to continue the fight—and to defeat Diomedes—he will prove in the end unable to save the honor of Hecuba or to prevent the queen from weeping at the death of Hector. Equally unable to defeat Diomedes or to found a new Troy, Troilus effectively symbolizes a dogmatic discoverer of antinomies who fails to resolve them critically. The baton must pass to Aeneas.

Kant is the critical Aeneas. Each of the antinomies pits a dogmatic metaphysical thesis against a skeptical antithesis. Kant critically resolves them by distinguishing the empirical world of appearances from a transcendent world of things in themselves. Nothing can be known about things in themselves, but we are obliged to represent ourselves as members of a kingdom of ends presided over by an empirically absent "king of kings." Such is the comfort Kant offers his queen. After restricting her domain to this moral sphere, Kant once again personifies her as Hecuba. The words he gives her this time are those of Virgil rather than Ovid. Reflecting on the futility of a belated defense of the old dogmatic metaphysics, he repeats the words that Hecuba utters to Priam just before he is killed: *Non defensoribus istis tempus eget* ("The time does not need these defenses").[76] This is not an admission of defeat but a reiteration of the need for a *critical* defense of the Trojan cause. The *Critique of Pure Reason* is a philosophical *Aeneid*—an epic account of the continuation of the spirit of Troy through the founding of a new legal order.

Kant regarded Virgil as a more polished poet than Shakespeare: "Genius is for the most part coarse like Shakespeare—he lacks polish; Homer, too. The virtuoso polishes it away; Virgil is like this."[77] Despite this remark, Kant's very admiration for Virgil makes him less an antique Roman than a Dane. Like the author of the *Critique of Pure Reason*, Hamlet is led by the perception of a contemporary crisis to think (as so many of Shakespeare's characters do) of "Aeneas' tale to Dido, and thereabout of it especially when he speaks of Priam's slaughter" (2.2.446–448). Just as Troilus is troubled by the painful discovery that the empirical Cressida doesn't match his idealized image of her, so Hamlet is troubled by the painful realization that Gertrude is not an inconsolable queen like Hecuba. Moreover, just as Troilus reasons from Cressida's perceived infidelity to the besmirching of Hecuba's honor, so Hamlet reasons from Gertrude's perceived infidelity to that of Ophelia, as if the empirical Ophelia ("Diomed's" Ophelia) could no longer be the Ophelia he has idealized (the one of whom he can say "I lov'd Ophelia" [5.1.269]).[78] Hecuba is to Hamlet precisely what she is to Troilus and Kant: the model of a faithful queen, one who would never let a second husband kiss her in bed. What grieves him is the fact that Gertrude's mourning wasn't perpetual, that she remarried after following his "poor father's body, / Like Niobe, all tears" (1.2.148–149).[79] He is inconsolable because she isn't. It is he rather than she who, brooding on an absent king, is visited by the Thing that, when gazed upon directly (as she looks upon it in the closet scene), is nothing.[80] Imploring the dry-eyed queen to look at the spirit of his father through the anamorphizing prism of his own melancholy tears, he asks: "Do you see nothing there?" (3.4.131).

The fact that Hamlet wishes Gertrude's mourning were as interminable as Hecuba's doesn't preclude his wanting to comfort her. If he is cruel, it is only to be kind. But first she must renounce her bestial lust: "Confess yourself to heaven, / Repent what's past, avoid what is to come, / And do not spread the compost on the weeds / To make them ranker" (3.4.149–152). In precisely the same manner, Kant wants to comfort his mobled queen, but first she must be rescued from all suggestion of empirical taint. "The birth of the purported queen" had been "traced to the rabble of common experience" by Locke and Hume.[81] According to Hume, the allegedly pure concept of causality was not her legitimate child but rather an empirical bastard:

> *Hume* ... called upon reason, which pretends to have generated this concept in her womb, to give him an account of by what right she thinks: that something could be so constituted that, if it is posited, something else necessarily must thereby also be posited. ... He concluded that reason completely and fully deceives herself with this concept, falsely taking it for her own child, when it is really nothing but a bastard of the imagination, which, impreg-

nated by experience, and having brought certain representations under the law of association, passes off the resulting subjective necessity (i.e., habit) for an objective necessity (from insight).[82]

Saving the honor of Hecuba is the first step toward comforting her. She need not despair, for although the king is absent his very absence is a sign that his kingdom is intelligible rather than sensible.

Charlotte von Knobloch seems to have been "the last young woman" with whom Kant corresponded in his precritical period.[83] Between the letter about Swedenborg and the publication of "Dreams," she married a Captain Friedrich von Klingsporn. Although there is absolutely no evidence that she and Kant were romantically involved, she disappears from Kant's correspondence at just about the time that he becomes a confirmed bachelor. We met the figure of an abandoned beloved in Kant's analogy with the mistress whom the poet places in a distant land. Somewhere along the way Kant abandoned the image of a metaphysical beloved whose favors he hoped to enjoy in favor of the image of a chaste mistress whose honor he could preserve. This conversion is similar to the one that Troilus undergoes when he renounces his love for Cressida while redoubling his commitment to the Trojan cause.[84] He doesn't allow his perception of Cressida's infidelity to call into question Hecuba's honor. In psychoanalytic terms, he responds to a trauma concerning feminine desire by dividing the feminine imago in two. Hamlet and Kant do something similar. Hamlet distinguishes two images of his mother (the one who married his father and the one who married Claudius) and two images of Ophelia (the one living and the one dead). For Kant, the good mother is a "veiled goddess": "The veiled goddess, before whom we bow the knee, is the moral law within us in its inviolable majesty."[85] The bad mother is nature in her "stepmotherly" aspect.[86] These two images are both present in an experience of the sublime. When we encounter something in nature that overwhelms our sensibility, we are reminded of the purely rational idea of something absolutely great or sublime. Reason asks the imagination to exhibit an object adequate to this idea, but the imagination is unable to comply with the demand. This failure on the part of our imagination—the failure, as it were, of the poet in us—causes us pain, but we quickly pass from aesthetic disappointment to aesthetic satisfaction at this very failure.[87] The basis of this satisfaction is the "feeling of spirit."[88] Our inability even to *imagine* (let alone perceive) an intelligible world of spirits confirms rather than disconfirms our ability to *think* and *enact* one.

The negative task of the *Critique of Pure Reason* is to prevent human reason from dogmatically affirming metaphysical illusions. The illusions themselves cannot be eradicated, and are even required as objects of faith. Coleridge provides an aesthetic "Analogon" of this metaphysical picture when he distinguishes poetic illusions from delusions, representing the former as objects of an essentially negative faith. Contrasting the "merely *suggested*" images of *Paradise Lost* with the fantastic images that Klopstock "*derived* from Scripture history," he writes:

> That *illusion*, contradistinguished from *delusion*, that *negative* faith, which simply permits the images presented to work by their own force, without either denial or affirmation of their real existence by the judgment, is rendered impossible by their immediate neighbourhood to words and facts of known and absolute truth. A faith, which transcends even historic belief, must absolutely *put out* this mere poetic Analogon of faith, as the summer sun is said to extinguish our household fires, when it shines full upon them. What would otherwise have been yielded to as pleasing fiction, is repelled as revolting falsehood.[89]

Coleridge is here applying to poetry the philosophical distinction that Kant draws between metaphysical illusion and delusional fanaticism. The critical belief or faith that Kant espouses in the *Critique of Pure Reason* is grounded in a suspension of knowledge claims about the illusions of reason. In this precise sense, critical faith is equivalent to the negative faith that Coleridge associates not only with Milton's images but with Shakespeare's representation of the Ghost in *Hamlet*.[90] For Coleridge, who recognized Kant's affinity with Hamlet, negative faith—or "poetic faith," or the "willing suspension of disbelief"—is a way of responding to images or "shadows of imagination."[91] For Kant, the negative faith of the judgment of the sublime not only suspends all judgment about images; it suspends the images themselves. As Coleridge knew, however, this result is achieved only through the positing of the very images that reason discards as inadequate to its idea. As he explains in a lecture summarized by John Payne Collier: "These were the grandest effects, where the imagination was called forth, not to produce a distinct form, but a strong working of the mind, still producing what it still repels, and again calling forth what it again negatives; and the result is what the poet wishes to impress, to substitute a grand feeling of the unimaginable for a mere image."[92] Sublime poets such as Milton negatively represent ideas of reason by providing images that show themselves to be inadequate to the very objects they represent. Such images function as negative symbols. For Kant, symbolism is one of two forms of "hypotyposis," a term that he transliterates from the Greek ὑποτύπωσις, meaning "under a sketched form or figure," and that he equates with the Latin *exhibitio* and the German *Darstellung*.[93] During the Renaissance, Protestants criticized Catholics for resorting to poetic devices such as hypotyposis, prosopopoeia, and prosopographia in their representations of Purgatory.[94] For Kant, hypotyposis is the act of "making something sensible." It is "schematic" if the thing we wish to make sensible is an object of a concept of understanding. It is symbolic if the thing we wish to make sensible is the object of an idea of reason.[95] Objects of understanding can be directly intuited, but objects of reason can only be indirectly intuited via symbols.[96] Beauty symbolizes "the morally good" because aesthetic judgments of taste are formally analogous to moral judgments.[97] Sublimity *negatively* symbolizes the concept of moral duty. Mother Nature verges on the sublime when she appears to be not merely indifferent to our moral purposes but actively malevolent toward them. Yet nothing in nature is truly sublime. The only thing truly sublime is the moral vocation of man to subdue the nature within and outside him. Mother Nature awakens in him the sense of the sublime that culminates in his esteem for that within him which transcends and controls her. In this action she can be regarded as objectively purposive, but only insofar as she prepares him to break with her influence over his will. In this Kantian sense of the term, Lear's reaction to the storm would be more sublime than the storm itself:

> Blow, winds, and crack your cheeks! rage, blow!
> . . .
> Singe my white head!
> . . .
> But yet I call you servile ministers,
> That will with two pernicious daughters join
> Your high-engender'd battles 'gainst a head
> So old and white as this.
> (3.2.1, 6, 21–24)

Like the pessimistic Lear and Gloucester, Kant takes the value of bare life to be "less than zero."[98] It is only by giving our lives moral value that we make them worth living.

No less sublime than moral duty is what Kant calls "diabolical evil," or a principled commitment to evil for evil's sake.[99] Satan in *Paradise Lost* is sublime in this sense.[100] Christ's "holiness of will" is a moral ideal to which we ought to aspire even though the most we can hope to achieve is a virtuous commitment to subordinate our desire for happiness to our respect for the moral law. Analogously, we can be tempted to aspire to Satan's diabolical evil even though it too would be an unattainable (evil) ideal. Human evil is merely "radical" in the sense that we are constitutionally susceptible to subordinating our respect for the moral law to a narcissistic principle of self-love.[101] Lady Macbeth aspires to diabolical evil when she bids the "spirits that tend upon mortal thoughts" to "unsex" her and "fill" her with "direst cruelty" (1.5.41–43). Her sublime incantation negatively symbolizes the evil to which she aspires.[102] By contrast, Macbeth is haunted by *positive* symbols of evil such as the air-drawn dagger that points him toward his first crime—a deed that he performs, in the words of A. C. Bradley, "as if it were an appalling duty." [103] As noted by the nineteenth-century English grammarian William Chauncey Fowler, "Is this a dagger which I see before me?" is an example of hypotyposis ("sometimes called vision"). [104] Macbeth's horror at the projections of his own imagination shows that he too falls short of diabolical evil. Whereas Lady Macbeth unsuccessfully "bullies" her conscience, Macbeth tries to look forward rather than backward: "I am in blood / Stepp'd in so far that, should I wade no more, / Returning were as tedious as go o'er" (3.4.135–137). [105] In committing himself to future deeds "which must be acted ere they may be scann'd" (3.4.139)—that is, before they can be registered as appalling—he acknowledges that he still has a conscience that he is trying to evade. [106] Diabolical evil is associated with the Weird Sisters and fully personified in Hecate. Only a morally sublime hero "not of woman born" can defeat their human surrogate.

From the diabolical sublime of *Macbeth*, Shakespeare eventually passed to the ethereal enchantment of *The Tempest*. Kant's own view of nature underwent a similar shift in his late writings. In the *Critique of Pure Reason*, he compared "the land of pure understanding" to "an island ... enclosed in unalterable boundaries by nature itself": "It is the land of truth (a charming [*reizender*] name), surrounded by a broad and stormy ocean, the true seat of illusion, where many a fog bank and rapidly melting iceberg pretend to be new lands." [107] In his final work, the unfinished *Opus Postumum*, he discovered that the isle was full of noises. It was permeated by an all-encompassing ether whose internal vibrations unified the material world. [108] Fichte, he suggests, may have been right after all to think that by positing ourselves as subjects we became capable of a kind of intellectual intuition. [109] Perhaps we could know ourselves to belong to a realm of spirits. Just before drowning his book, the other Magus of Königsberg, like Prospero, cast one final spell. It would be left to his heirs to spell out the philosophical—and Shakespearean—terms of this romantic vision. In their eyes, Kant had remained stuck at the Hamlet stage of the history of spirit. The "Northern philosopher" and the "Northern Prince" were melancholy consciousnesses whose negative faith had to be converted into a positive philosophy of revelation. [110] Fichte had shown how to complete Kant's Copernican Revolution. Inspired by Fichte, Schiller argued that the French Revolution had to be completed through aesthetic *Bildung*. [111] Together these two tasks would constitute "the unfinished project of modernity." [112] The difficulty of completing each task would come to be symbolized, respectively, by Hamlet's nihilism and his tarrying.

"He is a nihilist."
"What?"
Ivan Turgenev, *Fathers and Sons*, trans. Richard Freeborn

One hasn't grasped what is nevertheless readily at hand to be grasped: that
pessimism isn't a problem but a symptom,—that the name must be replaced
by the term "nihilism,"—that the question whether not-to-be is better than
to-be is itself already an illness, a decline, an idiosyncrasy …
Friedrich Nietzsche, *Nachgelassene Fragmente*

F. H. Jacobi was the first writer to use the word *Nihilismus* in a philosophical
context. In a letter to Fichte in 1799, he complained that Kant had spectral-
ized reality by reducing empirical objects to mere appearances. Fichte had
only exacerbated Kant's nihilistic tendency by doing away with the thing in
itself.[1] Mendelssohn had dubbed Kant "the all-destroyer" (*Alleszermalmer*), but
for Jacobi he was the *all-spectralizer*.[2] As he explained in his 1787 essay, "David
Hume on Faith, or Idealism and Realism, A Dialogue":

> Suppose … our understanding only relates to a sensibility … that exhibits
> *nothing of the thing themselves* and, *objectively speaking, is absolutely empty*. … Suppose
> all this, and then tell me what kind of life this sensibility and this under-
> standing would afford me. What would it be, at bottom, but the life of an
> oyster? I am all there is, and outside me there is, *strictly speaking, nothing.*
> Yet the "I," this "I," this all that I am, is in the end also nothing but the *empty
> illusion of something.* It is the *form of a form*, just as much of a ghost [*Gespenst*]
> as the other appearances that I call things, a ghost like the whole of nature,
> its order and its laws.[3]

Nihilism thus signified for Jacobi not the literal obliteration of reality but the seeping of negation into it. Fichte had only exacerbated the problem by making Kant's ghostly transcendental subject the very foundation of his philosophy.

In 1785, Jacobi had inaugurated the so-called Pantheism controversy by claiming that the recently deceased Lessing had once admitted to sharing Spinoza's view that God and nature were one and the same.[4] Mendelssohn, Lessing's friend, denied the charge, and took the fideistic Jacobi to task for rejecting rationalist proofs of the existence of God. The one thing that Jacobi and Mendelssohn could agree on was that Spinoza was an atheist. According to Jacobi, Spinoza arrived at his atheism by following to its logical conclusion the rationalist principle that Leibniz called the *Satz vom Grund* (the principle of sufficient reason or ground): *ex nihilo nihil fit*: Lear's claim to the silent Cordelia ("Nothing will come of nothing, speak again" [1.1.90]).[5] Kant intervened in the Pantheism controversy not by defending Mendelssohn's rationalism against Jacobi's fideism but by developing his own conception of rational (or negative) faith. Beyond the bounds of possible experience, reason had to orient itself by a moral compass of its own devising. Having once seen through the illusions of rational theology, the Kantian subject stands before an undiscovered country from whose bourn no traveler returns. Instead of puzzling the will, this predicament should prompt us to adopt practical postulates that make it possible to achieve the highest good.[6]

Jacobi wasn't convinced. In his eyes, Kant had merely projected a ghostly moral coordinate system onto the noumenal void. If the central ethical problem of Spinoza's philosophy had been to give meaning to a fully real but ultimately purposeless world that hadn't been created *ex nihilo* by a transcendent God (the underlying problem posed in *King Lear*), Kant's problem was akin to Hamlet's. Having first made nothing out of something (*potest aliquid in nihilum*), he now had to make something out of nothing. From here, Jacobi felt, it was a short step to *moral* nihilism. The pagan Lear is comforted by his dying vision of the resurrected Cordelia, but the Wittenberg-schooled Hamlet is not so sure that he would prefer resurrection to oblivion. Kant's moral optimism protects him from moral nihilism, but only if his practical postulates (faith in God and the immortality of the soul) are accepted. Since these postulates rested on nothing more than a subjectively felt need of reason, Jacobi could foresee their rejection.

Sure enough, there soon appeared a philosopher who accepted Kant's transcendental idealism but rejected his practical postulates. As Jacobi predicted, this philosopher explicitly embraced nihilism, though he called it something different:

> The essential purport of the world-famous monologue in *Hamlet* is, in condensed form, that our state is so wretched that complete non-existence

would be decidedly preferable to it. Now if suicide actually offered us this, so that the alternative "to be or not to be" lay before us in the full sense of the words, it could be chosen unconditionally as a highly desirable termination ("a consummation devoutly to be wish'd"). There is something in us, however, which tells us that this is not so, that this is not the end of things, that death is not an absolute annihilation [*absolute Vernichtung*].[7]

Schopenhauer advocates *pessimism*. From the Latin *pessimus*, or "worst," pessimism is the doctrine that the world in which we live is not, as Leibniz held, the *best* of all possible worlds but, on the contrary, "the *worst* of all possible worlds."[8] Schopenhauer reached this position by way of Kant's transcendental idealism. In *The World as Will and Representation* (first edition 1818), he argues that Kant misunderstood the metaphysical implications of his discovery that space and time are nothing but forms of human sensibility. The first readers of the *Critique of Pure Reason* had equated Kant's transcendental idealism with Berkeley's immaterialism. In response, Kant insisted that his idealism concerned only the forms of experience and not (like Berkeley's) their empirical content.[9] Schopenhauer, the first philosopher to emphasize the differences between the first and second editions of the *Critique of Pure Reason*, objected to Kant's backpedaling. Berkeley had discovered the fundamental truth that Kant went on to elaborate, namely, that "the world is my representation."[10] Unlike Berkeley, however, Kant rightly distinguished worldly appearances from things in themselves. Kant insisted that the thing in itself couldn't be known, while Fichte countered that it could be known through an intellectual intuition of the self. Schopenhauer disagreed with both Kant and Fichte: for him, the thing in itself was neither an inaccessible X, nor an intuitable noumenon, but rather an unintelligent will that could be known through the immediate awareness of our practical striving. The will's blind endeavor to manifest itself had given rise to the natural world. Every spatiotemporally distinct object was an avatar of the same metaphysically undifferentiated ground. Empirical objects appeared to be metaphysically distinct, but this was an illusion that only aggravated the will's suffering. Suicide was ineffective because suicidal acts were only further manifestations of the will. The most they could accomplish was the destruction of particular appearances. As an alternative to suicide, Schopenhauer recommended disinterested contemplation of beauty, which temporarily lowered the will's intensity. It was theoretically possible to lower it to absolute zero, that is, to annihilate the will.

Schopenhauer was not the least bit perturbed by Kant's alleged spectralization of the empirical world. Indeed, he believed that the difference between the world of appearances and the all-too-real will made communications with genuine specters possible. In his 1851 "Essay on Spirit-Seeing and Everything Connected Therewith," he revisited the supernatural experiences that

Kant had dealt with in "Dreams of a Spirit-Seer." Since the *principium indi-viduationis* extended no further than spatiotemporal appearances, distance in space and time shouldn't be an obstacle to direct communication between phenomenally distinct individuals. Kant had been right to reject *spiritualistic* explanations of so-called spirit-seeing, but he had failed to recognize that his transcendental idealism (coupled with Schopenhauer's doctrine of the will) left room for an alternative explanation of such phenomena.[11] While conceding that he couldn't prove "the reality of ghostly apparitions [*Geisterers-cheinungen*]," Schopenhauer invokes "the consistency of hundreds of cases of the most trustworthy evidence" of "somnambulistic clairvoyance."[12]

When Lessing observed that the nocturnal ghost in *Hamlet* was more con-vincing that the diurnal ghost in *Sémiramis*, his reasons were psychological and aesthetic. According to Schopenhauer, however, it is simply much more likely for ghosts to be noticed at night. During the day our attention is directed toward worldly appearances. At night we withdraw our perceptual "feelers" from the world, making us more attentive to supernatural communications.[13] Such communications can take place while we are awake, but they more com-monly occur when we sleep.[14] Most dreams are too consistent and rich in detail to be mere products of the dreamer's fancy. This argument resembles that of Hippolyta, for whom the "great constancy" of the dreams of the lovers in *A Midsummer Night's Dream* makes them "strange and admirable" (5.1.26–27). Schopenhauer doesn't mention Hippolyta's observation, but he does refer to "the pleasant remark that while dreaming everyone is a Shakespeare."[15]

Besides providing Kantian grounds for Hamlet's nihilism and the veracity of spirit-seeing, Schopenhauer associates Kant with Shakespeare. In his 1851 essay "On Judgement, Criticism, Approbation, and Fame," he writes:

> Soon after Shakespeare's death, his dramas had to make way for those of Ben Jonson, Massinger, Beaumont and Fletcher, and for a hundred years had to yield supremacy to these. In the same way, Kant's serious philosophy was supplanted by Fichte's humbug, Schelling's eclecticism, and Jacobi's mawkish and pious drivel, until in the end things went to such lengths that an utterly wretched charlatan like Hegel was put on a level with, and even rated much higher than, Kant.[16]

This double comparison—of Kant to Shakespeare, and his idealist succes-sors to usurping Shakespearean offspring—is a recurring theme in Scho-penhauer's works. In the preface to the 1844 edition of *The World as Will and Representation* he calls Hegel "a spiritual [*geistigen*] Caliban."[17] If Hegel is Caliban, then Kant must be Prospero—whom Coleridge calls "the very Shakespeare himself, as it were, of the tempest."[18] In fact, to highlight the idealistic char-acter of Kant's philosophy, Schopenhauer cites Prospero's words "We are such stuff / As dreams are made on."[19] By implication, Schopenhauer would be Ariel, the genial spirit called upon by Kant/Prospero/Shakespeare to thwart Hegel's monstrous plot to usurp his rule.

Elsewhere Schopenhauer associates Hegel not with Caliban but with Claudius.[20] Against sycophantic admirers of "that scribbler of nonsense and destroyer of minds," he writes, "we should like to exclaim what Hamlet said to his infamous (*nichtswürdigen*) mother: 'Have you eyes? have you eyes?'"[21] Here Schopenhauer plays the part of Hamlet, implicitly casting Kant in the role of the Ghost—a role first played by Shakespeare, according to Nicholas Rowe.[22] In chastening the reading public, Schopenhauer implies that the specter of Kant has called upon his rightful heir to avenge his supplanting by the "three sophists" (Fichte, Schelling, and Hegel).[23] Given his views about spirit-seeing, Schopenhauer might very well have believed that Kant had summoned him from beyond the grave.

Because he repudiates Kant's practical postulates, Schopenhauer requires a different basis for his moral philosophy. When he criticizes Kant in *On the Basis of Morality* (1841), he identifies with Cordelia, implicitly casting Kant in the role of Lear. In the introduction, he contrasts the modest basis of his own ethical theory with the "broad foundations" of those of his "competitors": "The position is like that of Cordelia before King Lear, with her weakly worded assurance of dutiful affection compared with the extravagant assertions of her more eloquent sisters."[24] Kant based his conception of duty on respect for the categorical imperative, an unconditional moral command issued by pure practical reason.[25] Schopenhauer denies that there is such a thing as a categorical imperative. Reason can only generate hypothetical imperatives whose function is to assist us in seeking ends set by our inclinations. He also rejects the terms of Kant's moral optimism, his faith in the attainability of the highest good conceived as happiness commensurate with virtue. Kant had effectively made Leibniz's conception of "the best of all possible worlds" a practical ideal. For Schopenhauer, the best we can hope for is what Gloucester yearns for, namely, speedy annihilation. Unfortunately, death may not be an absolute end. Edgar teaches Gloucester this pessimistic lesson when he stages his father's symbolic resurrection after his supposed leap off Dover Cliff. Like Lear, we are all "bound" to a "wheel of fire" (4.7.45–46), and the best thing we can do is show compassion for one another. Compassion, not duty, is the true basis of morality: "The weight of this sad time we must obey, / Speak what we *feel*, not what we *ought* to say" (5.3.324–325, my italics). It is rare to encounter someone who is genuinely moral, so "Hamlet does not exaggerate when he says, 'To be honest, as this world goes, is to be one man pick'd out of ten thousand."[26] Compassion cannot be commanded but arises, when it does, from a dim awareness that everything is fundamentally identical with everything else.

Schopenhauer is not the only philosopher to associate Kant with Lear. Apropos Thomas De Quincey's "The Last Days of Immanuel Kant," Deleuze remarks: "This is the Shakespearean side of Kant, who begins as Hamlet and winds up as Lear, whose daughters would be the post-Kantians."[27] Deleuze doesn't assign specific parts to the various post-Kantians, but Schopenhauer's identification with the compassionate Cordelia would leave the roles of Goneril and Regan for Fichte and Hegel to play.[28] In *The World as Will and Representation*, Cordelia and Coriolanus are singled out as the only truly "noble" characters in Shakespeare.[29] Even more than Cordelia, Coriolanus is a role that the haughty Schopenhauer—who opposed the democratic revolutionaries in Frankfurt in 1848—could easily have played.[30] Doing so would have left Fichte and Hegel (or, by 1848, Marx and Engels) the roles of the opportunistic tribunes Sicinius Velutus and Junius Brutus to play.

Finally, in his essay "On the Will in Nature" (1836), Schopenhauer marvels that no one has offered "as an appropriate motto" for Hegel's "philosophy of absolute nonsense" Posthumus Leonatus's puzzled characterization of the mysterious text that he discovers upon awakening from his dream: "Such stuff as madmen tongue and brain not."[31] Unfortunately for Schopenhauer, this particular insult backfires, for here Hegel is implicitly identified with Jupiter, author of the message that Posthumus *mistakes* for textual nonsense but which the Soothsayer later shows to have been divinely conceived and prophetic. Jupiter personifies the power of absolution and thus the truth of absolute knowing.

Whether Hegel is Philip Massinger, Caliban, Claudius, Goneril, a Roman tribune, or a pagan god, he is Schopenhauer's rival for the inheritance of the Kantian legacy. Schopenhauer's vitriol toward Hegel is like that of Marx toward Stirner. Marx accused Stirner of misappropriating the legacy of Hegel, just as Schopenhauer criticized Hegel for misappropriating Kant's. Both polemics bear on the nature of spirit, and both have Hamletian overtones.[32] In representing Hamlet as a pessimist rather than as a beautiful soul or unhappy consciousness, Schopenhauer reconceives his negativity. Hegelian negativity traverses the way of despair, but it culminates in the revelation of absolute spirit. For Schopenhauer, the negativity of pessimism represents the highest truth—an endpoint rather than a midpoint. Hamlet passively accepts his suffering—passively rather than actively, because any activity would represent a return to the false optimism that underlies all willing.

What Schopenhauer overlooks is the fact that Hegel's philosophy of absolute nonsense equates spirit with negativity, or the "night of the world":

> The human being is this Night, this empty nothing which contains everything in its simplicity—a wealth of infinitely many representations, images, none of which occur to it directly, and none of which are not present.

This [is] the Night, the interior of [human] nature, existing here—*pure Self*—[and] in phantasmagoric representations it is night everywhere: here a bloody head suddenly shoots up and there another white shape, only to disappear as suddenly. We see this Night when we look a human being in the eye, looking into a Night which turns terrifying. [For from his eyes] the night of the world hangs out toward us.[33]

Like Joyce's *Finnegans Wake*, the *Phenomenology of Spirit* is Hegel's Book of the Night. The task of spirit is to convert the night of the world into day: "Tarrying with the negative is the magical power that *converts it into being*."[34] In the preface Hegel criticizes Schelling for representing the "Absolute as the night in which … all cows are black."[35] Converting night into day requires the labor of the negative, not whistling in the dark. Toward this end, the chapter on sense-certainty begins, literally, at night: "If we take the 'This' in the twofold shape of its being, as 'Now' and as 'Here,' the dialectic it has in it will receive a form as intelligible as the 'This' itself is. To the question: 'What is Now?,' let us answer, e.g. 'Now is night.'"[36] If we write down the statement "Now is night" and look at it the following day we will see that it is false, since the new now will be day. This simple truth—that night eventually gives way to day—encapsulates the overall movement of the dialectic from the positing of being (day) to the negation of being (night) to the negation of that negation (the new day). When Hegel likens the journey of world-spirit to the tunneling of Hamlet's "old mole," he does so because the mole *cum* ghostly shade begins digging at dusk (when the Owl of Minerva takes flight) and *surfaces* at dawn (the speculative meaning of Marcellus's remark "It faded on the crowing of the cock" [1.1.157]).[37] The infinite judgment, "the *being of Spirit is a bone*," bears not only on Hamlet's contemplation of the skull of Yorick, but also on the infinite judgment of sense-certainty, namely, that the being of day is night.[38] Once again it is Marcellus who perceives that "sweaty haste / Doth make the night joint-laborer with the day" (1.1.78). Night and day are out of joint in the ethical collision between the realm of nocturnal shades (defended by Antigone) and the realm of the diurnal gods (represented by Creon). To reach the light, spirit must pass not only through the realm of shades, but through Absolute Terror—a night in which all *deeds* are black ("Thoughts black, hands apt" [3.2.255]). When the negative faith that sustains Kant's moral view of the world is converted into revealed religion, the truth that appears in the light of day is that of negativity itself. If the resurrected Hermione symbolizes absolute knowing better than the Ghost in *Hamlet* it is only because she, like Antigone, *embodies* negativity.

So, however, does Hamlet. In his lectures on aesthetics, Hegel criticizes those who represent Hamlet as a ghostly character lacking solidity and a sense of purpose.[39] The Ghost itself is just a projection of Hamlet's conscience;

Hegel would have agreed with Freud that there is nothing uncanny about it. In the same context in which he criticizes contemporary portrayals of Hamlet, Hegel represents the Hoffmannesque uncanny as a kind of spiritual sickness: "From the sphere of art, however, these dark powers are precisely to be banned, for in art nothing is dark; everything is clear and transparent. With these visionary notions nothing is expressed except a sickness of spirit; poetry runs over into nebulousness, unsubstantiality, and emptiness, of which examples are provided in Hoffmann and in Heinrich von Kleist's *Prince of Homburg*."[40] Freud derived his conception of the uncanny from Schelling: "Uncanny is what one calls everything that was meant to remain secret and hidden and has come into the open."[41] For Schelling, the purpose of art is to cover over the "abyss" with "flowers."[42] For Hegel, however, the abyss is precisely what art manifests. The closest that he comes to granting the uncanny a place in his aesthetics is in the symbolic art of ancient Egypt. Symbolic art is sublime in the Kantian sense of indicating its own inability to provide an adequate sensible form for its intelligible content. For Hegel, such art falls short of its proper vocation, namely, to allow the negativity of spirit to shine forth in the light. Classical art is pure *Schein*: art that casts no shadows. Romantic art reintroduces a crack within the work of art. It does so not to keep something in the shadows but rather to allow the intelligible light of spirit to illuminate *itself* through the sublation of its sensible medium. Shakespearean drama represents the highest form of Romantic art, which passes the torch of absolute spirit to religion. In the realm of art there is no room for such "perverse" (*verkehrte*) phenomena as "magic, magnetism, demons, the superior apparitions of clairvoyance, the disease of somnambulism, etc."[43] Had Hegel read Schopenhauer's "Essay on Spirit-Seeing" he would have regarded it as symptomatic of the same sickly culture that represented Hamlet as a ghost. On the basis of his characterization of a work of art as "a thousand-eyed Argus" whose every aspect allows the light of spirit to shine through, he might have turned around Schopenhauer's question and asked, "Have *you* eyes?"[44] Had he done so, Schopenhauer would surely have retorted that Hegel was like Shakespeare's Ajax, whom the Trojan servant Alexander describes as "purblind Argus, all eyes and no sight" (*Troilus and Cressida*, 1.1.29–30).[45]

Kierkegaard's critique of Hegel also has Hamletian overtones. While agreeing with Hegel that *Hamlet* represents a spiritual transition from art to religion, Kierkegaard disagrees with him about the significance of this fact. In *Stages on Life's Way* (1845), his pseudonymous author Frater Taciturnus depicts Hamlet's religious interiority as an unfathomable secret that cannot be brought into the light of day. In "A Side-Glance at Shakespeare's *Hamlet*," Taciturnus generates an anamorphic perspective on the play. Looking directly at it, the German literary critic Ludwig Börne had seen "a Christian drama" (*ein christliches Trauerspiel* in Börne's original essay).[46] Taciturnus characterizes this as "a most excellent comment," adding only that he would prefer to call it "religious" rather than Christian.[47] He goes on to suggest, however, that the very idea of a religious drama is a contradiction in terms. Insofar as Hamlet's doubts are religious they involve an inexpressible spiritual conflict that cannot be staged, but insofar as they are merely signs of waffling the play belongs to the aesthetic rather than the religious sphere.[48] In brief, both the play and the character are betwixt and between. If Taciturnus's side-glance represents an anamorphic distortion of Börne's direct gaze, the parallax that it generates is not just the difference between the religious and aesthetic points of view, but a difference internal to the religious point of view itself. The paradox is that it is the anamorphic perspective rather than the direct one that reveals the truth about religion, and about *Hamlet*.

In *Richard II*, Bushy discloses a similar paradox when he tells Queen Isabel that her side-glance at the absent king has generated an anamorphic distortion. From her perspective, an apparent nothing is something; from his, an apparent something is nothing. Taciturnus's oscillation between the two perspectives on *Hamlet* generates a similar parallax. On the one hand, Hamlet's negativity is merely aesthetic insofar as it negates the external world ("a foul and pestilent congregation of vapors" [2.2.302–303]). On the other hand, it is religious insofar as it is internally self-negating ("To die, to sleep— / No more" [3.1.59–60]). These two perspectives, however, are not on a par. In *Either/Or* the aesthetic and *ethical* points of view stand in an antinomial relation to each other, but in *Stages on Life's Way* the religious point of view represents an essentially higher perspective than the other two. Religious negativity, or despair, is of incomparably greater significance than aesthetic (or ethical) negativity. The fact that *Hamlet* falls short of being a religious work is a sign of its failure, but Kierkegaard implies that Shakespeare's greatness consists in his ability to depict this very failure—that is, to depict the difficulty of attaining a genuinely religious point of view.[49] This interpretation explains Johannes Climacus's apparently offhand reference to Hamlet in *Concluding Unscientific Postscript* (1846). Commenting on Luther's observation that it is difficult to pray without letting extraneous thoughts intrude, the pseudonymous Climacus writes: "So one could almost think that to pray is just as difficult as to play the role of Hamlet, of which the greatest actor is supposed to have said that only once had he been close to playing it well; nevertheless he would devote all his ability and his entire life to the continued study of this role."[50] Ironically, the moment when Claudius is trying to pray without letting extraneous thoughts intrude is the very moment when, for Taciturnus, Hamlet *may* pass from the aesthetic to the religious point of view. Claudius's failure is apparent—"My words fly up, my thoughts remain below" (3.3.97)—but Hamlet's success or failure is essentially inscrutable. Perhaps it is no accident that Climacus's self-reported age (thirty) is the same as the one that the Gravedigger ascribes to Hamlet.[51] Purporting to have that within which passes show, Hamlet and Kierkegaard both prize reticence.[52] For Kierkegaard, reticence is not just an ethical virtue but an essential aspect of a religious life, as he makes clear in a journal entry from 1846:

> When Hamlet dies, his sorrow, almost to despair, is that no one will come to know his life. And this is most certainly true, for anyone who has had one single idea, but by desperate efforts has concealed it in the form of a deception, becomes aware of this contradiction in the moment of death, for now in death he dares to speak, and now death comes so suddenly. ... But he who has willed to endure such a martyrdom in order to sense the idea of truth ought never be inconsistent, he must never secretly provide people with an explanation. The more consistent he is in this respect, the more true he is to his idea, which will reward him with inner happiness. Just as in life he repudiated the world's honor, so should he also do it in death and after his death continue to be the riddle he was in life.[53]

The impossibility of giving voice to a genuine interior monologue is indicated by Kierkegaard's Vigilius Haufniensis, the pseudonymous author of *The Concept of Anxiety* (1844): "Here I shall endeavor only to give all 'an understanding but no tongue,' as the inclosed [*indesluttede*] Hamlet admonishes his two friends."[54]

For Nietzsche, as for Kierkegaard, Hamlet's reticence had personal significance: "The rest is silence" was his final word about his friendship with Wagner. What had once appealed to him in *Tristan und Isolde* was Tristan's desire to join Isolde in the "wondrous realm of night" (*Wunderreicht der Nacht*).[55] With his "night-seeing" (*nachtsichtig*) eye, Tristan transcends the "deceptive appearance" (*täuschenden Schein*) of day.[56] Wagner's dramatization of this metaphysical vision was itself a deceptive appearance that compensated for the agony that his music expressed. When Nietzsche said that no "true musician" could listen to the third act of *Tristan und Isolde* without the balm of "words and images," he meant that only a god—Apollo—could save Wagner's followers from the slippery slope that led from pessimism to nihilism.[57] Eventually, he concluded that nothing could save them. Wagner had shown his true colors in *Parsifal*, a desperate attempt to revive the Christian values whose decline marked the onset of modern nihilism. Overcoming nihilism had been Nietzsche's implicit aim when he wrote *The Birth of Tragedy*. By the time he began to use the word *Nihilismus* around 1880 (evidently borrowing it from Turgenev and Prosper Mérimée rather than Jacobi), he had come to regard Wagner's art and Schopenhauer's philosophy as symptoms of a much broader cultural malaise.[58]

In "Schopenhauer as Educator," Nietzsche praises his erstwhile mentor for his Hamletlike pursuit of "a picture of life as a whole": "Schopenhauer is, as I said, great in that he pursues this picture as Hamlet pursues the ghost."[59]

When looked at awry, this ghostly picture turned out to be nihilism. In *Beyond Good and Evil*, Nietzsche characterizes the specter haunting Europe as a

> menacing sound from afar, as if some new explosive were being tested somewhere, a dynamite of the spirit, perhaps a newly discovered Russian *nihiline*, a pessimism *bonae voluntatis* which does not merely say No, will No, but—dreadful thought! *does* No. Against this kind of "good will"—a will to the actual active denial of life—there is today confessedly no better sedative and soporific than scepticism, the gentle, gracious, lulling poppy scepticism; and even *Hamlet* is prescribed by the doctors of our time against the "spirit" and its noises under the ground.[60]

Having identified Schopenhauer's pessimism as a form of nihilism, Nietzsche seeks to overcome it by casting Hamlet's nighted color off. Elsewhere he identifies nihilism with the loss of a sense of purpose, a frame of mind that recalls Hamlet's "How weary, stale, flat, and unprofitable / Seem to me all the uses of this world" (1.2.133–134): "*Nihilism: the goal is lacking; an answer to the 'Why?' is lacking. What does nihilism mean?—That the highest values are devaluated.*"[61] Nietzsche's solution wasn't to reaffirm the highest values, as Jacobi did; on the contrary, he regarded their decline as a necessary step on the way to the creation of new values. The previously existing values were the ones that Christianity had inherited from Platonism, and they themselves were inherently nihilistic. To create new values, it was necessary to accelerate their decline by practicing an active rather than a passive nihilism. Active nihilism was a sign of health. Passive nihilism was symptomatic of the enervation of the will. Since, however, it was impossible for the will *not* to will, the history of passive nihilism had culminated not in the cessation of willing but in "*a will to nothingness*."[62] Modern nihilism had arisen through the decline of Christian values that had been only *relatively* nihilistic insofar as they devalued life but compensated for this loss by providing the will with theoretical and practical goals.[63] With the decline of these transcendent values, the specter of *absolute* nihilism appeared for the first time.[64] As Jacobi had anticipated, Kant's Copernican revolution, coupled with the loss of Kant's moral compass, left human beings spinning in the void:

> Who gave us the sponge to wipe away the entire horizon? What were we doing when we unchained this earth from its sun? Where is it moving to now? Where are we moving to? Away from all suns? Are we not continually falling? And backwards, sidewards, forwards, in all directions? Is there still an up and a down? Aren't we straying as though through an infinite nothing? Isn't empty space breathing at us? Hasn't it got colder? Isn't night and more night coming again and again?[65]

In *Twilight of the Idols* (1888), Nietzsche reconstructs the rise and fall of Christian values. The starting point was Plato's distinction between the "true world" and the "'apparent' world." In modernity, Kant reduced the true world to a moral postulate. When this postulate lost its justification, the very idea of a true world became nugatory. The only question left was whether there still existed an apparent or illusory (*scheinbare*) world—the world that Jacobi had characterized as having become ghostly. If the answer was yes, then we were still in the grip of nihilism. If the answer was no—if in destroying the true world we had also destroyed the apparent world—then we were on the verge of creating new values. Nietzsche identifies this second possibility with the coming of Zarathustra: "Noon; moment of shortest shadow; ... incipit zarathustra."[66] In *Thus Spoke Zarathustra*, he pursues this picture as Hamlet pursues the Ghost—or, rather, as Hamlet *is pursued by* the Ghost. To overcome nihilism, Zarathustra must provide a negative answer to Jacobi's question: "Am I some kind of ghost?"[67] The fact that Zarathustra is haunted by precisely this question suggests that he too is struggling to cast Hamlet's nighted cloak off. Hegel thought it was a mistake to play Hamlet as if he were a ghost, but Nietzsche seems to have felt that there was no other way to play him. His equivalent to Kierkegaard's choice between aesthetic and religious nihilism was that between Hamlet's passive nihilism and Brutus's active nihilism. Zarathustra would *overcome* nihilism.

When Heidegger characterized Zarathustra as Nietzsche's *Fürsprecher*, he recognized that Zarathustra's fundamental task was to overcome nihilism. But according to Heidegger, Nietzsche misunderstood nihilism's true nature. Properly understood, it involved not the loss of value, but, more fundamentally, the interpretation of "being *as* a value."[68] Nihilism had originated with the affirmation of transcendent values, and it culminated in the apotheosis of the value-creating will. When Zarathustra celebrates the ideal of a perpetually self-revaluating overman, he doesn't overcome nihilism but rather brings it to completion. Nietzsche had been right to associate the advent of nihilism with Platonism, but the nature of that association had to be completely rethought. Toward this end, Heidegger develops an entirely different picture of early Greek thought and its relationship to Greek tragedy. The new picture shows that it was a mistake to associate Hamlet with Dionysian man. Hamlet was a nihilist, but not for the reasons Nietzsche had thought.

Heidegger's critique of Hamlet's negativity—and it is nothing less—represents a radical shift in the German reception of Shakespeare. From Herder's "Shakespeare" to Friedrich Gundolf's *Shakespeare und der deutsche Geist* (1911), Shakespeare had been regarded as a spiritual mediator between Sophocles and Goethe.[69] That perception began to change during the First World War, when international relations between Germany and England weren't what they had been in the days of the Seven Years' War.[70] In his 1935 lecture course,

Introduction to Metaphysics, Heidegger characterizes the Germans as "the metaphysical people" caught between the "pincers" of "Russia and America," which "seen metaphysically, are both the same: the same hopeless frenzy of unchained technology and of the rootless organization of the average man." The Germans were in the grip of a world-historical nihilism, and the question was how to overcome it. Echoing both Jacobi and Nietzsche, Heidegger laments, "There still looms like a specter over all this uproar [*ein Gespenst über all diesen Spuk*] the question: what for?—where to?—and what then?"[71] To reclaim "the inner truth and greatness" of German National Socialism, it was necessary to repose the fundamental question of metaphysics. Only in this way could nihilism be overcome.

When Heidegger published his lecture course in 1953, he glossed the phrase "inner truth and greatness of this movement [*innere Wahrheit und Größe dieser Bewegung*]" as "the encounter between global technology and modern humanity."[72] Unappeased by this retroactive editing, Jürgen Habermas sent a letter of protest to the *Frankfurter Allgemeine Zeitung*.[73] Lost amid the ensuing controversy was any awareness that Heidegger's original remark had something to do with Hamlet. Yet it did. The entire lecture course represented an argument with Nietzsche about the true nature of Greek tragedy and whether Hamlet's "To be or not to be" was the fundamental question of metaphysics. Bizarre as it may seem, Heidegger regarded the fate of National Socialism as turning on this question.

In a study of Sophocles that appeared in 1933, the German classicist Karl Reinhardt argued, *contra* Nietzsche, that Shakespeare was "not a descendant" of either Aeschylus or Sophocles. Via Seneca, he was closer in spirit to Euripides.[74] Alluding to the passage from *The Gay Science* in which Nietzsche praises the melancholy of Brutus, Reinhardt remarks that Sophocles's Ajax shows "no hint of melancholy, not even the melancholy of a Brutus." Likewise, "The tragedy of Ajax does not take place in a world which is out of joint."[75] Heidegger picks up on this theme in a 1942–43 lecture course on Parmenides, remarking that "Greek tragedy is still entirely sealed off to us. Aeschylus-Sophocles on the one side, and Shakespeare on the other, are incomparable worlds."[76] A few years earlier, in "The Age of the World Picture" (1938), he dismissed the idea that "modern science" was "more exact than that of antiquity" with this analogy: "Nobody would presume to maintain [*Niemand läßt sich beikommen zu behaupten*] that Shakespeare's poetry is more advanced [*fortgeschrittener*] than that of Aeschylus."[77] This remark (which appeals to the authority of idle talk [*Gerede*]) conveniently overlooks the fact that Lessing explicitly professed to be such a Nobody, and that Schopenhauer rated Shakespeare "much greater than [*viel größer als*] Sophocles" on the grounds that Shakespeare's tragic characters achieve a "spirit of resignation."[78] In a similar vein, Hegel and Kierkegaard took Shakespeare to exceed the ancient dramatists in his portrayal of subjectivity.[79] Heidegger would readily have agreed that Shakespearean drama was more "subjective" than ancient Greek drama (at least prior to Euripides). What he rejected was the idea that this made Shakespeare more spiritually advanced than the Greeks. On the contrary, he suggests in his 1935 lecture course that *Hamlet* is nihilistic in a way that Sophoclean tragedy isn't.

The course begins with a question: "Why are there beings at all instead of nothing? That is the question [*Warum ist überhaupt Seiendes und nicht vielmehr Nichts? Das ist die Frage*]."[80] Although he doesn't say so explicitly here, Heidegger's purpose is to distinguish the question that he takes to be fundamental ("Why are there beings at all instead of nothing?") from the question that Hamlet represents as fundamental ("To be or not to be"). That this is his aim is indicated by an explicit remark from his 1944 summer course on Heraclitus: "The question about being itself and nothing is by right, however, infinitely deeper than—that is, it is in an essentially different realm from—the familiar question, 'To be or not to be,' as usually understood in connection with the word of Shakespeare's Hamlet."[81] When Heidegger uttered the words "*Das ist die Frage*" in 1935, he must have emphasized the word *Das* to point out the contrast. If the Germans were going to overcome nihilism, their task was not to brush up their Shakespeare but to brush him aside.

According to Heidegger, the question "Why are there beings at all instead of nothing?" is fundamental not only philosophically but historically. It guides Parmenides's distinction between being and nonbeing. Some commentators take this distinction to be exhaustive, but on Reinhardt and Heidegger's interpretations, Parmenides's goddess of truth distinguishes three ways or paths that mortals can travel: the path of being, the path of nonbeing, and the path of seeming or illusion (rendered by Reinhardt and Heidegger as *Schein*). Of the three, only the first is said to be viable. It is also said to be unavoidable. One of the paradoxes of the poem is that the goddess commands Parmenides to remain on the path of being despite the fact that doing so is unavoidable (as if "ought" were compatible with "cannot not"). The path of nonbeing, though inaccessible, remains dangerous, while the path of seeming is represented as the commonly trod path of opinion (*doxa*). Since seeming and nonbeing both "belong" to being, the three paths ultimately converge.[82] Since "the place where three paths meet" is the locus of the Oedipus myth, it is a short step to interpret *Oedipus Tyrannus* as a dramatization of Parmenides's poem.

Reinhardt characterizes *Oedipus Tyrannus* as a "tragedy of seeming [*Schein*]": "In the *Oedipus* the danger to man lies not in the *hybris* of human self-assertion but in the *hybris* of seeming as opposed to being that is innate in his nature—a deeper danger."[83] Oedipus is the victim of divine powers who control his fate. After the disclosure of his crime he is required not to take responsibility for his actions but to accept his submission to the *daimon* that has ruled his course from the very beginning. Hegel had taken Oedipus's unconscious crime to make his tragedy "less spiritually advanced" than that of Antigone, who deliberately flouts Creon's decree. Oedipus's deed has to be "brought out into the light of day," but since Antigone's is carried out in broad daylight it can serve as the basis for an ethical collision between her self-assertion and that of Creon.[84] Contra Hegel, Reinhardt denies that the concept of an ethical collision was central to Sophoclean tragedy. What is tragic in *Antigone* isn't Antigone's defiance of Creon but Creon's self-righteous defiance of Tiresias. Like Oedipus, Creon succumbs to a "deeper danger" than that of self-assertion, namely, the danger of mistaking the path of seeming for the path of being.

Taking Reinhardt's interpretation one step further, Heidegger argues that seeming is dangerous because it "covers itself over *as* seeming."[85] Having come to the place where three paths meet, Oedipus thinks he has correctly chosen the path of being when in fact he has taken the path of seeming. What eventually leads him back to the path of being—a path that in another sense he never left—is his perseverance in seeking the truth. When he discovers the truth, its blinding light is unbearable: "To unveil what is concealed … he must, step by step, place himself into an unconcealment that in the end he can endure only by gouging out his own eyes—that is, by placing himself outside all light."[86] By gouging out his eyes he prevents himself from seeing what belongs to the realm of seeming—to human-all-too-human appearances. He doesn't turn away from being, that is, from the horrifying truth he has disclosed. His resoluteness in unveiling being is, for Heidegger, characteristic of Greek Dasein.

In *The Birth of Tragedy*, Nietzsche had equated Oedipus's revulsion at "the horror and absurdity of existence" with that of Hamlet.[87] Only Apollonian *Schein*, "illusion," could make existence bearable. Thus Nietzsche had himself chosen the path of seeming over the path of being. In *Twilight of the Idols*, he even represents the path of being as the path toward nihilism. Against the "error of being" he defends Heraclitus's affirmation of the sensory flux of becoming.[88] "Being" (*Sein*) was nothing more than "an empty word" or "unreal vapor"—in fact, it was nothing.[89] Parmenides's reification of this nothing marked the onset of nihilism. Plato accentuated Parmenides's error by dividing reality into a true realm of being and a merely apparent realm of becoming.

Heidegger rejects this interpretation of the history of metaphysics. Far from standing opposed to each other as thinkers, respectively, of being and becoming, Parmenides and Heraclitus both think of being as *phusis*, a term that Heidegger renders not as "nature" (*Natur*) but as "the coming-into-appearance [*Erscheinung-Treten*]" of "the emerging-abiding sway [*das aufgehend-verweilende Walten*]."[90] Only with Plato do the distinctions between being and becoming, on the one hand, and being and seeming, on the other, harden into metaphysical dualisms. Against Parmenides, Plato also introduces a sharp distinction between being and thinking—a distinction which, as we have seen in connection with the figure of the Sophist, makes the path of nonbeing viable in a certain way. This is the true root of nihilism. In modernity, a fourth distinction arises: between being and "the Ought." It arises through Descartes's representation of Dasein (human being) as a thinking subject. A direct line leads from the self-positing Cartesian subject to Kant's self-determining moral agent to Schopenhauer's will to Nietzsche's will to power—the metaphysical position that in 1935 was being "peddled about … as the philosophy of National Socialism."[91] While other Nazi philosophers were arguing about whether there were objective, transcendent values (Bruno Bauch) or whether all values were rooted in will to power (Alfred Baeumler), Heidegger maintained that both conceptions were fundamentally nihilistic.[92] To overcome nihilism it was necessary to inquire into the nature of the nonbeing or nothing that Parmenides had warned against. It was necessary to return to the place where the three paths meet.

In a 1940 lecture course devoted to Nietzsche's conception of nihilism, Heidegger claims that "the essence of nihilism consists in not taking the question of the nothing seriously." By not taking it seriously, "one remains obstinately fixed in the interrogative scheme of that familiar either-or."[93] This particular either/or isn't Hamlet's "To be or not to be," for it concerns the status of the nothing itself. Is nothing? Or can we not even say that nothing is? The problem with this either/or is that although nothing isn't a being, neither is it "purely null."[94] To respond to the question, "Why are there beings at all instead of nothing?" one has to think the nothing—that is, think the *being* of nothing even though nothing isn't a being. According to Heidegger, this question hadn't been properly posed since antiquity, just as the question about the essence of being hadn't been properly posed since Parmenides and Plato distinguished being from nonbeing. Against Nietzsche's contention that nihilism resulted from the pursuit of the path of being, Heidegger maintains that it arose through a failure to think both being and nothing. Paradoxically, modern nihilism involves not the thought of nothing but a failure to think the nothing: "Nihilism would then be the essential nonthinking of the essence of the nothing."[95] Returning to the question of the essence of the nothing is Heidegger's equivalent to tarrying with the negative. More precisely, it is his way of going back to the source of that which came to be represented in modernity as the negativity of subjectivity. Going back to the source leads him not to Hamlet but to Oedipus, *who tarries not with the negative but with the nothing.*

According to Heidegger, the early Greek thinkers had "to tear Being away from seeming and preserve it against seeming."[96] This is what Oedipus does when he perseveres in his quest for the truth of his being. When he discovers the truth, he doesn't commit suicide, as Jocasta does. Blinding himself is Oedipus's way of both turning away from the light and submitting himself to it. He confronts the nothing yet remains in being. When the Chorus in *Oedipus at Colonus* says that "not to be born surpasses thought and speech"—or, as Heidegger renders it, "never to have stepped into Dasein triumphs over the gatheredness of beings as a whole [*niemals ins Dasein getreten zu sein, obsiegt über die Gesammtheit des Seienden im Ganzen*]"—it recommends the very path that the goddess had warned Parmenides to shun.[97] Alluding to *The Birth of Tragedy*, Heidegger warns us that it would be anachronistic to equate the words of the Chorus with Schopenhauer's pessimistic thesis that "life is a business that does not cover its costs."[98] Schopenhauer's thesis assumes that human existence has a value that can be calculated by weighing its costs and benefits. But the Chorus says nothing about value. When it asserts that the path of nothing triumphs over the path of being, it signals the birth of nihilism out of the division of thinking and being: "*Logos* and *phusis* disjoin, step apart from each other."[99] This disjoining—the becoming out of joint of thinking and being—is not yet subjectivity in the modern Cartesian sense, for thinking has not yet been identified with negativity. But the way to modernity has been opened up. The danger that Dasein henceforth faces is that of forfeiting its status *as* Dasein, that is, as being-in-the-world. The Chorus in *Antigone* names this danger when it characterizes man as *to deinotaton*. Heidegger translates this expression as *das Unheimlichste*, "the uncanniest." Man is the uncanniest of beings in the same way that nihilism is "the uncanniest of guests."[100] Man is uncanny because he not merely *has* but *is* the "audacity … to overwhelm the appearing sway by withholding all openness toward it."[101] He is a "counter-violence" against the violence of the "overwhelming sway" of being.[102] Dasein triumphs over the violence of the overwhelming sway not by surviving, but by dying: "Not-being-here is the ultimate victory over Being." This is the danger not of *suicide* but of *ontocide*. Nihilism begins from the moment Dasein exists as this possibility of forfeiting its status as Dasein. It is in this sense that Dasein is "held out into the nothing."[103]

If Oedipus reverses the words of the Chorus (what Nietzsche called "the wisdom of Silenus"), he does so by persevering on the path of being. Persevering in being doesn't consist in affirming the value of life but in standing forth as Dasein in the face of the emerging-abiding sway. To stand at the crossroads where three paths meet is to be faced with a decision for or against being. Every Dasein must confront this truly universal Oedipus complex: "The human being must distinguish among these three paths and, accordingly, come to a decision for or against them."[104] For Heidegger, the first modern poet to revive Sophoclean tragedy wasn't Shakespeare but Hölderlin, who translated all three Theban plays (though he never finished his version of *Oedipus at Colonus*). In "Hölderlin and the Essence of Poetry" (1936), Heidegger claims that unlike "Homer or Sophocles, … Virgil or Dante, … Shakespeare or Goethe," Hölderlin's "whole poetic mission" was "to make poems solely about the essence of poetry."[105] To make poems about the essence of poetry is to confront the "danger that beings pose to being itself."[106] Hölderlin bears witness to the "flight of the gods" while preparing for a new "decision" about being. In his poem "In lovely blueness …" ("In lieblicher Bläue …"), he represents "King Oedipus" as having "One eye too many [*ein Auge zu viel*]." "One eye too many" suggests to Heidegger the poet's madness, the penalty that Hölderlin had to pay for "poetically think[ing] through to the ground and center of being."[107] It might also make us think of King Lear, who offers both his "too many" eyes to the blinded Gloucester ("If thou wilt weep my fortunes, take my eyes" [4.6.176]).[108] Hölderlin's poem continues:

> And hence the sons of the earth now drink
> Heavenly fire without danger.
> Yet us it behooves, you poets, to stand
> Bare-headed beneath God's thunderstorms,
> To grasp the Father's ray, itself, with our own hands
> And to offer to the people
> The heavenly gift wrapt in song.[109]

"Bare-headed beneath God's thunderstorms [*Mit entblößtem Haupt, unter / Gottes Gewittern*]" recalls Lear on the heath bidding the heavens to "let fall / Your horrible pleasure" (3.2.18–19), but such parallels are not on Heidegger's radar. In his eyes, the link between Hölderlin and Sophocles is unmediated. Had he tarried with Shakespeare as Nietzsche did, he might have read both Sophocles and Hölderlin differently. But he was more haunted by Shakespeare than he allowed. Ned Lukacher observes that Heidegger seems to allude to Hamlet (or Edgar) when, in his posthumously published *Der Spiegel* interview, he advocates the "preparation of readiness [*die Vorbereitung der Bereitschaft*]" "so that we do not, simply put, die meaningless deaths, but that when we decline, we decline in the face of the absent god."[110] *In Bereitschaft sein ist alles* is Schlegel's translation of Hamlet's "the readiness is all" (5.2.222). It is possible too that Heidegger's conception of "letting-be [*Gelassenheit*]" was inspired by Hamlet's remark to Horatio, "Since no man, of aught he leaves, knows what is't to leave betimes, let be" (5.2.223–224).[111]

In *Specters of Marx*, Derrida detects a further echo of Hamlet in Heidegger's commentary on the Anaximander Fragment. Heidegger translates the Greek αδικία—conventionally rendered as "injustice" or *Ungerechtigkeit*—as "*aus den Fugen*" or "out of joint," an apparent echo of Schlegel's "*Die Zeit ist aus den Fugen*."[112] According to Derrida, however, Hamlet's line doesn't simply equate time's being out of joint with injustice; as a response to the appearance of the Ghost it also suggests that the diachronic welcoming of strangers is a condition for the possibility of justice. As an alternative to Heidegger's Parmenidean conception of fundamental ontology (or the questioning of being) Derrida advocates a Hamlet-inspired "hauntology" (or the questioning of ghosts).[113]

In *Time and the Other* (1948), Levinas argues that prior to *Hamlet* the distinctive feature of classical tragedy was the hero's ability to commit suicide.[114] From *Antigone* to *Romeo and Juliet*, suicide represented a "triumph over fatality." In their respective tombs, both Antigone and Juliet lie (in the words of Lacan) in "the zone between-two-deaths": symbolically dead but not yet actually dead, they are able to triumph over fatality by killing themselves.[115] As Juliet puts it before she faces this horrifying predicament: "If all else fail, myself have power to die" (3.5.242).[116] According to Levinas, Shakespeare goes "beyond tragedy or the tragedy of tragedy" when he has Hamlet discover in the "To be or not to be" soliloquy that annihilation may be impossible. This discovery is said to contradict Heidegger's representation of death as the "possibility of impossibility," for if annihilation is strictly impossible it cannot be possible in any sense.[117] This criticism is somewhat confusing because Levinas himself represents the impossibility of dying as merely hypothetical and thus as theoretically possible, but his main point seems to be that self-annihilation is *existentially* impossible. Like Schopenhauer, he derives the (possible) impossibility of annihilation from our phenomenological access to a prepersonal condition, one that he characterizes as that of unremitting, impersonal existence: *Il y a* ("there is"). In *Existence and Existents* (1947), he indicates several ways in which this level of existence can be disclosed. Each is a path of stalled negation: imagining the destruction of the world, contemplating (à la Pascal) the silence of infinite space, being plunged into total darkness—or encountering ghosts.[118] When Hamlet and Macbeth meet their ghosts, they experience "horror of being" rather than (*pace* Heidegger) "anxiety over nothingness":[119]

> Spectors [sic], ghosts, sorceresses are not only a tribute Shakespeare pays to his time, or vestiges of the original material he composed with; they allow him to move constantly toward this limit between being and nothingness where being insinuates itself even in nothingness, like bubbles of the earth ("the Earth hath bubbles"). Hamlet recoils before the "not to be" because he has a forboding [sic] of the return of being ("to dye, to sleepe, perchance to Dreame"). In *Macbeth*, the apparition of Banquo's ghost is also a decisive experience of the "no exit" from existence, its phantom return through the fissures through which one has driven it. ... It is the shadow of being that horrifies Macbeth; the profile of being takes form in nothingness.[120]

Standing in relation to death isn't a matter of being "held out into the nothing," as Heidegger would have it, but of confronting an enigmatic *something*. Macbeth is sufficiently courageous to face any living creature that might threaten him with death, but he quakes when confronted with the *undead* Banquo ("Avaunt, and quit my sight! ... Or be alive again, / And dare me to the desert with thy sword" [3.4.92, 102–103]). When he learns that Birnam wood has come to Dunsinane, he longs for an impossible escape from being: "There is nor flying hence, nor tarrying here." Beginning "to be aweary of the sun," he wishes that "th' estate o' th' world were now undone" (5.5.47–49).[121] All he can do is "try the last" against Macduff (5.8.32). Levinas concludes that it is "not death" that Shakespeare's postclassical "heroes seize," but only this "last chance" "prior to death."[122] The intimation that nothingness is a screen covering over the horror of interminable existence "deprives suicide, which is the final mastery one can have over being, of its function of mastery."[123] *Hamlet* and *Macbeth* turn out to be "more advanced" than classical tragedies because they portray "the fatality of irremissible being."[124]

Levinas is right to observe that there is something about Shakespeare's ghosts that Heidegger is unable to think, but it isn't clear that it has to do with the impossibility of committing suicide. Heidegger would have agreed with Levinas that being is irremissible, a debt that we can never fully discharge. This is one implication of his claim that even nothing "belongs" to being.[125] Dasein's capacity to confront the overwhelming sway isn't the kind of self-mastery that Kant invokes in the judgment of the sublime. In standing forth as a counterviolence against the sway of being, Oedipus isn't raised above nature in dignity; rather, he is shown to be in default of his proper essence as Dasein. In representing Oedipus as resolute, Heidegger acknowledges the impossibility of masterful dying and even implicitly criticizes Shakespeare for granting to Hamlet the same capacity for death that Juliet claims for herself. Levinas may have come to realize this, for he later criticizes Heidegger on a completely different score, namely, for privileging ontology over ethics. In "Ethics as First Philosophy" (1984) he argues that "To be or not to be" is *not* the fundamental question of philosophy.[126] Although he doesn't seem to realize that Heidegger had made the same point (albeit with a different intent), he implies that Heidegger (like Nietzsche) remains within the *moral* nihilism that has held sway since Schopenhauer, if not Parmenides. If, for Lukacher, Heidegger's Shakespeare is "the poet of the end of the *Gestell* and the beginning of the *Ereignis*" (i.e., the poet of the end of the nihilistic sway of being as will to power and the inception of a new form of being), Levinas's Shakespeare is the poet of the end of ontology and the beginning of ethics.[127] If Hamlet remains on the cusp of this transition, it is not by virtue of the "To be or not to be" soliloquy but by virtue of his response to the Ghost: "Speak, I am bound to hear" (1.5.6). This is what Heidegger doesn't think: Hamlet's tarrying—not with the nothing, but with the spectral.

In the signs that bewilder the middle class, the aristocracy and the poor prophets of regression, we do recognise our brave friend, Robin Goodfellow, the old mole that can work in the earth so fast, that worthy pioneer—the Revolution.

Karl Marx, "Speech at the Anniversary of the *People's Paper*"

Yet the critic declares that "Hamlet tarries too long in this state of passive emotion." Too long? In what way? In relation to what consequence or what action?

Karl Werder, *The Heart of Hamlet's Mystery*[1]

In what sense does Hamlet tarry?

In act 3, scene 3, Hamlet comes upon the kneeling Claudius. Having seen the king "blench" (2.2.597) at "The Mousetrap," he knows his course. Now he has a perfect opportunity. He draws his sword ... and *does nothing*, just as Pyrrhus did when his sword, poised above the "milky head" of "reverent" King Priam, "seem'd i' th'air to stick":

So as a painted tyrant Pyrrhus stood,
And, like a neutral to his will and matter,
Did nothing.
(2.2.478–482)

Pyrrhus does nothing as the "flaming top" of "senseless Ilium" (2.2.474–475) comes crashing down, as if in sympathetic response to his first, ineffectual blow against King Priam. In the First Player's description—"Then senseless Ilium, / Seeming to feel this blow, with flaming top / Stoops to his base, and with a hideous crash / Takes prisoner Pyrrhus' ear" (2.2.474–477)—Ned

Lukacher discerns both the encrypted signature of Shakespeare ("*sh* / ... *akes* ... *Pyr* ... *ear*") and the stirring of Pyrrhus's conscience.[2] Pyrrhus does nothing as he hearkens to the inarticulate noise that almost seems to call out to him. After the interrupted line of verse "Did nothing," the First Player continues:

> But as we often see, against some storm,
> A silence in the heavens, the rack stand sill,
> The bold winds speechless, and the orb below
> As hush as death, anon the dreadful thunder
> Doth rend the region; so after Pyrrhus' pause,
> A roused vengeance sets him new a-work,
> And never did the Cyclops' hammers fall
> On Mars's armor forg'd for proof eterne
> With less remorse than Pyrrhus' bleeding sword
> Now falls on Priam.
>
> (2.2.483–492)

Like Pyrrhus, Hamlet does nothing when he pauses with his sword poised above the declining head of irreverend Claudius. What precipitates his interruption isn't an external noise but the internal sounding of his own conscience. He worries about the prospect of a Pyrrhic victory—not the triumphal sort won by the son of Achilles, but the self-defeating sort that we associate with the King of Epirus, whose "triumphs" over Roman armies cost him far more than they did Rome. Were Hamlet to kill Claudius while he is praying, the king's soul might go to Heaven rather than to Purgatory or (as Hamlet would prefer) to Hell. Weighing this possible outcome against the fact that his father was "Cut off ... Unhous'led, disappointed, unanel'd" (1.5.76–77), he asks himself if this would be an adequate form of revenge. His answer is the simplest of negations: "No!" (3.3.87). Like the First Player's "Did nothing," Hamlet's "No!" is an entire line of verse that bears comparison with Lear's repeated trochaic negations when he realizes that Cordelia will "come no more": "Never, never, never, never, never" (5.3.308–309). For Hamlet, a single syllable suffices. Instead of killing Claudius, he sheathes his sword. Like the son of Achilles, he will avenge his father's death, but only after following a far more tortuous path.

Since the eighteenth century, this moment in the play has been known as that of Hamlet's "delay." I prefer to characterize it as his "tarrying." According to the *Oxford English Dictionary*, one sense of "tarry" is "to delay or be tardy in beginning or doing anything, esp. in coming or going." The OED also glosses Shakespeare's use of "delay" in a passage from 1 *Henry IV* as "To put off action; to linger, loiter, tarry." This conflation of the two terms is misleading, for Shakespeare seems never to use "tarry" as a synonym for "delay."[3] The primary sense of "tarry" in Shakespeare is to linger in a place without having to mind the clock. To "delay," by contrast, means to be guilty of tardiness, especially from the standpoint of the court or law. When Hamlet numbers "the law's delay" among "the whips and scorns of time" (3.1.69, 71) he gives this sense a reflexive twist, observing that the law itself can fail to achieve justice.[4] Hamlet seeks justice, but despite his acceptance of the role of heaven's "scourge and minister" (3.4.175), he isn't an agent of the law. It is Claudius who personifies the law, no more so than when he admonishes Rosencrantz, Guildenstern, and Laertes not to "delay" their respective charges. Were we to say, with the critics, that Hamlet delays, we would have to agree with Claudius when he warns Laertes:

> That we would do,
> We should do when we would, for this "would" changes,
> And hath abatements and delays as many
> As there are tongues, are hands, are accidents,
> And then this "should" is like a spendthrift's sigh,
> That hurts by easing.
> (4.7.118–123)

On the surface, this seems like good advice. But it expresses a fundamentally different attitude toward time and circumstance than the one that Hamlet conveys when he laments, "How all occasions do inform against me, / And spur my dull revenge!" (4.4.32–33), and "I do not know / Why yet I live to say, 'This thing's to do'" (4.4.43–44). While resolving to have none but "bloody" thoughts, he continues to do nothing as he leaves for England.[5] Claudius, by contrast, is always doing something in "hugger-mugger" (4.5.84) fashion. He has killed his brother and married his queen while the memory of his death is still "green" (1.2.2). The impropriety of this interruption of the time reserved for mourning is acknowledged not only by Claudius but by Gertrude ("our o'erhasty marriage" [2.2.57]) and Horatio ("Indeed, my lord, it followed hard upon" [1.2.179]). It torments Hamlet, as is indicated by his progressive compression of the actual period of time that has passed since his father's funeral: "But two months dead, nay, not so much, not two" (1.2.138); "within a month" (1.2.153); "within's two hours" (3.2.127).[6] Just as Hamlet always prefers to tarry, so Claudius always prefers not to delay. His advice to Laertes not to delay his revenge turns out to be bad advice. Laertes would have done better to tarry.

Like Hamlet, Socrates tarries. In Plato's *Theaetetus*, Socrates tells Theodorus that unlike lawyers and rhetoricians, whom the water-clocks of the court urge to hurry (i.e., not to delay), philosophers are able to take their time (i.e., to tarry): "Philosophical men always have what you spoke of just now: leisure.

They conduct their arguments in peace and at leisure. ... Meanwhile, the man of rhetoric always has to speak under pressure of time; for the water clock harries him onwards."[7] To suggest that Socrates would have been better off preparing for his trial than discussing the nature of knowledge with Theodorus and Theaetetus would be to recommend the kind of advice that another uncle associated with the law gives Josef K. in Kafka's *Trial*: "And you sit there calmly with a criminal trial hanging over your head?"[8] Like Josef K., Socrates and Hamlet have both been summoned before the law, but they respond to a higher calling (the decree of the Delphic oracle; the command of the Ghost). Though neither escapes the court alive, their deaths—like the tarrying that led to those deaths—transfigure the worlds they leave behind. Their final words to their respective friends—"We owe a cock to Asclepius"; "the rest is silence"—underscore the ultimate effectiveness of their tarrying.[9]

The word "tarry" doesn't appear in *Hamlet*, but Socrates's characterization of leisurely abiding outside the court fits Shakespeare's typical usage. When the Fool says that he "will tarry" (2.4.82) with King Lear, he implies not just that he will spend time with the ostracized king but that he will do so outside the court. In *2 Henry IV*, Falstaff tells Justice Shallow that he would happily share a drink with him but that he "cannot tarry dinner" (3.2.191–192). In this context "tarry" means "make time for." Falstaff implies that he must hurry to join Prince John at York, but he has been doing everything he can to postpone that appointment. King Henry admonishes Hal: "Our hands are full of business, let's away, / Advantage feeds him fat while men delay" (*1 Henry IV* 3.2.179–180). The implied jibe at the fattening Falstaff goes hand in hand with the king's wording. No one is better at tarrying than Falstaff, as is indicated by Hal when he pokes fun at Sir John for having no "reason" to "be so superfluous to demand the time of the day" (*1 Henry IV* 1.2.11–12). The emphasis in this passage should be put on the word "day," for as Kant reminded us, day is the time for urgent business, whereas night is the time most apt for tarrying. Falstaff would like the prince and himself to be known not as "thieves of the day's beauty" (that would make them delayers by the King's reckoning) but as "gentlemen of the shade, minions of the moon" (1.2.25–26). "We have heard the chimes at midnight," he tells Justice Shallow (*2 Henry IV* 3.2.215). If he cannot tarry dinner now, he nevertheless looks forward to tarrying long enough with Shallow on his return trip to "make him a philosopher's two stones" (3.2.329–330).

In *Henry VIII*, Queen Katherine refuses to "tarry" in the divorce court at Blackfriars (2.4.132). Doing so would grant the court a legitimacy she doesn't acknowledge. She will tarry elsewhere. Conversely, in the courtroom scene in *The Merchant of Venice*, Portia, disguised as Balthazar, orders Shylock not to leave the court: "Tarry a little. ... Tarry, Jew, / The law hath yet another hold on you" (4.1.305, 346–347).[10] Here Portia turns the tables on Shylock, who a moment before had refused to release Antonio from the hold the law had on him. Only after failing to convince Shylock to show mercy does Portia bid him to tarry in the name of the law. Her interpellation of him as a Jew—"Tarry, Jew"—functions as an interpellation precisely insofar as he himself stands for (Jewish) law. The claim that the law makes on him to tarry is essentially temporary, lasting only as long as it will take Shylock to (be forced to) convert to Christianity. Thus, although tarrying is here associated with the law, it is so only insofar as the law is in the process of being suspended by an agent not of law but of mercy. Something similar happens in *Measure for Measure* when Duke Vincentio's temporary refusal to pardon Angelo for ordering Claudio's execution is converted not just into legal exoneration but into a kind of ethical-religious forgiveness.[11] "Tarry, Jew" similarly marks the promise of a messianic suspension of the law despite the fact that Portia ironically announces it in the name of the law. Her two other uses of the word are in keeping with Shakespeare's usual practice. In 3.2 she bids Bassanio to "tarry, pause a day or two" (3.2.1) before undergoing the test of the caskets, lest he choose the wrong one and be forced by the quasi-legal decree of her father to abandon his hope to marry her.[12] Invoking two different types of torture, she wants to "peize the time" (3.2.22)—that is, lengthen it by pressing it with weights—while he wants to shorten it: "For as I am, I live upon the rack" (3.2.25). The alternatives of stretching and shrinking time are associated by Portia with tarrying and acting precipitately. She would prefer that Bassanio tarry now, while he would prefer to choose quickly so that they can tarry together afterwards. It is as if the two lovers were trying to follow the paradoxical maxim *Festina lente* (Make haste slowly) and had to choose between two ways of doing so.[13] A similar division between hastening and tarrying occurs in Portia's directive to Nerissa: "Away, make haste. Thou know'st where I will tarry" (4.2.18).

Another instance of tarrying lovers can be found in *Much Ado About Nothing*, when Beatrice and Benedick linger in the church after Claudio denounces Hero:

> Benedick   Come, bid me do any thing for thee.
> Beatrice   Kill Claudio.
> Benedick   Ha, not for the wide world.
> Beatrice   You kill me to deny it. Farewell.
> Benedick   Tarry, sweet Beatrice.
>
> (4.1.288–292)

Benedick wouldn't kill Claudio for the wide world—but Beatrice exceeds the wide world in value.[14] When he bids her to tarry, he indicates his readiness to challenge his friend if she is convinced that Claudio has wronged her cousin. After she confirms her conviction he again bids her to tarry: "Tarry, good

Beatrice. By this hand, I love thee" (4.1.324–325). Soon Benedick is "engag'd" (4.1.331) in more senses than one. Eventually the two lovers will counter-sign the signs of love they exchange here, completing the conversion of their habitual verbal parrying into mutual tarrying by marrying.[15]

One final example is worth noting because of the suggestive way in which it contrasts tarrying with delaying. In *The Comedy of Errors*, Dromio of Syracuse tries to remind the baffled Antipholus of Ephesus how he was "hind'red by the sergeant to tarry for the hoy *Delay*" (4.3.39–40)—that is, prevented from boarding the ship that would have taken Antipholus of Syracuse away from Ephesus. Dromio's complicated thought seems to be that an agent of the law has taken from Antipholus the time he would have needed to await the paradoxically named ship that would have sped him away *without* delay. To "*tarry for the hoy Delay*" is not to *await* a delay but to *circumvent* one.

Perhaps I have tarried too long in this lexical detour.[16] By way of excuse, I offer my reading of the tarry–delay distinction in the same spirit in which Foucault offers his identification of a provisional distinction in Nietzsche's use of *Herkunft* ("descent") and *Ursprung* ("origin") in *The Genealogy of Morals*.[17] While conceding that Nietzsche may not always adhere to the terminological distinction his text broaches, Foucault puts it to good philosophical use. We can do something similar with the distinction between tarrying and delaying. To represent Hamlet as tarrying rather than as delaying is to represent him as standing outside the law as Socrates does in the *Theaetetus*. When he interrupts himself in 3.3 with the word "No!" he literally "tarries with the negative" (*verweilen beim Negativen*). Tarrying with the negative is a way of doing nothing—not in the sense of remaining inactive, but in the sense of performing a negative act or nonact that gains extra time or "surplus" time. The character of surplus time is aptly described by Derrida in his remarks on a letter from Madame de Maintenon, the wife of King Louis XIV, to Madame de Brinon, the superintendent of a boarding school at Saint-Cyr: "The king takes all my time; I give the rest to Saint-Cyr, to whom I would like to give all."[18] The *rest* of Madame de Maintenon's time is the part that is excluded from the totality of the time of the court. It is equivalent to the "interim" that Hamlet claims for himself when Horatio says, "It must be shortly known to [the king] from England / What is the issue of the business there": "It will be short; the interim's mine" (5.2.71–73).[19] *The king takes all of Hamlet's time; he gives the rest to the memory of his father, to whom he would like to give all.* The rest of Hamlet's time after 3.3 will be used to end the reign of Claudius and send him to Hell.

Critics in the eighteenth century were horrified at Hamlet's professed intention not just to kill Claudius but to damn him. Dr. Johnson regarded his speech as "too horrible to be read or to be uttered."[20] By the end of the century the critics had decided that Hamlet couldn't really mean what he was saying; he must be rationalizing his inability to act. In this way, his negative act was reinterpreted as inactivity, his tarrying as delaying.

How should we understand Hamlet's negative act? In the *Critique of Pure Reason*, Kant identifies four ways of *cognizing* nothing. Perhaps we can extrapolate four corresponding ways of *doing* nothing and so zero in on what is peculiar to Hamlet's tarrying. We cognize nothing when the supposed object of a representation involves (1) an "empty concept without [an] object, *ens rationis*"; (2) an "empty object of a concept, *nihil privativum*"; (3) an "empty intuition without an object, *ens imaginarium*"; or (4) an "empty object without [a] concept, *nihil negativum*."[21] An *ens rationis*, or being of reason, is a problematic object of a non-contradictory concept—something we can consistently think, but not cognize, like a noumenon. A *nihil privativum* is an absence or lack, like a shadow. An *ens imaginarium*, or imaginary entity, is, for Kant, a pure form of intuition, empty space or time. Finally, a *nihil negativum*, or negative nothing, is something impossible, whether because its concept is inherently self-contradictory or because it is incompatible with the spatiotemporal form of the empirical world.[22] Trading concepts for maxims (rules of action) and intuitions for inclinations (desires) yields four corresponding types of negative activity. We perform a negative act when the supposed object of our activity involves (1) an empty maxim without an object, (2) an empty object of a maxim, (3) an empty inclination without an object, or (4) an empty object without a maxim. These possibilities can be identified, respectively, as (1) a "noumenal" act that lacks a phenomenal object, (2) a "privative" act that falls short of acting in a positive manner, (3) an "imaginary" act that merely exhibits the conditions for the possibility of acting in a positive manner, and (4) an "impossible" act—one that is either inherently self-contradictory or incompatible with the existing conditions for the possibility of acting in a positive manner.

Aspects of Hamlet's nonactivity have been characterized in each of these four ways.

(1) To act on an empty maxim without an object—to perform a noumenal act—is to engage in pointless activity. Often, the secret purpose of pointless activity is to delay the performance of an effective act. From a psychoanalytic perspective, such is the character of an obsessive act. An obsessional neurotic "does nothing" not by sitting around like "John-a-dreams" but by following maxims that defer effective action. Coleridge takes Hamlet to behave in this manner when he postpones killing Claudius for the sake of sending his soul to Hell: "Hamlet seizes hold of a pretext for not acting, when he might have acted so effectually."[23] This pretext is his empty maxim.[24]

(2) To pursue the empty object of a maxim—to perform a privative act—is to behave in an "antic" or hysterical manner. Hamlet tells Horatio and

Marcellus that he will *put on* an antic disposition, but many critics have felt that he actually does behave hysterically. This interpretation is consistent with his remark to Laertes that it was his madness, and not he himself, that wronged his brother. Some critics find this apology to be hypocritical, but it is in keeping with the "rash and bloody" (3.4.27) character of his slaying of Polonius. Unlike noumenal activity, which *postpones* an effective act, privative or hysterical activity *preempts* one.[25] Ella Sharpe picks up on this dimension of Hamlet's situation when she argues that "the impatience of Hamlet, not procrastination, is the central problem of the play." According to Sharpe, Hamlet is unable to "tolerate" the "waiting time" required by his melancholia.[26] Always on the verge of self-destruction or madness, his procrastination is a means of self-defense, an "ekeing-out of time."[27] Whenever he does act, he does so prematurely, as when he slays Polonius.[28] This isn't a delaying tactic, but it has a similar postponing effect; as Friar Laurence warns Romeo: "Too swift arrives as tardy as too slow" (2.6.15). Rosencrantz conjectures that the cause of Hamlet's melancholy is ambition, "the very substance" of which "is merely the shadow of a dream" (2.2.257–259). His diagnosis is incorrect, but his characterization of ambition could be applied to privative activity, the very substance of which is merely the shadow of *fantasy*.

(3) An empty inclination without an object is an imaginary act or fantasy. Taking his cue from Kant, Coleridge distinguishes productive "imagination" from reproductive "fancy."[29] Imagination, or fantasy in its productive sense, frames our perception of reality in much the same way that an empty intuition without an object reveals the formal structures of space and time. What Lacan adds to this idea is that the cognitive and practical dimensions of imagination are always intertwined so that fantasy frames both perception and desire. For Lacan, Shakespeare's play is primarily about Hamlet's overproximity to the desire of his mother.[30] His irrepressible fantasies about Gertrude's desire for Claudius prevent him from locating Ophelia in the fantasy frame of his own desire.[31] All he can do is impotently fantasize (now in the Coleridgean sense of fancying) about killing Claudius. His self-reproaches—such as "I do not know / Why yet I live to say, 'This thing's to do'" (4.4.43–44)—show that he is well aware of the merely fantasmatic structure of his empty intention. Coleridge concludes that Hamlet suffers from "perpetual solicitation of the mind to act, but as constant an escape from action."[32] As André Gide observes, however, Hamlet's fantasies are not completely idle, for they prepare the way for effective action: "In *Hamlet*, from one end to the other, nothing bolder, more skilful, than that shift which takes place by which each decisive action is preceded by a sort of tryout of that action, as if it had trouble fitting into *reality*."[33] Hamlet's problem is to pass from an imaginary act to an

effective act. As Deleuze observes, he needs time to become "capable" of this passage.[34]

(4) Finally, an empty object without a maxim is an impossible act. Kant characterizes an empty object without a concept as a "monster" or *Unding*. Analogously, we can characterize an impossible act as a monstrous act or *Unhandlung* (i.e., an "un-act" or "nonact," the practical analogue of an infinite judgment).[35] One type of *Unhandlung* is inherently impossible. Another is impossible only given the existing conditions for the possibility of acting in an effective manner. The first is self-defeating, but the latter could involve striving to transform the existing conditions for effective action. In the latter case, the object would be utopian if the conditions in question were practically necessary and thus insuperable, but it would be revolutionary if these conditions were practically contingent and so capable of being transformed. *Pace* Deleuze, a revolutionary nonact needs time to develop because it exceeds the order of what is currently possible. Deleuze invites us to think of Hamlet's nonact as revolutionary when he observes that, unlike Oedipus, whose effective act belongs essentially to the past, Hamlet's belongs essentially to the future.[36] We can say of a revolution what Hamlet says of death: "If it be now, 'tis not to come; if it be not to come, it will be now; if it be not now, yet it will come—the readiness is all" (5.2.220–222).

Hamlet's tarrying is revolutionary in this precise sense. Insofar as he tarries, he is not an obsessional neurotic whose true aim (repetition) differs from his ostensible goal (revenge).[37] Nor does his tarrying make him a hysteric whose true aim is preemption and provocation. Nor does he remain stuck at the level of fantasy when he tarries, as if he were incapable of a *passage à l'acte*. Nor, finally, is his tarrying utopian. It is revolutionary in that it seeks to make possible an effective act whose object, at the present moment, is impossible.

Since the nineteenth century, Hamlet's tarrying has been associated both with revolutionary potential and with revolutionary failure. At the end of his lectures on the history of philosophy, Hegel compares the historical activity of spirit to the subterranean tunneling of the Ghost: "Spirit often seems to have forgotten and lost itself, but inwardly opposed to itself, it is inwardly working ever forward (as when Hamlet says of the ghost of his father, 'Well said, old mole! canst work i' the ground so fast?'), until grown strong in itself it bursts asunder the crust of earth which divided it from the sun, its Notion, so that the earth crumbles away."[38] Marx gives this passage a materialist twist in his "Eighteenth Brumaire of Louis Bonaparte": "But the revolution is thorough-going. It is still preoccupied with journeying through purgatory. It does its work methodically. By 2 December [1851] it had completed half its preparatory work, and now it is completing the other half. … And when it has brought this second half of its preparatory work to completion the whole of Europe will jump up and cry: Well grubbed up, old mole!"[39] Marx's modification of "Well said" (*Brav* in the Schlegel-Tieck translation) to "Well grubbed up" (*Brav gewühlt*) suggests that the medium of revolutionary activity is economic rather than philosophical.[40] It is the mole qua animal, not qua spirit, that tunnels toward the light. The implication is that Hegel's mole is a mere ghost or shade, a shadow lacking sufficient *material* reality to be the cause of the objective reality of historical events: "When we criticize the *œuvres posthumes* of our ideal history, i.e. philosophy, instead of the *œuvres incomplètes* of our real history, our criticism stands at the centre of those problems of which the present age says: *That is the question* [*Das ist die Frage*]."[41] In one of his earliest writings on Hegel's *Philosophy of Right*, Marx recasts "To be or not to be" as the question of the success or failure of the revolution: "Sovereignty of the monarch or of the people—that is the question."[42] Replacing the ghost of *Geist* with a puckish spirit, he identifies the revolution with "Robin Goodfellow, the old mole that can work in the earth so fast."[43]

Before the French Revolution, Shakespeare was reviled in Paris not only for violating the classical dramatic unities (*pace* Voltaire) but for his perceived political subversiveness. After the Revolution, he was championed as the poet of the people. As Richard Wilson summarizes:

> In the decades before 1789 the graveyard scene in *Hamlet*—with its workers gloating over the skulls of the great—came to symbolise the popular justice that the savants of the salons thought had been suppressed in France. But after the Terror, this "Gothic Shakespeare," with his theatre of animality and blood, haunted the imagination of nineteenth-century Paris as the "Man of the Crowd," and a forecast of the return of repressed revolutionary crimes.[44]

Marx shared Victor Hugo's enthusiasm for the revolutionary dimension of Shakespeare. The Marx household in London was described by one contemporary as "a Shakespearean cult."[45] Marx frequently recited Shakespeare to his children, while his wife Jenny reviewed contemporary Shakespeare performances.[46] She called him "the Moor," apparently an allusion to Othello since he once said in a letter that he loved her "more than the Moor of Venice ever loved." In the same letter he went on to allude to Hamlet, imagining his critics comparing a picture of Marx the social critic to a picture of Marx lying at Jenny's feet: "'Look to this picture and to that!'—that's what they should have written underneath."[47]

Marx's admiration for Shakespeare is evidenced in his response to Ferdinand Lassalle's tragedy *Franz von Sickingen*. He told the young dramatist that he should have let "the most modern ideas … speak in their purest form. … You would then have found yourself compelled to *Shakespearize* more, while now

I see *Schillerizing*, the transformation of individuals into mere mouthpieces for the spirit of the time."[48] Shakespeare's characters come from all walks of social life, a feature that Marx admired in Balzac as well. Marx's own writings are filled with miniature Shakespearizings in which not only Hamlet and Othello but Dogberry, Lysander, Malvolio, Shylock, Benedick, Mistress Quickly, Falstaff, Pistol, Thersites, Timon, and others are associated with contemporary political figures. From the frequency of his use of the phrase *Das ist die Frage*, it is evident that he enjoyed playing the revolutionary Hamlet.[49] As Peter Stallybrass notes, he would have relished multiple levels of "subversive activity" in Hamlet's reference to the old mole: "The modern German for subversive activity—*Maulwurfsarbeit*—means literally the work of the mole. In figuring his father as mole, Hamlet enacts a radical metamorphosis: from human to animal; from omnipotent monarch to blind burrower; from ideological figurehead to a worker in the ground."[50]

Like Hegel, Marx knew that it takes time to make a revolution. His awareness of time makes him a thinker of history as well as of politics—or, rather, of political history and historical politics. The nature of historical politics is pithily summarized in the *Eighteenth Brumaire*: "Men make their own history, but they do not make it just as they please in circumstances they choose for themselves; rather they make it in present circumstances, given and inherited."[51] Circumstances given and inherited are the conditions for the possibility and impossibility of effective actions. The crucial question for a would-be revolutionary is how to transform existing conditions that are unjust.

Hannah Arendt criticizes both Hegel and Marx for allegedly conflating history and politics. She observes that the Hegelian theme of the "cunning of reason" ultimately derives from Kant and Hamlet: "It was Kant, not Hegel, who was the first to conceive of a cunning secret force in order to find meaning in political history at all. The experience behind this is no other than Hamlet's: 'Our thoughts are ours, their ends none of our own,' except that this experience was particularly humiliating for a philosophy whose center was the dignity and the autonomy of man."[52] For Hegel and Marx, there was nothing humiliating about the fact that political agents had to reckon with history. Nor did reckoning with history mean reducing politics to teleology. According to Arendt, a historically minded politics conflates the incompatible stances of a cognizing spectator and an engaged actor. As political agents we are free, but only on the condition that we suspend judgment about our place in history; as soon as we try to observe ourselves from the retrospective standpoint of a future historian, we lose our sense of freedom and have no other choice but to represent ourselves as mere instruments of historical necessity.[53] Hamlet's distinction between the ends we set ourselves and the ends we actually achieve is recast by Arendt as the difference between political objectives and historical results. While she resists any appeal to a historical divinity that shapes our political ends, she also emphasizes the Hamlet-like character of politics. In "Personal Responsibility under Dictatorship" she observes: "Whoever takes upon himself political responsibility will always come to the point where he says with Hamlet: 'The time is out of joint: O cursed spite / That ever I was born to set it right!" Implicitly emphasizing the word "born," Arendt equates our capacity to set the time right with our "natality": "To set the time aright means to renew the world, and this we can do because we all arrived at one time or another as newcomers in a world which was there before us and will still be there when we are gone, when we shall have left its burden to our successors."[54] Natality is not just our beginning at birth, but our ever-present possibility—indeed necessity—of beginning anew.

Despite her worry about the conflation of history and politics, Arendt's conception of natality as the charge to set right an out-of-joint time is not incompatible with Hegel's and Marx's belief that there is a dialectical relationship between the standpoints of the historical spectator and the engaged political agent. On their understanding of Hamlet's pronouncement, our relationship to the present is always mediated by our relationships to the past and the future. Far from overdetermining politics, historical consciousness is a condition for the possibility of our freedom. In a sense, we are constantly faced, as is Hamlet, by the choice between actions that are "too early" or "too late." We must choose whether to tarry (as the Mensheviks argued should be done before the Russian Revolution) or to perform a precipitate act (as the Bolsheviks insisted). Since time is always out of joint, there is never a "right" time to act. This is compatible with our constantly being beginners.[55] A greater danger than that of the mixing of history and politics is that of a one-sided political passivism that does nothing but delay and the converse conflation of a one-sided political activism that treats all tarrying as delaying.

Over the years, militants on both the Left and Right have accused their opponents of suffering from a political Hamlet complex. In his History of the Russian Revolution, Trotsky labeled Julius Martov, the leader of the Mensheviks, "the Hamlet of democratic socialism," and he castigated Nikolai Sukhanov for "his Hamlet temperament."[56] In 1844, the poet Ferdinand Freiligrath, who like Marx wrote for the Neue Rheinische Zeitung and took part in the temporarily impossible revolutionary acts of 1848, identified the fledgling German nation with an indecisive Hamlet: "Germany is Hamlet. ... Its boldest act is only thinking [Deutschland ist Hamlet! ... Sein bestes Tun ist eben Denken]."[57] In Mein Kampf, Hitler warned: "When the nations on this planet fight for existence—when the question of destiny, 'to be or not to be,' cries out for a solution—then all considerations of humanitarianism or aesthetics crumble into nothingness."[58] In 1933, the year he came to power, a new "activist Hamlet" began to appear on the German stage. In 1936, the actor Gustaf Gründgens performed Hamlet in Berlin in a blond wig. He was "full of responsibility" and "ready to act."[59] In 1940, the poet Hermann Burte, celebrating "the extraordinary work of Adolf Hitler," declared of the future German poet: "He will not be a Hamlet who flees from himself, because he will set aright the times that are out of joint!"[60] In France, Jean-Louis Barrault was "attacked in the Vichy press for playing Hamlet as someone who 'lacks fire, and thinks rather than feels.'"[61] After the war, the Freiligrathian Hamlet resurfaced on the Left, notably in Heiner Müller's Hamletmachine, in which a Red Brigade Ophelia takes over the role of an effective revolutionary from a Hamlet whose Oedipus complex has reached crisis proportions.[62]

A Marxist defense of the tarrying Hamlet can be found in Walter Benjamin. In The Origin of German Tragic Drama (1928) Benjamin argues that the seventeenth-century Trauerspiel, or mourning play, has an entirely different political significance from that of classical tragedy. Whereas tragedy is associated with myth, Trauerspiel is allegorical. Mythical time is circular, whereas allegorical time is linear and historical. Thus on Benjamin's account, the cultural shift from tragedy to Trauerspiel reflects the same becoming-out-of-joint of time that Deleuze associates with Kant's Copernican revolution. Allegorical time is out of joint not only because it has ceased to measure the eternal motion of the cosmos around a stable center, but because it establishes virtual correspondences between distinct historical time-slices. In classical tragedy, human beings are subject to the blows of fate, but they acquire a kind of sublime dignity by struggling against them. In the Trauerspiel, human suffering loses all meaning. Yet precisely by "signifying nothing," the Trauerspiel negatively signifies the foreclosed promise of redemption. Its martyred princes display neither the beauty of Michelangelo's David nor the sublimity of his prisoners, but the melancholy that Benjamin associates with Dürer's engraving Melencolia I and which is well expressed by the elderly Niños in Michelangelo Antonioni's film The Passenger when he says (calling "tragedy" what apart from the suggestion of circular time befits Benjamin's conception of Trauerspiel): "Other people look at the children and they all imagine a new world. But me, when I watch them I just see the same old tragedy begin all over again. They can't get away from us. It's boring."[63] As Benjamin observes, the German Trauerspiel is in fact boring: being boring rather than beautiful or sublime is its intrinsic aesthetic feature. The only Trauerspiel that managed to "strike Christian sparks" from the genre was Hamlet. Hamlet redeems allegorical time not by passing from indecision to decision but by tarrying with the negativity of the Trauerspiel itself:

> Whereas tragedy ends with a decision—however uncertain this may be—
> there resides in the essence of the Trauerspiel, and especially in the death-scene,
> an appeal of the kind which martyrs utter. ...

For the *Trauerspiel* Hamlet alone is a spectator by the grace of God; but he cannot find satisfaction in what he sees enacted, only in his own fate. His life, the exemplary object of his mourning, points, before its extinction, to the Christian providence in whose bosom his mournful images are transformed into a blessed existence. Only in a princely life such as this is melancholy redeemed, by being confronted with itself. The rest is silence.[64]

After the war, Carl Schmitt accused Benjamin of depoliticizing *Hamlet* by representing it as a *Trauerspiel*.[65] Drawing on the work of Lilian Winstanley, Schmitt's *Hamlet or Hecuba?* (1956) takes the political significance of *Hamlet* to derive from the Elizabethan succession crisis.[66] When *Hamlet* was first performed around 1601, King James VI of Scotland hadn't yet been named Elizabeth's successor, but he had many political supporters in London, including Shakespeare's patron the Earl of Southampton. Gertrude's marriage to Claudius would have reminded audiences of the 1567 marriage of James's mother, Mary Queen of Scots, to the Earl of Bothwell, the man suspected of murdering James's father. Schmitt takes the play's silence concerning the question of Gertrude's complicity in Claudius's crime to be a kind of compromise formation that gingerly avoided the question concerning Mary's guilt. Another aspect of the play that Schmitt focuses on is what he calls "the distortion of the avenger that leads to the Hamletization of the hero."[67] This represented a coded message to James that he should not, like Hamlet, *delay* his claim to the English crown. Schmitt characterizes these historical "intrusions" (*Einbrüche*) as more than mere "*allusions*" and "*mirrorings*."[68] While granting that the play contains passing allusions to minor events and well-delineated mirrorings of significant events such as the rebellion and execution of the Earl of Essex, he discerns something different in kind in the Jacobean intrusions or incorporations, namely, the politicization of the play and its transformation into "an authentic myth."[69] *Hamlet* was a modern tragedy that had living significance for Shakespeare's contemporaries and lasting significance for later audiences who might no longer recognize its historical significance in the context of the Elizabethan succession crisis but could readily appreciate its political significance in their own historical contexts. Only when the theater lost its public/political status and became a private/cultural site for mere entertainment was it possible for *Hamlet* to be played as a "mere" *Trauerspiel*. By reducing *Hamlet* to the sad story of the death of a prince, Benjamin, like Schiller before him, occluded its political significance.

The political significance of *Hamlet* lies for Schmitt in its underwriting of a modern conception of sovereignty according to which the sovereign is "he who decides on the exception."[70] The tragedy of *Hamlet* is that Hamlet *delays* his claim to sovereignty. For Benjamin, by contrast, *Hamlet* is a *Trauerspiel*—and a political one at that—because the prince *tarries.* In the messianic terms that Benjamin later develops, Hamlet's tarrying can be likened to the effort of a passenger aboard "the locomotive of world history … to activate the emergency break." The task of the historical materialist is not to serve history as an instrument but to release the "messianic force" that disrupts it from within.[71] Hamlet's reference to the divinity that shapes our ends is messianic in this precise sense. Far from depoliticizing the play, Benjamin brings out its revolutionary potential. Thus, the debate between Benjamin and Schmitt isn't about a political versus an apolitical Hamlet; it is about the character of Hamlet's politics. Schmitt, a conservative jurist whose assistance in rewriting the Weimar constitution helped to justify the Nazis' claim to sovereignty, professes to understand both *Hamlet* and the nature of political theology better than the Marxist Jew who took his own life to avoid being sent back to Germany. His representation of *Hamlet* as a modern myth rather than an out-of-joint allegory not only masks the play's revolutionary character but retrospectively justifies the Nazis' representation of themselves as resolute Hamlets who had to overcome the aestheticizing tendencies that they attributed to Jews, and which Schmitt now attributes to the martyred Benjamin. Apart from this offensive subtext, Schmitt's identification of Hamlet with James unconvincingly reduces Hamlet's melancholy to the disappointment of a dawdling heir—an interpretation worthy of the clueless Rosencrantz.

According to Benjamin, Hamlet's tarrying opens up a type of messianic politics that had been unknown to classical tragic protagonists. This crucial claim is overlooked not only by Schmitt but by Alain Badiou when he develops a theory of political subjectivity around the figures of Orestes and Antigone. Picking up on the phrase *prince amer de l'écueil* ("bitter prince of the reef") in Mallarmé's *Un coup de dés*, Badiou characterizes Hamlet as "the master of the undecidable act."[72] ("Only a decision! [*Nur ein Entschluß!*]" is the imploring first line of the last stanza of Freiligrath's poem.) Appropriating Marx's critique of Hegel, Badiou writes: "It is only in drama, as in *Hamlet,* that specters cast a semblance of efficacy."[73] Instead of looking to Shakespeare for a model of revolutionary agency, as Marx and Benjamin did, Badiou turns in his *Theory of the Subject* to Sophocles and Aeschylus.

Like Hegel, Badiou takes Antigone's collision with Creon to represent a structural deadlock that she is unable to resolve. Instead of transforming the social coordinates that make her burial of Polyneices impossible, Antigone is herself buried alive. Unable to grub her way back to the surface, the poor mole hangs herself. For Hegel, this result symbolized the decline of ancient Greek ethical life, but Badiou takes it to symbolize the inadequacy of Hegel's own idealist philosophy to resolve the materialist contradictions of capitalist society. With an eye toward identifying a form of political subjectivity that would be capable of resolving such contradictions, he turns from Sophocles's

Antigone to Aeschylus's *Oresteia*. What Antigone is unable to accomplish, namely, the founding of a new order, Orestes achieves.

Together, the Antigone–Creon and Orestes–Athena dyads represent for Badiou complementary aspects of a fourfold theory of political subjectivity. Sophocles's coordinates are characterized as both idealist (prefiguring Hegel) and structuralist (prefiguring Lacan), whereas Aeschylus's are said to be historical and materialist. Structuralism and idealism privilege "place" over "force," whereas historical materialism privileges force over place. To privilege place is to reduce politics to the art of mere realignment. Despite Hegel's insistence that Antigone's defiance of Creon anticipates the destruction of the Greek ethical world, Badiou maintains that her negative act changes nothing essential. In the context of the *Phenomenology of Spirit*, it would be equivalent to the termination of a struggle for recognition not in the institution of a master–slave relationship but in the immediate death of one who refused to be enslaved. Such a death may be heroic, even sublime, but it is also completely ineffective. Identifying Creon's subjective position with that of the superego and Antigone's with that of anxiety, Badiou acknowledges that the play ends with the mutual defeat of both parties but without bringing about a positive transition to a more just society. For such a transition to take place, the subjective affect of anxiety would have to be transformed into courage, and the superegoic character of state law would have to give way to justice. Absent such a double transformation, the mutual defeat of Creon and Antigone leaves the basic structural conflict between anxiety and the superego in place. Hegel himself takes the decline of Greek ethical life to lead to the various forms of anxious servility under tyranny that he finds writ large in ancient Rome. Thus, even for Hegel, Antigone's act, while it changes something, fails to resolve the fundamental social antagonism. But according to Badiou, Hegel fails to appreciate the evanescent character of Antigone's act. She temporarily embodies the excess of force over the structural place to which she is assigned in Thebes, but her act reveals this excess only in the same way that a flash of lightning reveals both itself and the night to which it immediately returns. Antigone's surplus-force is symmetrical to that of Creon. The collision between them plays itself out like the mutual annihilation of matter and antimatter. Genuine liberation from the superego–anxiety pair requires *effective* destruction, or what Badiou calls a "disruptive inception."[74]

It is this force that Badiou finds shared between Orestes and Athena in Aeschylus's trilogy. Orestes destroys the old order, while Athena founds the new. Like Antigone, Orestes is no stranger to anxiety, but he experiences it differently. Antigone is never in doubt that she must bury her brother's corpse, so her anxiety has nothing to do with uncertainty about the task to which she is called. If anything, she experiences anxiety because she does *not* doubt, because there is no symbolic buffer separating her from the real force that her act manifests. In this respect, Antigone exemplifies what Lacan calls the "lack of lack." By contrast, Orestes is anxious because he *does* doubt, because he questions Apollo's command to avenge his mother's murder of his father. Badiou suggests that it is precisely because Antigone doesn't doubt that her resolve to defy Creon's edict takes the form of a blind will to destruction. Conversely, Orestes's doubt enables him to perform a deliberate act. Such an act requires that anxiety be transformed into courage. It takes courage for Orestes to commit matricide deliberately rather than in a frenzy, as Agave kills Pentheus in Euripides's *Bacchae*. Yet even the courage of Orestes isn't sufficient to bring about the disruptive inception of a new order. For this, Athena's intervention is necessary. To break the cycle of retribution to which Orestes's crime belongs, Athena must placate the unleashed Erinyes. Just as, for Nietzsche's Zarathustra, the destructive act of the lion must be supplemented by the innocent affirmation of the child, so Orestes's matricide must be supplemented by the absolution he is granted by the Athenian jurors.[75] By casting the tie-breaking vote and relegating the Erinyes to the cellarage (evidently to play the role of tunneling moles), Athena retroactively justifies Orestes's act. In the same way that Orestes passes from anxiety to courage, Athena represents the passage from the superego to justice. Together they accomplish what Antigone and Creon could not, namely, the institution of a new political order. Because courage originates in anxiety, and justice in the superego, Badiou's model of political subjectivity requires all four of these tragic coordinates.

One problem with this model has to do with the confinement of the Erinyes to the cellarage. As Žižek points out, Badiou effectively equates justice with the advent of a "patriarchal Law" beneath which there lurks barely repressed (maternal) "superego fury."[76] Another problem is that it is odd to think of Aeschylus as solving problems posed by Sophocles. As Aristotle reports, Sophocles went beyond Aeschylus by adding a third actor.[77] This enabled him to mediate the tragic protagonist's relationship to his or her antagonist. The collision between Antigone and Creon is dyadic, but it is mediated by the crucial figure of Ismene. It is she, rather than Antigone, who represents anxiety in the face of the Creonic superego. Indeed, Antigone steels her own icy resolve against her sister's fear of punishment.[78] Badiou makes no reference to Ismene, an omission that makes his reading of the Antigone–Creon dyad strangely Aeschylean rather than Sophoclean.

Only once does Aeschylus introduce a third actor, in another scene that Badiou doesn't mention. When Orestes comes to kill Clytemnestra in *The Libation Bearers*, he is accompanied by his friend Pylades. Discovering her son's purpose, Clytemnestra implores him to remember that it was she who gave birth to him and nursed him as an infant. Suddenly, Orestes is filled with self-doubt. He hesitates in precisely the same manner that Pyrrhus hesitates in the First

Player's narration in *Hamlet*. Instead of replying directly to Clytemnestra, he turns to his friend: "What shall I do, Pylades? Be shamed to kill my mother?" Until this moment, Pylades has been silent, as if waiting for Orestes to address him. By giving Pylades a voice, Aeschylus represents the birth of conscience as the voice of the friend. But this birth—again, like that of Pyrrhus's conscience—turns out to be a stillbirth, a missed opportunity, a nonevent cut off by the authoritative voice of the gods. Like Ismene, Pylades bids Orestes to remember the decree of a superegoic father figure—in this case, Apollo. In Richmond Lattimore's translation: "What then becomes thereafter of the oracles declared by Loxias at Pytho? What of sworn oaths? Count all men hateful to you rather than the gods."[79] Orestes is satisfied; the die has been cast. The master of the *decidable* act kills Clytemnestra. At the end of the cycle, Athenian justice will put an end to the cycle of retribution, but only at the cost of a tenuous repression that will return, precisely, in *Hamlet*. On Badiou's troubling account of political subjectivity, Orestes's matricide is the revolutionary act *par excellence*. The fact that he kills Clytemnestra deliberately rather than in a fit of madness is hardly mitigating. After all, we pity Agave, but shudder at Medea.

Why does Badiou take the buried Antigone to pass the revolutionary baton *backward*, to Orestes, rather than *forward*, to Hamlet? Why does he Aeschylize rather than Shakespearize? As Žižek observes, both *Antigone* and *Hamlet* deal with the political stakes of an improper burial.[80] Critchley and Webster argue in Badiou's backward fashion that Antigone begins where Hamlet leaves off.[81] Following Benjamin, I would argue instead that Hamlet is a modern Antigone who, as a figure of *Trauerspiel*, is able to resolve a deadlock that she, as a figure of tragedy, cannot.

In 1803, Hegel believed that the *Oresteia* provided an ideal representation of the birth of ethical life. What he would later represent in *Antigone* as the collision between divine and human law, the law of the state and the law of the family, is portrayed in his essay on natural law as a conflict between Apollo, the god of light, and the Erinyes (or Eumenides), presiders over the hearth. This collision is resolved by Athena, whose Christlike embodiment of the divine in human form enables her to mediate between the two realms. What placates the Erinyes, for Hegel, is not simply that they are given a place in the cellarage, but that, outside it, they have a room with a view: "the Eumenides ... would now have their place in the city, so that their savage nature would enjoy (from the altar erected to them in the city below) the sight of Athene enthroned on high in the Acropolis, and thereby be pacified."[82] Thus for the early Hegel, Aeschylus's old moles have found their place in the sun. Why, then, did Hegel abandon this model of reconciled powers in favor of his later account of the destructive collision of Sophocles's *Antigone*? Why did he go in the opposite direction from Badiou, representing the crime of Antigone as more significant than that of Orestes?

The answer has to do with the fact that the *Oresteia* marks the advent of the Greek ethical world, as Hegel understands it, and *Antigone* the beginning of its decline. In 1803, Hegel believed that the Greek polis could be revived, albeit not in its original, "naive" form. As a "sentimental" modern, he knew that the inner spiritual life that Luther, Hamlet, and Descartes had disclosed made it impossible for Protestant Europe to return to Athens. But he agreed with Schiller that to complete the unfinished project of modernity—the project undertaken by the French Revolutionaries—it was necessary to create an aesthetic state in which modern subjects would become, as it were, Christian Athenians.[83] By 1807, Hegel had come to doubt the viability of any return to Greek ethical life. Accordingly, he turns his attention away from the *Oresteia* and toward *Antigone*. The properly Christian (i.e., for Hegel, Protestant) experience of subjectivity begins (both chronologically and dialectically) only after the destruction of the Greek world. In modernity, tragic collisions take the form of moral dilemmas within the souls of tragic protagonists. Within this constellation, what would a modern *Oresteia* look like?

Kierkegaard raises the same question about *Antigone*. He imagines a modern Antigone who is the only person to know her father's crimes. This shifts the focus of her drama from the performance of public deeds to the maintenance of private secrets. Instead of dutifully burying her brother, a modern Antigone would remain silent, as Cordelia does when Lear bids her to bare her soul. Having no external act to perform, Kierkegaard's modern Antigone would undergo an internal collision instead.[84] Kierkegaard reads *Hamlet* in the same way. What Schmitt represents as a "taboo" concerning the question of Gertrude's guilt is for Kierkegaard the necessity of Hamlet's keeping secret (even in soliloquy) his suspicion about her complicity in the regicide. What distinguishes Shakespeare's characters from those of Sophocles and Aeschylus is not only that they have inner lives, but that their inner lives are the true theaters of decisive happenings. A modern Orestes would be forced to ruminate—all the more if the question of his mother's guilt were left uncertain and if he were instructed by the spirit of his father *not* to kill her but rather to "leave her to heaven" (1.5.86).

Prior to Freud, it was customary to compare Hamlet to the Orestes of Aeschylus's *Choephori* and Sophocles's *Elektra* rather than to the Oedipus of *Oedipus Tyrannus*.[85] Although Freud insists that Hamlet unconsciously wants to do what Oedipus unconsciously does, a far more salient parallel is that Hamlet deliberately doesn't do what Orestes deliberately does, namely, kill his mother to avenge his father's murder. As Nicholas Rowe first observed in 1709: "Hamlet is represented with the same Piety towards his Father, and Resolution to Revenge his Death, as *Orestes*; he has the same Abhorrence for his Mother's Guilt, which, to provoke him the more, is heighten'd by Incest. But 'tis with wonderful Art and Justness of Judgment that the Poet restrains him from doing Violence to his Mother."[86] Eighteenth-century critics were divided as to whether Sophocles's *Elektra* or Shakespeare's *Hamlet* was a more accomplished tragedy.[87] For Herder, Hamlet was "the thoughtful Orestes [*der bedächtiger Orestes*]."[88] This characterization encapsulates what Hamlet represents for both Hegel and Kierkegaard, namely, an Orestes whose conflict is internal rather than external.[89] When the Ghost tells Hamlet not to kill Gertrude, his negative command—"Taint not thy mind, nor let thy soul contrive / Against thy mother aught" (1.5.85–86)—opens up the very possibility of its own transgression (like the Pauline law). Hamlet is *tempted* to kill his mother, if only in the sense of representing a repressed possibility as a rejected hypothetical ("I will speak daggers to her, but use none" [3.2.396]). Shakespeare shows us what Sophocles doesn't, namely, how conscience impedes impulsive actions. From a psychoanalytic point of view, it might seem as if Hamlet has internalized the external prohibition against matricide, that his conscience is nothing more, so to speak, than the incorporated law of the father. For Hegel, however, it is the other way around: the Ghost represents a projection or "objective form" of "Hamlet's inner presentiment." The reason Hamlet tarries isn't that he is unable to make up his mind; rather, "Hamlet hesitates because he does not blindly believe in the ghost."[90] His doubt—or, conversely, his negative faith—is radically different from the "childlike confidence [*kindlich Vertrauende*]" of Orestes, who never questions the authority of the gods.[91]

Once again the difference is that Orestes doesn't have a conscience, at least not in the modern sense. Apollo and the Erinyes are equally external agencies, primal forces that *precede* the formation of a superego. Whereas the Ghost is a projection of Hamlet's conscience, the Erinyes haven't yet been introjected or incorporated by Orestes; likewise, if Orestes personifies courage, it is a courage that precedes the advent of conscience. Hamlet's lament that "conscience does make cowards of us all" (3.1.82)—like his self-deprecating remarks about being "pigeon-liver'd" (2.2.577) and "thinking too precisely on th' event" (4.4.41)—registers one of the costs of having a conscience, namely, that what passed for courage in antiquity (the courage of Pyrrhus) is no longer available in modernity. From this it doesn't follow that to disavow an acquired conscience is to acquire courage, no more than does getting drunk before going into battle (although it might be expedient). If anything, courage in the modern sense depends on not disavowing one's cowardly conscience. Laertes acts in a cowardly manner when he surreptitiously anoints his rapier with poison and continues to fight even while acknowledging that doing so is "almost against [his] conscience" (5.2.296). For Aristotle, cowardice was only one of the extreme opposites of the virtuous mean of courage, the other being rashness. Hamlet acts rashly when he slays Polonius—"O, what a rash and bloody deed is this!" (3.4.27)—but just as Laertes's cowardice is distinctively modern, so is Hamlet's rashness.

The courage of Fortinbras might be represented as a mean between these extremes. In Badiou's terms, Fortinbras would stand for justice insofar as he transforms the havoc of pure destruction into the inceptive disruption of a new political order. However, reconciliation in *Hamlet* is achieved not through the agency of Fortinbras but through the mutual forgiveness that Laertes and Hamlet extend to each other before he even arrives on the scene. By the time he arrives, he has nothing to do but play the part of a constitutional monarch, adding a formal signature to decisions already reached by parliamentarians. It is Laertes's request for mutual forgiveness that breaks the cycle of retribution, something unavailable in Orestes's clash with the Erinyes. At the end of *Hamlet*, no Erinyes have to be consigned to the cellarage. The old mole has been pacified ("Rest, rest, perturbed spirit!" [1.5.182]), and the body of Hamlet can be incorporated into the early modern state. Just as the statue of Athena was raised to a privileged place in Athens, so Hamlet's corpse is elevated to a privileged place on the modern stage.

What makes *Hamlet* a political allegory rather than a political myth is the fact that its subjective coordinates are those not of (classical) courage and justice (qua patriarchal law), but of conscience and justice (made possible through mutual forgiveness). *Hamlet*'s transformation of the unproblematic ancient virtue of courage into the problematizing experience of conscience subjects its hero to the dialectical zigzag between the extremes of inactive thought (cowardly conscience) and thoughtless action (rashness) as he struggles to act thoughtfully. This dialectic manifests itself in his painful longing to perform a classically courageous act like that of an Orestes or Pyrrhus or Hercules. But he cannot do so in good faith. Only by learning to act conscientiously does Hamlet accomplish his political objective.

The difference between Hamlet's problematizing conscience and the unproblematizing courage of Orestes is akin to that between Hamlet's melancholy and Antigone's mourning. For Antigone, the external ritual of sprinkling dirt on the corpse of Polyneices is a sufficient way of remembering the dead. For Hamlet, memorialization takes the form of interiorization (*Erinnerung*), a process that cannot be definitively concluded through the performance of rituals. Hamlet is melancholy because his grief is a wound that must not be healed. For Abraham and Torok, mourning is *effective* thought, thought that comes to terms with loss through the performance of a symbolic action, whether this be sprinkling dirt, burying, sharing "funeral bak'd-meats" (1.2.180), or talking with fellow survivors about the deceased. Melancholia is a kind of ineffective mourning. This is the condition from which Hamlet suffers but to which Antigone is strangely immune. Mania involves a leap from inactive thought to unthinking action, much as Hamlet leaps into the grave to fight Laertes.[92] It also involves a fantasized disavowal of conscience. Thus, the cowardice–rashness dialectic could be correlated with the oscillation between melancholia and mania. Mania would be melancholia's "false cure," a way of "acting out" instead of "working through" a deadlock. Like an act of mourning, a conscientious deed would effectively reunite thought and action.

Orestes isn't manic in the modern sense, for he doesn't have a conscience to disavow. But he could be described as manic in the ancient sense of being rash rather than courageous. As Socrates explains in the *Theaetetus*: "The clever ones rush about, carried away like ships with no ballast, and they tend to be manic [μανικώτεροι] rather than truly brave."[93] Those who are truly brave or courageous are able to tarry in the way that the philosopher tarries. If Orestes is manic, it is in this sense of being "unphilosophical." A modern Orestes would be manic if he disavowed his Hamletlike conscience. When Pylades bids Orestes to consider what the gods would say in response to his possible actions, he advises him well in the context of Greek ethical life, but as Hegel emphasizes, such advice seems alien to us. Closer to home is the scene in which Hamlet tells Horatio that the deaths of Rosencrantz and Guildenstern are not "near [his] conscience" and then asks if it is "not perfect conscience" to kill the king (5.2.58, 67). Were Horatio to respond to Hamlet as Pylades does to Orestes, he would not be the Wittenberg student we know him to be.[94] The challenge for Hamlet is to determine the nature of the weak messianic power with which the Ghost has invested him.

What would Badiou's theory of the subject look like if we substituted Hamlet for Orestes? Perhaps mourning and mania would be the principal coordinates of classical tragedy, while melancholia and conscience would be those of Shakespearean *Trauerspiel*. Over the course of the play, Hamlet passes through each of these coordinates. Insofar as the play bears witness to the birth of conscience, we can say, retrospectively, that when Pylades bids Orestes to consult the gods, a similar event *fails* to take place. By nostalgically celebrating this failure, Badiou shows a lack of fidelity to one of the signal events of modernity.

Seventeenth-century audiences seem to have felt that Hamlet epitomized the role of the successful avenger. Only in the eighteenth century did a perception of undue delay creep in. In 1736, the anonymous author of "Some Remarks on the Tragedy of Hamlet Prince of Denmark" (either Sir Thomas Hanmer or George Stubbes) argued that Shakespeare had been "obliged to delay his hero's revenge" for the sake of preventing his play from ending too quickly. By the end of the century, the question had shifted from "Why does Shakespeare delay?" to "Why does Hamlet delay?" What Hanmer or Stubbes took to be a deficiency in Shakespeare's plot was now perceived to be a motivational conflict in Hamlet's soul.[95] Like Johnson, Francis Gentleman was troubled by Hamlet's diabolical desire to damn Claudius. At approximately the same time that Kant was insisting that human beings were incapable of diabolical evil, literary critics were saying something similar about Hamlet. Instead of ascribing genuinely evil maxims to him, the critics decided that he must be self-deceived. Far from being cruel, he was so mild that he couldn't bring himself to kill Claudius at all. Dimly aware of this psychological limitation, he rationalized his inactivity by pretending to himself that he was waiting for an occasion when killing Claudius *would* amount to sending his soul to hell. From here it was a short step to Goethe's representation of Hamlet as a delicate vase and Freud's representation of his revived Oedipus complex. As long as his professed explanation for tarrying was taken at face value, he was the conscientious Orestes who leaves his mother's soul to the examination of her own conscience.

According to Hegel, "*Conscience* expresses the absolute entitlement of subjective self-consciousness to know *in itself* and *from itself* what right and duty are, and to recognize only what it thus knows as the good."[96] For just this reason, conscience can be arbitrary, solipsistic, and terroristic—in a word, diabolical. More to the point, there is no way for moral conscience to distinguish good from evil apart from relying on its own subjective convictions. When moral conscience seeks confirmation from others, it finds that its convictions are not universally shared. The rebuffed conscientious subject must either become a moral solipsist or else acknowledge the authority of ethical (*sittlich*) institutions that determine what counts as right and wrong. Making this transition from (Kantian) morality to ethics proper involves the acquisition of what Hegel calls "true conscience."[97] Hamlet enacts this transition not only by consulting Horatio, but by exacting his revenge in public, asking Horatio to submit his "cause aright / To the unsatisfied" (5.2.339–340).

In his essay on the structure of logical time, Lacan argues that every act of self-identification (such as "This is I, / Hamlet the Dane!") involves an essential moment of hesitation. In *Theory of the Subject*, Badiou agrees that "the time to conclude" must be preceded by a pause. Once again, however, he associates this moment with Orestes rather than with Hamlet, emphasizing that Orestes's hesitation is strategic and not a sign of indecisiveness. For Freud, procrastination (*Denkaufschub*) is a form of "experimental action," a mental activity halfway between pure contemplation and bodily movement.[98] Gide recognized this to be the kind of experimentation that Hamlet engages in when he sets out to test the veracity of the Ghost's report, and when he speculates about what might happen if he were to kill Claudius while the king is praying. Diabolical or not, his decision to tarry—to do nothing for now—is a conscientious deed and not a mark of indecision.

A more Oresteian Hamlet can be found in Saxo Grammaticus's *Historia Danica*, as well as in *Der bestrafte Brudermord, oder Prinz Hamlet aus Daennemark*, an adaptation of Shakespeare's play that was once thought to be its source (the so-called *Ur-Hamlet*, an Elizabethan revenge drama that may have been written by Thomas Kyd).[99] Just as the *Oresteia* is less "advanced" than *Antigone*, so *Der bestrafte Brudermord* (*Fratricide Punished*) is more primitive than *Hamlet*. It is also more Roman than Greek, beginning with a Senecan prologue in which the Queen of the Night summons the Furies to avenge the murder of the king ("*Ich bin die dunkle Nacht, die alles schlafend macht*").[100] When the Ghost appears, it is a strangely material mole with sufficient strength to knock down one of the sentinels. The action is not only brisker but somewhat farcical, as when Hamlet contrives to duck so that the two pirates who have been charged to kill him can shoot each other instead of him. Lacking six of Shakespeare's Hamlet's seven soliloquies, the avenging prince lacks the very thing that Hegel took from Herder's characterization of Hamlet as a "thoughtful Orestes," namely, *Metaphysische und Gewissensskrupel*—in a word, conscience. As in Shakespeare's actual sources—Saxo, Belleforest, and (probably) the *Ur-Hamlet*—the Hamlet of *Der bestrafte Brudermord* doesn't tarry at all. He is just as unthinking as Orestes and he has no properly messianic charge.

Derrida argues that a genuinely messianic politics involves the awaiting of *arrivants*—strangers and ghosts who never appear as such ("And therefore as a stranger give it welcome" [1.5.165]).[101] Awaiting in this sense would have the character of tarrying, but Žižek worries that Derrida's conception of the messianic as always "to-come" (*à-venir*) entails a politics of perpetual postponement or delay. Representing Derrida's model as fundamentally Judaic, Žižek advocates a Christian messianism according to which the Messiah has already come and gone.[102] He links this model to Benjamin's conception of the "weak" messianic power that the dead have bequeathed to the living. Habermas observes that the distinctive feature of Benjamin's messianism is that it "twists the radical future-orientedness of modern times in general so far back around the axis of the now-time that it gets transposed into a yet more radical orientation toward the past."[103] Instead of simply replacing future-oriented protentions with past-directed retentions, Benjamin treats the past as if it still belonged to an open future. What's done cannot be entirely undone, but perhaps it isn't fully done. By orienting us toward a past-that-is-still-to-come rather than toward a future-that-never-arrives, Benjamin, like Hamlet, strikes Christian sparks from a politics of tarrying. For Benjamin no less than for Hegel, the dying Hamlet is closer to Christ (and Socrates) than is the statue of the living Athena. Yet Derrida himself includes past objects and events under the heading of things to come—such are the *revenants* that he finds Marx theorizing in the "Eighteenth Brumaire" when he observes that historical consciousness and anachronistic role-playing are essential components of revolutionary activity. Conversely, Marx anticipates Derrida when he observes that whereas past revolutions drew their inspiration from more distantly past events, the coming revolution "cannot create its poetry from the past but only from the future."[104]

At issue for both Derrida and Žižek are historical intrusions of a sort different from the ones that Schmitt finds in *Hamlet*. Sartre observes that a properly Marxist intrusion takes place every time an actor plays Hamlet: "He crosses his mother's room to kill Polonius hidden behind the arras. But that is not *what he is actually doing*. He crosses a stage before an audience and passes from 'court side' to 'garden side' in order to earn his living. ... But one cannot deny that these *real* results are present in some way in his imaginary act."[105] Only in a communist society could an actor play Hamlet for the sake of playing him: perhaps this is what Marx is getting at when he envisions a revolution whose poetry will come from the future. In *Tarrying with the Negative*, Žižek suggests that Hamlet's exclamation "This is I, / Hamlet the Dane!" shows that he has acquired the capacity to act, but only when it is "too late."[106] However, he also observes that "in a way, we can say that the crucial thing takes place, that the mole does his work, before 'anything happens,' which is why the fall of a social edifice usually is not perceived as the overcoming of a mighty adversary."[107] Putting these two remarks together, Hamlet's capacity for positive action arrives "too late" only insofar as his tarrying has already accomplished the essential deed. To dream, with Badiou, of a more decisive Hamlet—an Oresteian James—would be to conflate what Benjamin calls the "divine violence" that no human agent is entitled to wield with the sort of "mythical violence" that is the prerogative of a Schmittian sovereign.[108]

Like Badiou, Arendt argues that every founding act (or "disruptive inception") exhibits a surplus of "force" over "place," or what Habermas would characterize as a surplus of the reason of force over the force of reason. Unlike Badiou, however, Arendt distinguishes force from violence. Force is an essential component of initiating action (*praxis*), whereas violence is a feature of creation and destruction (*poiesis* and anti-*poiesis*). Actions are beginnings that invite contestation. As such, they are conscientious in Hegel's ethical sense of the term. Morally conscientious acts preclude contestation and as such can be thought of as violent. What Arendt tends to downplay is the fact that we cannot necessarily know ahead of time whether a particular act will be received as violent or forceful—whether it will be regarded as "truly" conscientious in Hegel's sense or as falsely conscientious. This is why Orestes goes on trial and why Hamlet's story has to be reported to "the unsatisfied" (5.2.340). Like a Kantian judgment of taste, an act can only purport subjective universality. For this reason, Schmitt claims that a sovereign decision has to be retroactively ratified by acts of parliament, while Badiou argues that a revolutionary transformation must be retroactively acknowledged by faithful subjects of a new political order. The problem with their accounts lies not in their appeals to retroactive justification but in their reduction of tarrying to indecision. The flipside of this reduction is a fascination with violence. Žižek observes that Antigone's violent "passion for the Real" fascinated

Lacan, who was influenced by Bataille when he delivered his seminar on the ethics of psychoanalysis.[109] The only authentic act for Bataille is a violent transgression that paradoxically sustains rather than sublates the very law that it transgresses. Badiou is aware of this danger, which is why he turns from Antigone to Orestes, whose justification by Athena purports to break the cycle of transgression and retribution. But the only act that Orestes can perform is one that constitutes rather than sublates the superegoic foundation of the law. Perhaps this is why, in *Logics of Worlds*, Badiou modifies his account of the four coordinates of political subjectivity by replacing that of the superego with "terror."[110] Just as courage originates in anxiety, he now suggests, so justice can be achieved only by passing through terror—a point that Hegel himself makes regarding the French Revolution.

In *Less Than Nothing*, Žižek introduces a further modification of Badiou's theory of the subject, suggesting that "justice" should be replaced by "enthusiasm."[111] As he observes, one advantage of this substitution is that it desubjectivizes justice. Another is that it highlights the subjective effect of the idea of justice. In the *Critique of Judgment*, Kant defines enthusiasm (*Enthusiasm*) as "the idea of the good with affect," adding: "This state of mind seems to be sublime, so much so that it is commonly maintained that without it nothing great can be accomplished."[112] Enthusiasm without reason is "blind" (or manic), but practical reason without enthusiasm is melancholy. Žižek argues that "enthusiasm can only emerge against the background of terror," a claim that is in keeping with Kant's descriptions of both the feeling of the sublime and the reactions of spectators to the French Revolution.[113] Perhaps we can discern in Kant's privileging of the standpoint of the spectator not a refusal of revolutionary activity but a conception of revolutionary tarrying. The fundamental difference between Žižek and Badiou is how to conceive a "Bartleby politics," that is, a politics of nonparticipation in global capitalism.[114] Construing Bartleby's "I would prefer not to" as an infinite judgment that affirms a negative (political) predicate, Žižek distinguishes an ineffectual politics of resistance or destruction from an effective "subtraction" that "opens up the space for the New."[115]

Simon Critchley has accused Žižek of waffling in Hamletlike fashion between this "Bartleby act" of refusal and the dream of an Antigonelike act of divine violence:

> On the one hand, the only authentic stance to take in dark times is to do nothing, to refuse all commitment, to be paralyzed like Bartleby. On the other hand, Zizek [sic] dreams of a divine violence, a cataclysmic, purifying violence of the sovereign ethical deed, something like that of Sophocles's Antigone.

But Shakespearean tragedy is a more illuminating guide here than its ancient Greek predecessor. For Zizek is a Slovenian Hamlet, utterly paralysed but dreaming of an avenging violent act for which, finally, he lacks the courage. In short, behind its shimmering inversions, Zizek's work leaves us in a fearful and fateful deadlock: the only thing to do is to do nothing. We should just sit and wait. As the great Dane says, "Readiness is all." But the truth is that Zizek is never ready.[116]

Critchley criticizes Žižek for being both too Hamletlike and not Hamletlike enough. On the one hand, Žižek is the "Slovenian Hamlet" (or "master of the undecidable act"); on the other, he fails to grasp the true import of Hamlet's remark that "the readiness is all." Yet Hamletian readiness is precisely what Žižek thematizes in Bartleby's negative act. Moreover, to equate this act with paralysis is to conflate the various ways in which one can "do nothing." Like Hamlet's tarrying, the Bartleby act is neither obsessional, nor hysterical, nor fantasmatic, nor utopian (in the sense of demanding something absolutely impossible); it is (potentially) revolutionary in the sense of demanding something that is impossible only relative to contingent social coordinates.[117] To demand the impossible in this sense is to tarry with the negative as Hamlet does when he says "No!" and sheathes his sword. Perhaps the task for the Left today is to reinvent Marx's "Hamlet politics": "Here's fine revolution, and [or "an": "if"] we had the trick to see't" (5.1.90–91).

CHAPTER 5

HAMLET'S NONEXISTENCE

Do it, England.
Hamlet 4.3.65

In his *Metaphysical Disputations* (1597), the Jesuit philosopher Francisco Suárez reflects on the ontological status of *entia rationis*, or "beings of reason" (what Kant calls "thought-entities" or *Gedankendingen*). Though lacking in "real being," beings of reason have intrinsic natures by virtue of which they are possible or impossible beings.[1] Just a few years after the publication of Suárez's treatise, Richard Burbage's Hamlet posed a similar question about Queen Hecuba, wondering how the First Player can get more agitated over an *ens rationis* than he himself can about his murdered father (who, as murdered, lacks existence in a far more significant way):

> Is it not monstrous that this player here,
> But in a fiction, a dream of passion,
> Could force his soul so to his own conceit
> That from her working all the visage wann'd,
> Tears in his eyes, distraction in his aspect,
> A broken voice, an' his whole function suiting
> With forms to his conceit? And all for nothing,
> For Hecuba!
> What's Hecuba to him, or he to Hecuba,
> That he should weep for her? What would he do
> Had he the motive and the cue for passion
> That I have?
>
> (2.2.551–562)

In the same way that Hamlet puzzles about the ontological status of Hecuba, philosophers have puzzled about his ontological status. Commenting on Suárez's doctrine, Daniel Novotný writes:

> Suárez and other Baroque scholastic authors seem to assume without questioning that *consistent fictions*, such as Hamlet, might become real beings. This implies that Hamlet is a possible being and therefore that he is a real being. But is this a valid assumption? For several reasons I do not think that a consistent fiction as such is a possible being. First, Hamlet has "underdetermined features." Thus, for instance, it *cannot be said* whether he liked ham and eggs for breakfast. ... Second, it seems to be part of Hamlet's identity that he is a fictitious person made up by Shakespeare. If suddenly a person stood in front of us, claiming to be Hamlet, would he be *Shakespeare's* Hamlet? The same holds true of another world in which everything would be as Shakespeare described it. ... Third, there is an infinite number of possible Hamlet-like beings satisfying perfectly all of Shakespeare's descriptions. Which one is identical to the "real" Hamlet that Shakespeare and his readers have in mind?[2]

The example of Hamlet is by no means unique to Novotný. In philosophy, Hamlet's fictionality has acquired an exemplary status akin to that of Socrates's mortality in the syllogism, "All men are mortal. Socrates is a man. Therefore, Socrates is mortal." Since for Socrates the purpose of philosophy is preparation for death, it is fitting that his mortality should be regarded as exemplary. Since for Hamlet the purpose of playing is to hold, as 'twere, the mirror of fiction up to nature, it is no less fitting that his fictionality should be privileged. He frequently appears on philosophers' lists of fictional entities, as in C. K. Ogden's illustration of Jeremy Bentham's theory of fictions: "A centaur is as much a fiction as Hamlet or the golden age."[3]

Eva Brann suggests that the problem of nonexistent entities first arose in modernity.[4] In the *Sophist*, Plato puzzles about nonbeing and falsehood, but not about nonexistent entities per se. The Eleatic Stranger domesticates nonbeing by incorporating it within false statements about genuine entities—as in "Theaetetus flies"—but he doesn't deal with false existential statements of the form "Achilles exists." In the *Parmenides*, the young Socrates expresses puzzlement about privative entities such as "hair and mud and dirt" and about whether to say that the One is or is not, but again there is no discussion of nonexistent entities per se.[5] In the *Republic*, Plato's attack on the poets is based on the idea that the fictions they represent lead the soul further away from, rather than toward, ultimate reality, which consists of *genuine* beings of reason such as the forms and the objects of pure mathematics.[6] Yet even the fictions of the poets have (privative) being; they are not wholly nonexistent entities. In the *Poetics*, Aristotle argues that because poetry deals with things that are universal rather than particular it is more philosophical than history.[7] But fictional things that are universal are possible only in the sense of being potential, and Aristotle restricts his conception of potentiality to ways in which actual beings might be. The very universality of poetry implies that the fictional characters it depicts are not nonexistent entities but abstractions of a special sort. Only in late Scholasticism is the idea developed that besides potential being there are possible beings, each of which, in contemporary parlance, is a concrete, though nonexistent, individual.[8] This seems to be what Suárez is getting at when he distinguishes real beings from consistent beings of reason.

In his critique of the ontological argument for the existence of God, Kant claims that when we predicate being of a being of reason, we treat it as though it were a real being, but the reality of real beings isn't due to their possession of a special predicate, for being is not a real predicate at all. We cannot even predicate *real possibility* of beings of reason (that is, conformity to the conditions of possible experience) but only *logical possibility* (the non-contradictoriness of their concepts).[9] Thus, Kant not only undermines the ontological argument but strips arbitrarily conceived fictional entities of the minimal ontological standing that Suárez gives them. Yet because he reduces real beings to appearances, he is required to treat pure beings of reason (that is, noumena) as necessary metaphysical posits and thus as fictions of a special sort. In a similar vein, Jeremy Bentham divides unreal beings into "fictitious entities," which he regards as necessary discursive constructs (many of which are equivalent to Kant's categories), and "fabulous entities," which include nonactual concrete particulars such as Hecuba and Hamlet.[10] Thus, both Kant and Bentham distinguish "necessary" fictions from "imaginary" fictions. A stronger version of Suárez's thesis can be found in Alexius Meinong. In "The Theory of Objects" (1904), Meinong accords a special kind of being—*Sosein*, or "being-so"—to nonexistent entities. Not only do *possible* nonexistent entities such as the golden mountain have *Sosein*; so do *impossible* nonexistent entities such as round squares.[11]

Like Meinong, the young Bertrand Russell was willing to grant some kind of being to nonexistent entities, but by the time he published his landmark essay "On Denoting" in 1905 he had had a change of heart. Rejecting any ontological category wider than that of existence, "On Denoting" develops a metaphysically deflationary analysis of non-referring linguistic expressions the use of which seems to commit their speakers to the reality of things that don't actually exist. One of Russell's favorite examples is "Hamlet." The exemplary status that Russell bestows upon "Hamlet" in his theory of denoting is similar to the exemplary status that Freud gives to Hamlet in his theorization of the Oedipus complex. Since "On Denoting" was no less influential in shaping the history of analytic philosophy than *The Interpretation of Dreams* was in shaping the twentieth century's other analytic tradition, this coincidence is striking. Even more striking is the fact that Hamlet represents for Russell not only an exemplary fiction but, in the context of Shakespeare's fiction, an ideal to which Russell aspired to live up. This aspect of Russell's thought has been largely neglected by his philosophical heirs.

Russell first appeals to Hamlet in an 1897 paper entitled, "Seems, Madam? Nay, It Is" (published 1957). In this paper, he indicates his reasons for rejecting the metaphysical idealism of F. H. Bradley and John McTaggart. In somewhat different ways, both Bradley and McTaggart distinguish the world as it appears to us in time from atemporal reality. They maintain that atemporal reality is fundamentally good, despite appearances to the contrary (i.e., despite the fact that there is apparent evil in the world). Coming to know this fact couldn't liberate us from perceived evils, but it could provide some "consolation" for "adversity."[12] In "Seems, Madam?" Russell rejects this idea of metaphysical consolation in much the same way that Nietzsche eventually repudiated his own advocacy of it in The Birth of Tragedy. He ironically quotes the Panglossian transport of the Second Brother in Milton's Comus: "How charming is divine Philosophy! / Not harsh and crabbed, as dull fools suppose, / But musical as is Apollo's lute." Against McTaggart's charming conception of a perfect, atemporal reality, Russell observes, first, that it is impossible to form any definite idea of it. Second, we could only be comforted by the thought of a perfect reality if we could foresee our own participation in it at some future time—an idea Russell associates with Shakespeare's phrase "All's well that ends well."[13] But the perfection of an atemporal reality can be no more complete in the future than it is in the present. Like Hegel's unhappy consciousness, we must infer from our present misery that we are forever cut off from perfect reality. Perhaps we could be consoled by the bare thought of a perfect reality, but only by "persuading ourselves, for the moment, of the reality of a world we have ourselves created." But in that case, metaphysics would be closer to art than to religion: "What metaphysics does for us ... is essentially what, say, The Tempest does for us. ... It is not because Prospero's magic makes us acquainted with the world of spirits that we value the Tempest; it is not, aesthetically, because we are informed of a world of spirit that we value metaphysics."[14] Finally, even if there is an eternal reality, there is no way of knowing if it is benignly enchanted, like Prospero's island, or malignantly ruled by gods who torture and kill us for their sport.[15]

In the same year that he published "Seems, Madam?"—sixty years after its original presentation—Russell looked back on his early philosophical development: "At that time I preferred King Lear to all the rest of Shakespeare, even to Hamlet, and it was because of its vast cosmic despair that I liked it. ... There was a kind of bitter satisfaction in imagining that the tortures human beings endure give pleasure to the gods and are therefore not wholly purposeless."[16] In the paper itself, however, it was Hamlet rather than Gloucester who had the last—or rather first—word. When Gertrude asks Hamlet why the "common" death of a father seems so "particular" with him, Hamlet replies: "Seems, madam? nay, it is, I know not 'seems'" (1.2.72, 75–76). The title of Russell's paper effectively casts him in the role of Hamlet with respect to one or two of his philosophical "mothers." (Fathers and mothers are one flesh in atemporal reality—so, his mothers!) He knows not "seems," for "it is the lamentable prerogative of evil that to seem so is to be so."[17] What little comfort Russell had once been able to derive from imagining a realm of sadistic gods had been undercut by a sense of the finality of grief.[18] If philosophy really were capable of "affording a possibility of meeting again after death those whom [we] have loved," its consolation would be infinite ("we should be immeasurably grateful").[19] Unfortunately, philosophy couldn't make a plausible case for resurrection. To underscore the finality of death Russell gives the final word not to Lear (as he might have) but to Keats: "That I shall never look upon thee more, / Never have relish in the fairy power / Of unreflecting love."[20]

It was in this disenchanted frame of mind that Russell began to muse about the ontological status of fictions. In "On Denoting," he characterizes Meinong's theory of objects as "intolerable," not simply because it grants a kind of reality to things that don't exist, but because in so doing it violates the law of contradiction. It does so, first, by requiring us to attribute both existence and nonexistence to every nonentity alleged to exist (such as "the present King of France"), and, second, by requiring us to attribute contradictory predicates other than existence to intrinsically contradictory nonentities such as "the round square."[21] Positing nonentities also violates the law of the excluded middle. Since there is no present king of France, it would be just as false to include him in the class of things that aren't bald as it would be to include him in the class of things that are. "Hegelians, who love a synthesis," Russell quips, "will probably conclude that he wears a wig."[22] In point of fact, it was Kant rather than Hegel who argued that the infinite judgment "S is non-P" involves a kind of synthesis of affirmative and negative judgments. To say that the human soul is nonmortal is to exclude it not only from the class of mortal things but also from the class of immortal things. Although this doesn't violate the law of the excluded middle, it does make the soul "wear a wig" in a certain way.[23] Wearing a wig is the soul's manner of *conceivably* belonging to a realm of spirits.[24] In "Seems, Madam?" Russell denied that *The Tempest* could acquaint us with the reality, or even with the *possible* reality, of spirits. In "On Denoting" he returns to *The Tempest* for an example that presupposes the finality of death. Were the king of Naples to say, "If Ferdinand is not drowned, Ferdinand is my only son," his statement would be true even if Ferdinand were drowned and therefore no longer in existence.[25] But if

Ferdinand no longer exists, he cannot be the referent (or denotation) of the denoting phrase "my only son" unless we are prepared (as Russell is not) to grant him a posthumous kind of being in the company of the present king of France and the round square. This example, aimed at Frege's distinction between meaning and denotation (or sense and reference) reminds us that Russell was as much concerned about the ontological status of the dead as he was about the fictitious. The example of the king of Naples underscores the logical—and ontological—irrelevance of anything that *The Tempest* might have to say about the nonmortality of the soul.[26]

To avoid the paradoxes associated with the positing of nonentities, Russell reinterprets the logical function of denoting phrases. Unlike proper names, which denote objects of our immediate acquaintance, denoting phrases of the form "the such-and-such" (e.g., "the present King of France," "the round square") denote objects only when they can be expanded into true propositions of the form "There is one and only one entity that has the property of being such-and-such." When this cannot be accomplished, sentences containing a phrase of the form "the such-and-such" are generally false (except in special cases, such as when the phrase is mentioned rather than used). The correct logical analysis of "The present King of France is bald" yields "There is an entity which is now King of France and is bald." If this sentence is false because there isn't an entity which is now King of France (rather than because there is such an entity who happens not to be bald) then "we escape the conclusion that the King of France has a wig."[27] Russell concludes, "The whole realm of non-entities … can now be satisfactorily dealt with."[28] (There is a touch of irony in this remark, because "the whole realm of non-entities" has turned out to be a denoting phrase without a denotation.)

Hamlet (or rather "Hamlet") can be satisfactorily dealt with by noticing that linguistic items that look like names but don't refer to objects of anyone's acquaintance are not genuine names at all but denoting phrases in disguise. Like other denoting phrases, some such pseudo-names succeed in referring to actual objects and others don't. Russell's two examples of non-referring pseudo-names are "Apollo" and "Hamlet."[29] Although seemingly arbitrary, Apollo and Hamlet had both figured in the argument of "Seems, Madam?"— Apollo being associated with the idea that philosophy could provide metaphysical consolation, Hamlet with the repudiation of metaphysical consolation. Both examples frequently recur in Russell's later writings, but especially that of "Hamlet." In a sense, he had effectively turned Hamlet's negativity—or rather the negativity that Shakespeare fictionally attributes to Hamlet—on Hamlet himself. As he observes in his *Introduction to Mathematical Philosophy* (1919):

> To maintain that Hamlet, for example, exists in his own world, namely, in the world of Shakespeare's imagination, just as truly as (say) Napoleon

existed in the ordinary world, is to say something deliberately confusing, or else confused to a degree which is scarcely credible. There is only one world, the "real" world: Shakespeare's imagination is part of it, and the thoughts that he had in writing Hamlet are real. So are the thoughts that we have in reading the play. … There is not, in addition to them, an objective Hamlet. … If no one thought about Hamlet, there would be nothing left of him; if no one thought about Napoleon, he would have soon seen to it that some one did. The sense of reality is vital in logic, and whoever juggles with it by pretending that Hamlet has another kind of reality is doing a disservice to thought. A robust sense of reality is very necessary in framing a correct analysis of propositions about unicorns, golden mountains, round squares, and other such pseudo-objects.[30]

Likewise, in *An Inquiry into Meaning and Truth* (1940):

We experience "Hamlet," not Hamlet; but our emotions in reading the play have to do with Hamlet, not with "Hamlet." "Hamlet" is a word of six letters; whether it should be or not be is a question of little interest, and it certainly could not make its quietus with a bare bodkin. Thus the play "Hamlet" consists entirely of false propositions, which transcend experience, but which are certainly significant, since they can arouse emotions. When I say that our emotions are about Hamlet, not "Hamlet," I must qualify this statement: they are really not about anything, but we think they are about the man named "Hamlet." … The fundamental falsehood in the play is the proposition: the noise "Hamlet" is a name. (Let no one make the irrelevant remark that perhaps there was once a Prince of Denmark called "Hamlet.")[31]

Finally, in *A History of Western Philosophy* (1945):

Let us take an imaginary person, say Hamlet. Consider the statement, "Hamlet was Prince of Denmark." In some sense this is true, but not in the plain historical sense. The true statement is "Shakespeare says that Hamlet was Prince of Denmark," or, more explicitly, "Shakespeare says there was a Prince of Denmark called 'Hamlet.'" Here there is no longer anything imaginary. Shakespeare and Denmark and the noise "Hamlet" are all real, but the noise "Hamlet" is not really a name, since nobody is really called "Hamlet." If you say "'Hamlet' is the name of an imaginary person," that is not strictly correct; you ought to say "It is imagined that 'Hamlet' is the name of a real person." … All statements about Hamlet are really about the *word* "Hamlet."[32]

Russell makes this last point in the context of a discussion of Parmenides's equation of thought and being. On his interpretation, Parmenides reasons that every thought must be about something that exists in the present, and everything that exists must be capable of being thought. From this it follows that generation and corruption are both illusory, and that anyone who existed in the past must still exist. To avoid these implications, Russell reflects on the relationship between the apparent name of a dead person (this time "George Washington" rather than "Napoleon") and the apparent name of a fictional character (predictably, "Hamlet"). After rehearsing his reasons for thinking that "Hamlet" is a pseudo-name, Russell argues that "George Washington" was a real name while George Washington was alive, but only for those (like George Washington himself) who were directly acquainted with him. For everyone else, "George Washington" was and is a denoting phrase that could be used to refer to George Washington in true sentences about him. After he died, he no longer existed (period!) so no one could any longer claim (present) acquaintance with him.[33] Accordingly, no one (not even those previously acquainted with him) could continue to use "George Washington" as a name. Thus death coincides with the death of a name, or with the definitive mutation of what had once been a name for some people into a denoting phrase for all.[34] (This is somewhat different from the case in which the death of Ferdinand transforms the king of Naples's use of the phrase "my only son" from a denoting phrase with a denotation to a denoting phrase without one. Compare Othello's "My wife, my wife! what wife? I have no wife" [5.2.97].) Faced with the alternatives of granting some kind of present being to the dead and denying that we can speak of things that no longer exist, Russell bites Parmenides's bullet: when we purport to refer to the past, we are really referring to present traces of the past. This thesis avoids what he takes to be the more extravagant metaphysical hypothesis, namely, that there is no such thing as "*passing away*."[35] Passing away—and its corollary, coming into existence—should not be confused with *becoming*, understood as an intermediate state between being and nonbeing. As Russell observes apropos Zeno: "The only point where Zeno probably erred was in inferring … that, because there is no change, therefore the world must be in the same state at one time as at another."[36] Strict adherence to the law of noncontradiction requires Russell to reject the ontological category of becoming, which Parmenides had consigned to the path of opinion or seeming. To save the phenomena of coming into existence and passing away, he must represent them as instantaneous changes of state or as processes composed of instantaneous changes of state. Becoming in the strict sense is no less "wiggish" than nonmortality. Despite his assertion that the past no longer exists, Russell also suggests that it is forever fixed—a point that he makes by quoting Macbeth: "The past does not change or strive; like Duncan, after life's fitful fever it sleeps well."[37]

The doctrine that pseudo-names like "Hamlet" have no referents enables Russell to explain why the ontological argument fails. Proponents of the argument assume that "God" is the name of an essence from which fact the existence of a being that has that essence can be derived. This analysis derives its plausibility from the surface logic of ascriptions of properties to fictional entities such as Hamlet: "Any ordinary person or thing, it is held, on the one hand exists, and on the other hand has certain qualities, which make up his or its 'essence.' Hamlet, though he does not exist, has a certain essence; he is melancholy, undecided, witty, etc."[38] Russell agrees with Kant that existence isn't a real predicate that would add anything to being melancholy, undecided, or witty, as proponents of the ontological argument mistakenly believe, but he suggests that a more philosophically satisfying refutation is provided by his own theory of descriptions, which shows that "God" is no more a genuine name than is "Hamlet." There isn't even a real essence answering to the term "God," as Kant's refutation still implicitly allowed.[39] Despite Russell's perfunctory dismissal of the ontological argument, there was a time when he was fully convinced by it. While a student at Cambridge, he had an epiphany while returning home one day from the tobacconist's shop. Wonderstruck, he threw his tin into the air and, catching it, felt himself converted to the idealism of Bradley and McTaggart.[40] It was several years later that his reflections on Hamlet contributed to his change his mind.

In *Human Knowledge: Its Scope and Limits* (1948), Russell contrasts the pseudo-name "Hamlet" with "Stalin," which in 1948 could still acquire the status of a genuine name in the presence of the living Stalin:

> Suppose you are in Moscow and some one says "that's Stalin," then "Stalin "is defined as "the person whom you are now seeing"—or, more fully: "that series of occurrences, constituting a person, of which this is one."... I think it will be found that every name applied to some portion of space-time can have a verbal definition in which the word "this," or some equivalent, occurs. This, I should say, is what distinguishes the name of an historical character from that of an imaginary person, such as Hamlet.[41]

How, then, do we distinguish the nonexistence of those with whom we were never acquainted from the nonexistence of those who never existed? To answer this question Russell seems to allow, after all, that names can outlive their bearers. We can know that "Socrates" is (still) a genuine name through our acquaintance with true sentences in which it appears. But then how do we distinguish "Socrates" from "Hamlet"?

> We can define "Socrates" as "the person described in the *Encyclopaedia* under the name 'Socrates.'" Here the name "Socrates" is experienced. We can of course define "Hamlet" in a similar way, but some of the propositions used in the definition will be false. E.g. if we say "Hamlet was a Prince of Denmark who was the hero of one of Shakespeare's tragedies," this is false. What is true is: "'Hamlet' is a word which Shakespeare pretends to be the name of a Prince of Denmark." It would thus seem to follow that, apart from such

words as "this" and "that," every name is a description involving some this, and is only a name in virtue of the truth of some proposition. (The proposition may be only "this is a name," which is false if this is "Hamlet.")[42]

Despite his repeated insistence that Hamlet doesn't exist, Russell observes in On Education (1926) that it would be pedantic to keep reminding someone of this fact during a performance of the play: "We do not believe that Hamlet ever existed, but we should be annoyed by a man who kept reminding us of this while we were enjoying the play."[43] While enjoying the play, we willingly suspend our disbelief. Russell's conception of this state of mind seems to have changed over time. If "'Hamlet' consisted entirely of false propositions," as Russell claimed in An Inquiry into Meaning and Truth, then to appreciate the play we would have to pretend that what we know to be false is true. Brann suggests that such a frame of mind would involve a suspension of belief rather than of disbelief.[44] If, however, fictional sentences are neither true nor false—as Russell suggests in My Philosophical Development (1959)—then our attitude would be one of treating pseudo-propositions as true propositions: "When an actor says, 'This is I, Hamlet the Dane,' nobody believes him, but nobody thinks he is lying." (More precisely, nobody thinks either that Hamlet himself is there on the stage or that the actor is saying something false, whether the actor is lying or mistaken.) Russell concludes that fictional utterances have no truth-value at all since they don't purport to say something true.[45] To accept the play on its own terms, we must suspend our ordinary attitude toward uttered propositions.

Another possibility, not considered by Russell, is the dialetheic option that utterances in a play might be both true and false. On this account it would be the law of noncontradiction rather than our disbelief that would be temporarily suspended. Russell seems to rule out this option on the grounds that it would violate the ordinary logician's conception of truth. He also rejects any nonlogical conception of truth that we might be tempted to attribute to fictional utterances. As he says in An Outline of Philosophy (1927):

> There is a tendency to use "truth" with a big T in the grand sense, as something noble and splendid and worthy of adoration. This gets people into a frame of mind in which they become unable to think. But just as the grave-diggers in Hamlet became familiar with skulls, so logicians become familiar with truth. "The hand of little employment hath the daintier sense," says Hamlet. Therefore it is not from the logician that awe before truth is to be expected.[46]

While denying that utterances in fictions are true in any meaningful sense, Russell doesn't deny that they have existential significance. In On Education he writes, "To appreciate *Hamlet* ... will not be much use in practical life, except in those rare cases where a man is called upon to kill his uncle; but it gives a man a mental possession which he would be sorry to be without, and makes him in some sense a more excellent human being."[47] More explicitly existentialist is the question that he poses on the opening page of *A History of Western Philosophy*:

> Is man what he seems to the astronomer, a tiny lump of impure carbon and water impotently crawling on a small and unimportant planet? Or is he what he appears to Hamlet? Is he perhaps both at once? Is there a way of living that is noble and another that is base, or are all ways of living merely futile? ... Must the good be eternal in order to deserve to be valued, or is it worth seeking even if the universe is inexorably moving towards death?[48]

The word "crawling" suggests that the opposition between Hamlet and the astronomer is really a distinction between two attitudes that Hamlet expresses, for he himself (like Russell's astronomer) represents man as a beast "crawling between earth and heaven" (3.1.127–128). His loftier description of man as "noble in reason" and "infinite in faculties" culminates in the cosmologically mixed category "quintessence of dust" and the negative conclusion "Man delights not me" (2.2.304, 308–309). The figures of Hamlet and the astronomer had already converged in Russell's "Dreams and Facts" (1919), where he observes that from the astronomer's point of view human existence is insignificant and meaningless. Given the track record of human history, he adds, the best we can "hope" for is "mutual annihilation." In the past, people who found such a pessimistic view "intolerable" sought metaphysical comfort from doctrines teaching that man is the "culmination" of natural processes, the ultimate end for the sake of which everything else exists (he might have said "the paragon of animals" [2.2.307]). To illustrate the limited character of such a perspective on humanity's place in nature, Russell asks his reader to imagine a society whose members know nothing of *Hamlet* besides the First Sailor's line "God bless you, sir" (4.6.7) and have structured their entire existence around ritual performances of it.[49] If a member of that society were to discover the rest of the play and try to enlighten others about it, his fellows would wish to "punish" or "exile" him, as the prisoners in Plato's cave wish to kill the messenger who tries to correct their limited worldview.[50] In this analogy, acquired acquaintance with *Hamlet* as a whole represents the larger, *disenchanted* perspective of the astronomer. From another point of view, to become acquainted with *Hamlet* (if not with Hamlet) is to acquire a *nobler* perspective on the human condition. This implication is reinforced by a passing remark in Russell's *Power: A New Social Analysis* (1938): "Even if all actors received the same salary, a man would rather act the part of Hamlet than that of the First Sailor."[51] Presumably the pleasure or honor of playing Hamlet is a function not only of his having more lines than the First Sailor (indeed, more than any other Shakespearean character), but of his exemplification of nobility in reason and infinity in faculties.[52]

Taken together, Russell's two remarks about the First Sailor show that he didn't regard the perspectives of Hamlet and the astronomer as diametrically opposed; on the contrary, he contrasts both of them taken together with the imaginatively impoverished religious perspective whose sole text is "God bless you, sir."[53] The task of philosophy is to liberate us from all cultural and personal confinement, as Russell eloquently argues in The Problems of Philosophy (1912): "The man who has no tincture of philosophy goes through life imprisoned. ... Unless we can so enlarge our interests as to include the whole outer world, we remain like a garrison in a beleaguered fortress, knowing that the enemy prevents escape and that ultimate surrender is inevitable."[54] After completing The Problems of Philosophy, he set about working on a book to be called "Prisons." The title was meant to allude to Hamlet's remark, "Denmark's a prison" (2.2.243), remembered by Russell as "The world's a prison."[55] Apparently he finished an entire draft of the book, in which he argued that liberation from the "prison" of the "finite self" could be found in a "religion of contemplation," but according to Ray Monk he "became extremely dissatisfied with it and presumably destroyed it."[56] He could have counted himself a king of infinite space were it not that he had bad dreams.

In The Problems of Philosophy, Russell characterizes logic as "the great liberator of imagination." Contrary to Aristotle, for whom the purpose of logic is simply to formalize the laws of deductive reasoning, Russell takes logic to represent possibilities that might or might not obtain in the actual world. He criticizes Kant's transcendental idealism for having confined philosophers' imaginations within a Euclidean prison. Post-Kantian developments in mathematical logic made it clear that we could imagine a variety of non-Euclidean spaces any one of which could turn out to describe the structure of physical space.[57] Russell's analysis of the ability of mathematical logic to free us from the prison of transcendental idealism prefigures Quentin Meillassoux's account of "mathematics' ability to discourse about the great outdoors [grand dehors]" and so liberate us from Kantian "correlationism."[58] For Russell, this process has two modally distinct steps. First, mathematical logic discloses "an open world of free possibilities."[59] Second, empirical investigation determines which of these possibilities obtains in the actual world.[60] Thus, logic undermines "correlationism" not by leading our thoughts directly to "the great outdoors," but by directing them away from it toward the even greater outdoors of free possibilities. It then passes the baton to empirical investigation.[61]

Russell represents Hamlet as an eminent logician. Reflecting on the logical form of his remark that "one may smile, and smile, and be a villain"

(1.5.108)—"instead of 'there are smiling villains' we say: it is false that all values of 'either x does not smile or x is not a villain' are false"—Russell observes in *An Inquiry into Meaning and Truth* that it is by "an ironical pretence" that Hamlet infers from his discovery that Claudius is a smiling villain that not all smilers are not villains. Later, he observes, Hamlet applies this generalization to the novel particular cases of the smiling Rosencrantz and Guildenstern.[62] A few pages later, Russell reflects on the logical form of Gertrude's inference in the closet scene that because she doesn't see the thing that Hamlet professes to see, and because she sees all that there is to see, Hamlet must be hallucinating. Her second premise—"all that is I see" (3.4.132)—makes her inference logically valid but possibly unsound: "I have always wondered how she knew she saw 'all that is.' But she was right in regarding this as a necessary premiss for her denial of the ghost." Russell wonders whether Gertrude's claim to see all that is could be empirically justified. He compares her denial that there is a hidden object in her closet to the negative assertions "there is no cheese in the larder, and nobody in the village not called Williams."[63] He doesn't mention Hamlet's own response to her assertion, namely, that the cause of her denial of the existence of the Ghost is her wish to believe that Hamlet is mad: "Lay not that flattering unction to your soul, / That not your trespass but my madness speaks" (3.4.145–146). Presumably, Russell would have acknowledged that in the context of the play Gertrude doesn't see all that is. Although he doesn't remark here on Hamlet's suggestion that the relevant negative fact is not the nonexistence of the Ghost but Gertrude's lack of virtue, in *A History of Western Philosophy* he praises Hamlet's recommendation that she "assume" a virtue in the hope that doing so may actualize it (3.4.160), noting that this sound advice is in keeping with Aristotle's account of the role played by self-habituation in the acquisition of moral virtue.[64]

In "'Useless' Knowledge" (1935), Russell defends Hamlet against the charge of thinking without acting. He maintains that "action without thought" generally poses a greater danger than "thought without action": "Hamlet is held up as an awful warning against thought without action, but no one holds up Othello as a warning against action without thought."[65] In "Machines and the Emotions" (1924), he criticizes Bergson for preferring action to intellection: "Bergson, like the pragmatists, prefers action to reason, Othello to Hamlet; he thinks it better to kill Desdemona by intuition than to let the King live by intellect."[66] If "moving matter about" were among the "ends" of existence rather than the means to higher ends, he adds elsewhere, "we should have to consider every navvy superior to Shakespeare."[67] As examples of pseudo-revolutionary "rebellion," he mentions "smashing lamp-posts" and "maintaining Shakespeare to be no poet."[68] He laments the fact that Shakespeare's belief that "an age" could be "measured … by its style in poetry" is now regarded as "out of date."[69] In a later text he voices a similar complaint:

If *Hamlet* is to be interesting to a really modern reader, it must first be translated into the language of Marx or of Freud, or, better still, into a jargon inconsistently compounded of both. I read some years ago a contemptuous review of a book by Santayana, mentioning an essay on Hamlet "dated, in every sense, 1908"—as if what has been discovered since then made any earlier appreciation of Shakespeare irrelevant and comparatively superficial. It did not occur to the reviewer that his review was "dated, in every sense, 1936." Or perhaps this thought … filled him with satisfaction.[70]

Santayana's essay on *Hamlet*—republished in *Obiter Scripta* (1936)—originally appeared as the introduction to Sidney Lee's edition of the play.[71] Its focus on questions about character—for example, "The hero's character does not come out at first in its ultimate shape," "Some of Hamlet's actions and speeches seem anterior to his true character"[72]—would in fact have been regarded as "out of date" by Cambridge literary critics such as L. C. Knights and F. R. Leavis, who in 1937 attacked the recently deceased A. C. Bradley (the younger brother of the idealist philosopher) for his supposedly extravagant "character criticism." Bradley's *Shakespearean Tragedy* was first published in 1904. In 1940, Philip Blair Rice associated Santayana's Shakespeare criticism with that of Bradley, judging both to be dated: "'On the Absence of Religion in Shakespeare' (1896) and 'Hamlet' (1908) … were written at a time when a blind Shakespeareolatry was more prevalent than it is now, and when A. C. Bradley was convincing a considerable section of the scholarly public that Shakespeare was a great philosopher."[73] Russell's defense of Santayana suggests that he wouldn't have been sympathetic with this critical remark.[74] Nor would he have been sympathetic with Leavis's complaint that Bradley treated Shakespeare's characters as if they actually existed. As we have seen, Russell happily engaged in such criticism himself. Leavis's cavils were like those of the man bent on reminding someone enjoying the play that Hamlet doesn't really exist. The same could be said of L. C. Knights's ironic treatment of the mock-Bradleyan question, "How many children had Lady Macbeth?" Russell probably felt that Bradley had been right to represent Shakespeare as a great philosopher in certain respects. Beyond the logical sophistication of his characters (including not only Hamlet, but the Gravedigger, the Fool, Feste, Falstaff, Touchstone, Rosalind, and many others), Shakespeare addresses existential questions at least as important as the kind dealt with in mathematical logic. Russell regarded *Lear* and *Hamlet* as Shakespeare's two most philosophically significant plays, presenting complementary perspectives on the meaning of human existence. As he observes in "If We Are to Survive This Dark Time—" (1950):

It is easy to forget the glory of man. When King Lear is going mad he meets Edgar, who pretends to be mad and wears only a blanket. King Lear moralizes: "Unaccommodated, man is no more but such a poor, bare, forked animal as thou art."

This is half of the truth. The other half is uttered by Hamlet:

"What a piece of work is a man! how noble in reason! how infinite in faculty! In form and moving how express and admirable! in action how like an angel! in apprehension how like a god!"

Grimly—yet optimistically—Russell concludes, "Soviet man, crawling on his knees to betray his friends and family to slow butchery, is hardly worthy of Hamlet's words, but it is possible to be worthy of them. ... Every one of us can enlarge his mind, release his imagination, and spread wide his affection and benevolence."[75] In his autobiography, he remarks that a friend from his student days once likened him to Cordelia.[76] In aspiring to live nobly "even if the universe is inexorably moving towards death," he himself identified more closely with Hamlet.

The existentialist side of Russell's engagements with Hamlet has received far less attention than his theory of descriptions. It is almost as if his elimination of the referent of the pseudo-name "Hamlet" had rendered nugatory his writings *about* Hamlet. This effect can be seen in the way in which the theory of descriptions was reworked by Quine. In his 1948 essay "On What There Is," Quine largely accepts Russell's way of paraphrasing apparent talk about fictional entities. Using slightly different terminology, he distinguishes two types of "seeming names."[77] Descriptive names, such as Russell's example "the author of *Waverly*," are incomplete sentence fragments, as Russell demonstrated in "On Denoting." But what of nondescriptive singular terms such as "Pegasus"?[78] Quine tells us that they can be treated in precisely the same way. Taking the noun "Pegasus" to be a reified form of the predicate "*being Pegasus*" enables us to translate "Pegasus exists" into the logically regimented $\exists xFx$—that is, "There exists an x such that Fx," where F means "is-Pegasus" or "pegasizes."[79] Taking the existential quantifier to be a univocal indicator of ontological commitment, Quine concludes that "to be is to be the value of a variable."[80]

The first question for us to ask about this extension of Russell's theory of descriptions is how Quine's analysis of "Pegasus" differs from Russell's analysis of "Hamlet." The answer is "Not by much." In "On Denoting," the theory of definite descriptions deals not only with denoting phrases such as "the present King of France" and "the author of *Waverly*" but also with apparent names such as "Apollo" and "Hamlet," which Russell treats as disguised definite descriptions.[81] What Quine adds is the simplicity and elegance of using the existential quantifier and the trick of predicatization to do all of the necessary paraphrasing in one fell swoop. A second question to consider is whether there is any philosophical significance in Quine's preference for the example of "Pegasus" over that of "Hamlet." This time the obvious answer would be "Surely not; the whole point of an example is that it is just an example."

The very obviousness of this answer should give us pause. Before assessing it, let me give a brief indication of the range of exemplary roles that the fictional Hamlet has come to play in analytic philosophy. On the first page of *Much Ado about Nonexistence* (the cover of which sports an illustration of Hamlet contemplating the skull of Yorick), A. P. Martinich and Avrum Stroll ask, "How … is it possible to talk about such fictional entities as Sherlock Holmes and Hamlet, given that the nonexistent is nothing at all?"[82] Elsewhere, Stroll groups Hamlet with the present king of France and Atlantis; with the present king of France and Santa Claus; with the present king of France, Medusa, and Santa Claus; with Odysseus and Santa Claus; and with Sherlock Holmes and Lancelot.[83] In homage to both Russell and Quine, Christopher Hookway and James Cargile pair Hamlet with Pegasus.[84] For some philosophers, such as Martinich and Stroll, fictional characters such as Hamlet and Pegasus really do exist—in fiction. For others, such as Alvin Plantinga, Hamlet exists in possible but nonactual worlds.[85] Saul Kripke, in the course of explaining how his theory of rigid designation represents an alternative to Russell's theory of descriptions, credits Russell with indicating how "one can say … with propriety that the author of *Hamlet* might not have written *Hamlet*."[86]

This is just the tip of the iceberg. In each of these philosophical texts, Hamlet (or "Hamlet" or *Hamlet* or "*Hamlet*"!) is treated as an arbitrary example. Every example must be arbitrary to count as an example, but the fact of its being singled out *as* arbitrary makes it minimally exemplary—and thus nonarbitrary—in at least this one respect. Let us call this "Agamben's paradox," since according to Giorgio Agamben every example "stands out" from the set whose members it "stands for." One way to resolve this paradox would be to invoke an analogue of Russell's theory of types, the technical device by which he and Whitehead tried to avoid paradoxes of self-reference.[87] Instead of saying that examples are arbitrary and nonarbitrary on the same "level," we could say that arbitrariness is a requisite first-order property that a member of a set must possess in order to qualify as an example of a member of that set, and that the nonarbitrariness associated with exemplarity is a second-order property that the example acquires by being singled out. The problem with this solution is that the two-level analysis is artificial and/or begs the question, as critics of the theory of types argue. We can see this by comparing Agamben's paradox to a paradox about exemplification noted by F. H. Bradley. To say that an object exemplifies a property is to say that the relation of exemplification holds between that object and that property. But if exemplification is itself a relational property, we must then say it is exemplified as well, and so on, *ad infinitum*. Theoretically, Bradley's regress could be avoided by representing exemplification as a primitive fact. Analogously, it could be argued that being an example doesn't endow an object with a special property but is just a primitive fact about it. This would only be the case, however, if everything with a common property were on the same footing. Agamben's question is about what happens when an object's exemplification of a property is represented *as* a special (first-order) property of that object—that is, when it is *singled out* as an example. Recourse to our analogue of the theory of types won't be able to resolve this level-crossing dimension of the paradox.

In the end, Agamben's paradox may be more existentially than logically perplexing. When a person is arbitrarily singled out, the obvious question is "Why me?"[88] Even if we know that no satisfying answer can be given to this question (on the grounds that our "election" is truly arbitrary), we seek to give some meaning to the special status we have acquired. Leibniz couldn't bear the thought that God would arbitrarily place qualitatively identical monads in different places: there had to be a "sufficient reason" for the placement of everything that existed. Even Samuel Clarke, defending the Newtonian view that matter was composed of qualitatively identical parts, believed that God must have had good reasons for distributing them in space as he did. Both philosophers denied the possibility of divine arbitrariness, but Clarke was willing to accept the paradox that God might have a sufficient reason for locating two qualitatively identical parts of matter in different places.[89] This apparent absurdity exasperated Leibniz, but one way to make it intelligible would be to add a performative twist to Clarke's argument, namely, that each of God's initially arbitrary choices was made nonarbitrary after the fact. Each "chosen" individual would be retroactively endowed with a property by virtue of which its initial selection wouldn't be arbitrary after all. *Contra* Clarke, this retroactivity would be a function not of God's wisdom but simply of his power of choice. It would apply to his election of persons no less than to his "election" of parts of matter. Outside of an explicitly theological context we should acknowledge, with Lacan, that the possibility of election in general is grounded in the fiction of the "big Other." By virtue of being selected to play a particular role, a nondescript individual acquires a kind of "justification" in the eyes of the big Other. Žižek argues that this is how names acquire their referential force. According to Kripke and Ruth Barcan Marcus, names aren't disguised descriptions, as Russell maintained, but meaningless tags arbitrarily assigned to their referents.[90] Žižek accepts this analysis up to a point, but he adds that once an object has acquired its arbitrary name it thereby acquires the additional property of *being* the bearer of that name. Only by virtue of this now nonarbitrary property does the "arbitrary" tag stick to its bearer: "A name refers to an object *because this object is called that.*"[91] Names begin life as arbitrary tags, but thereafter they function as disguised descriptions of a special sort.

A similar point would hold for the selection of examples. The retroactive nonarbitrariness of exemplification is illustrated in the scene from

Shakespeare's 1 *Henry VI* in which King Henry arbitrarily plucks a red rose rather than a white: "I see no reason, if I wear this rose, / That any one should therefore be suspicious / I more incline to Somerset than York!" (4.1.152–154). What the King fails to realize is that his arbitrary choice immediately becomes nonarbitrary, as is recognized by the Duke of York: "I like it not, / In that he wears the badge of Somerset" (4.1.176–177). When Warwick notes the arbitrariness of the King's choice—"Tush, that was but his fancy"—York doesn't disagree, but he remains unappeased: "And if I wist he did—but let it rest" (4.1.178, 180). York knows that Henry now wears a red rose *because it is his color*: the Wars of the Roses have already begun. In precisely the same way, Quine's arbitrary choice of Pegasus over Hamlet was "but his fancy." Nevertheless, I contend, Russell *should have* "liked it not." Though originally "just" an example in "On Denoting," "Hamlet" had become exemplary not only by virtue of having been singled out (in this sense it was "minimally" exemplary), but by the way in which Hamlet—the character rather than the pseudo-name—exemplified Russell's larger philosophical vision. Quine's perfectly arbitrary choice of "Pegasus" rather than "Hamlet" didn't precipitate a philosophical schism. Nor did Russell *consciously* ascribe any special significance to the example of "Hamlet" in his theory of descriptions. On the contrary, he seems to have seen no philosophically interesting connection between the Hamlet he thought *about* and the Hamlet he thought *with*—and he believed that he saw all there was to see. Yet whenever he insisted on the nonexistence of the fictional Hamlet he was effectively playing the Hamlet who insists on the nonexistence of the fictional Hecuba.

Like Russell, Quine occasionally mines Shakespeare for sentences to subject to logical regimentation, but unlike Russell, he has nothing to say about their literary dimension.[92] Like the puzzled Audrey in *As You Like It*, he could almost have said to Russell: "I do not know what 'poetical' is. ... Is it a true thing?" (3.3.17–18).[93] Yet as José Benardete has brilliantly demonstrated, there is a "Quinean poetics" nestled within Quine's treatment of the existential quantifier. Equating "poetics in the broad sense" with "the study of the non-literal, as opposed to the literal, use of language," Benardete points out that Quine's rejection of the analytic–synthetic distinction—his denial that we can definitively distinguish sentences that are true or false by virtue of the meanings of their terms from sentences that are true or false by virtue of the way the world is—leaves ontological commitment to be the deciding factor in telling the two apart.[94] He goes on to show how Quinean poetics can be brought to bear not just on the ontological commitments of philosophers, but on the ontological commitments of poets, elucidating an ambiguous passage in Shakespeare's Sonnet 99, where the poet, having chided "the forward violet" for stealing its "sweet that smells" from his lover's breath, reports: "The roses fearfully on thorns did stand, / One blushing shame, another white despair." Reflecting on the debate between those critics who read "blushing" as an adjective and those who read it as a participle, Benardete shows how the rejection of analyticity deepens our understanding of what it might mean for roses to blush shame and white despair.[95] Although Quine himself may never have read Shakespeare this way, Benardete convincingly shows that a sophisticated poetics can be derived from "On What There Is." The same can be said of "On Denoting." The difference between Quinean and Russellian poetics is that the former is based on the rejection of analyticity (a doctrine not advocated by Russell), the latter (exclusively) on the distinction between names and pseudo-names, a distinction that Hamlet—or rather Shakespeare—foreshadows. While excluding Hamlet from his ontology, Russell not only includes *Hamlet* but suggests that the world would be greatly impoverished without it. G. E. Moore expresses a similar thought when he observes in *Principia Ethica* (1903) that while "the sufferings of Lear, and the vice of Iago" would be genuine evils if they actually existed, the contemplation of their imaginary existence in Shakespeare's plays is something good "as a whole."[96]

Perhaps T. S. Eliot, who wrote a dissertation with Russell on the idealism of F. H. Bradley, appreciated the Shakespearean side of his thought. Wittgenstein, by contrast, seems to have been suspicious of Russell's enthusiasm for Shakespeare. He believed that most praise of Shakespeare was merely "conventional." Only the "authority" of a Milton could convince him that Shakespeare was a truly great poet.[97] For most people, he surmised, Shakespeare's greatness had to be accepted on faith: "It may be that the essential thing with Shakespeare is his ease and authority and that you just have to accept him as he is if you are going to be able to admire him properly. … My *failure* to understand him could then be explained by my inability to read him *easily*."[98] Echoing eighteenth-century characterizations of Shakespeare as an inspired genius, he hypothesized that the English poet was "a *creator of language*" whose drama obeyed "a law of its own."[99] Like Voltaire, he nevertheless stuck to his own neoclassical instincts: "The reason why I cannot understand Shakespeare is that I want to find symmetry in all this asymmetry. … I understand how someone can admire that and call it *supreme* art, but I don't like it."[100] While disturbed about his inability to appreciate Shakespeare ("I could only stare in wonder at Shakespeare; never do anything with him"), he remained "*deeply* suspicious of [*Ich habe ein tiefes Mißtrauen gegen*] most of Shakespeare's admirers."[101]

In "The Elements of Ethics" (1910), Russell, following Moore, claims that despite the apparent truth of Hamlet's remark that "there is nothing good or bad but thinking makes it so," goodness is an objective property of those things that possess it.[102] In his "Lecture on Ethics" (1929), Wittgenstein rejects the terms of this opposition. Goodness isn't an objective property that can be found in the world; it is a value that transcends the world. We should therefore repudiate both Russell's and Moore's objectivism and Hamlet's subjectivism: "What Hamlet says seems to imply that good and bad, though not qualities of the world outside us, are attributes to our states of mind. But what I mean is that a state of mind, so far as we mean by that a fact which we can describe, is in no ethical sense good or bad."[103] Expressions of psychological preference are ultimately meaningless: "To say *Lear* is agreeable is to say something nondescriptive."[104] By 1935, Russell had rejected moral objectivism in favor of a position closer to the one that he had previously associated with Hamlet.[105]

Like Quine and Russell, Wittgenstein has a distinctive poetics that is grounded in the analysis of ordinary language. Stanley Cavell has brought it to bear on Shakespearean tragedy. According to Cavell, Wittgenstein thinks that the possibility of raising skeptical doubts about the existence of the external world is a permanent feature of the human condition. In *Othello*, this possibility manifests itself as jealousy: "What philosophy knows as doubt, Othello's violence allegorizes (or recognizes) as some form of jealousy."[106] Just as Nietzsche said it was certainty rather than doubt that made Hamlet melancholy, so Cavell suggests that Othello is tormented not by genuine doubt but by disavowed knowledge: "Nothing could be more certain to Othello than that Desdemona exists ... is separate from him; other. This is precisely the possibility that tortures him."[107] Othello's tragedy consists not in his being deceived by Iago, but in his disavowal of his awareness that Iago's allegations are false.[108] This interpretation leads Cavell to downplay Iago's agency, reducing him to a convenient pretext akin to Descartes's evil genius.

While indebted to Wittgenstein, Cavell's account of the link between jealousy and skepticism in *Othello* is foreshadowed by Russell. In *The Problems of Philosophy*, Russell observes that only Desdemona can be directly acquainted with her feelings for Cassio. Others can know her feelings only indirectly, by description.[109] Russell thereby implies that Shakespeare locates the potential for jealousy in the difference between knowledge by acquaintance and knowledge by description. No matter how sincere and forthcoming Desdemona might be in describing her feelings, Othello can never be directly acquainted with them. Russell goes on to observe that anything that can be known only by description is subject to doubt. The link between jealousy and skepticism would then concern Othello's *genuine* lack of certainty about the state of Desdemona's heart, a lack that Iago masterfully exploits by supplying Othello with false descriptions and direct acquaintance with something other than Desdemona's heart, namely, his perception of Cassio's possession of Desdemona's handkerchief. The moral of *Othello* would be that we must come to terms with the fact that no one can be directly acquainted with anyone else's mental states. Russell applies this moral not just to our knowledge of other people but to our knowledge of everything distinct from ourselves: "Knowledge is a form of union of Self and not-Self; like all union, it is impaired by dominion, and thereby by any attempt to force the universe into conformity with what we find in ourselves."[110]

Russell argues that if Desdemona really does love Cassio, then the object of Othello's belief would be, precisely, Desdemona's love for Cassio. But what if Othello is mistaken? The theory of descriptions tells us that pseudo-names like "Hamlet" don't need referents to be used in meaningful sentences, but the intentional structure of false beliefs seems to require that they be about nonobtaining states of affairs. This, however, would be just as intolerable: "When Othello believes that Desdemona loves Cassio, he must not have before his mind a single object, 'Desdemona's love for Cassio,' or 'that Desdemona loves Cassio,' for that would require that there should be objective falsehoods, which subsist independently of any minds; and this, though not logically refutable, is a theory to be avoided if possible." Russell circumvents this implication by representing Othello's belief as a fourfold relation between himself, Desdemona, the universal relation of loving, and Cassio: "The actual occurrence, at the moment when Othello is entertaining his belief, is that the relation called 'believing' is knitting together into one complex whole the four terms Othello, Desdemona, loving, and Cassio."[111] If Desdemona loves Cassio, then over and above this fourfold relational complex is a threefold relational complex linking Desdemona, loving, and Cassio in the right way. If Desdemona doesn't love Cassio, then there is no such complex, but there is still the fourfold complex constituted by Othello's belief. Other beliefs constitute other sorts of n-tuple relations. Russell eventually abandoned this analysis, having come to believe that there were no such things as believing subjects or irreducible relational terms.[112]

Following Wittgenstein, Cavell resists the idea that each of us has privileged access to our own private mental states, and that we have to infer from others' outward behavior what their internal states might be. Skepticism is possible because our fundamental relationship to the world is not epistemic. The key to quieting the skeptic within us lies not in knowing others but in acknowledging them. We acknowledge others by engaging in conversation with them. Othello's loss of the ability to converse, especially with Desdemona, reaches an extreme when he collapses into incoherent "babbling" in 4.1.[113] His radical skepticism manifests itself as jealousy. Emilia observes that "jealous souls … are not ever jealous for the cause, / But jealous for they're jealous" (3.4.159–161)—a formulation reminiscent of Socrates's suggestion in the *Phaedo* that beautiful things are not beautiful for the cause, but beautiful for their participation in beauty.[114] Emilia isn't positing a form of jealousy, but rather a "monster / Begot upon itself, born on itself" (3.4.161–162). Her psychological insight into the solipsistic and self-generating character of jealousy is fully compatible with her additional surmise that Othello is being "abus'd by some most villainous knave" (4.2.139). Thus, she chides two forward violets: the one blushing green jealousy, the other "blackest sins" (2.3.351). Under the pretense of warning Othello of "the green-ey'd monster which doth mock / The meat it feeds on" (3.3.166–167), Iago incites him to engender it. Cut off from Desdemona, the only object with which Othello is truly acquainted in Russell's sense is his jealousy. Were he to acknowledge that he cannot be directly acquainted with anyone else's thoughts or feelings but his own he would be less, rather than more, alienated.

Unfortunately, Cavell doesn't engage with Russell's remarks about *Othello*. Nor does he address Russell's comments about *Hamlet*, despite their relevance to his interpretation of the dumb show as a displaced representation of the "primal scene" of Hamlet's birth.[115] According to Cavell, the question that Hamlet is trying to answer in staging the dumb show is not whether Claudius killed his father but how Hamlet came to be the person he is: "Why of all the ones I might have been am I just this one and no other, given this world and no other, possessed of exactly this mother and this father?" *Pace* Arendt, "To be or not to be" turns out to be as much about the mystery of birth (and election) as it is about the mystery of death. Hamlet's existential brooding leads him to discover that "human existence has two stages … birth and the acceptance of birth." By taking on the mystery of his own existence, Hamlet embraces rather than solves the so-called problem of the external world. Like Russell, Cavell attributes to Hamlet (along with Descartes and Emerson) the insight "that to exist the human being has the burden of proving that he or she exists, and that this burden is discharged in *thinking* your existence."[116]

In *Human Knowledge: Its Scope and Limits*, Russell imagines an experiment that might enable one to prove the independent reality of the external world:

> You could, if you were a philosophic millionaire, have *Hamlet* performed in a theatre in which you were the only live occupant and every other seat was occupied by a cine-camera. When the performance was over you could have the various records thrown upon the screen, and you would find them closely resembling each other and your own memory; you would infer that during the performance something happened at each of the cine-cameras which had the same structure as what was happening at you.[117]

In its exclusive reliance on empirical data, this thought experiment differs from the far more poetic approach to cinema that Cavell takes in his discussion of the Hollywood comedy of remarriage.[118] Yet the reference to Hamlet suggests that Russell is trying to do precisely what Cavell takes Hamlet to be doing when he stages the dumb show, namely, to confirm his own existence by thinking about it. From a psychoanalytic point of view, it cannot be a mere coincidence when, to illustrate a point about probability, Russell observes that "the 8,oooth word of *Hamlet*" probably doesn't contain the letter Z.[119] Such examples point not only toward Agamben's paradox, but toward the workings of the unconscious. Russell agreed with Freud that seemingly irrational mental phenomena could be explained by appeals to unconscious thoughts. A remark to this effect in *The Scientific Outlook* (1931) pointedly alludes to Hamlet: "modern psychologists, … like Hamlet, 'must be edified by the margent.'"[120] Taken literally—and self-reflexively—Russell is saying that to explain an author's psychological motives for writing a text, we must factor in the text's margins. Marginal phenomena include not only slips and lapses but seemingly arbitrary asides such as Russell's allusion to Horatio's remark that Hamlet must be edified by marginal supplements to Osric's inscrutable discourse. Russell all but tells us that his own text contains marginal phenomena that would edify a Hamletlike modern psychologist who paid close attention to them.

In a letter from the period when he was wrestling with Meinong's theory of objects, Russell described his personal struggle to come to terms with a past that was all too present: "Yes, one must learn to live in the Past, and so to dominate it that it is not a disquieting ghost or a horrible gibbering spectre stalking through the vast bare halls that once were full of life, but a gentle soothing companion, reminding oneself of the possibility of good things, and rebuking cynicism and cruelty."[121] Around the same time, he wrote in his journal, "Then came that strange life in the Past … where the real world seemed a dream, and only the dead appeared real. And I sat alone, reading ghostly books; and I worked at Frege, Meinong, and proofs, feeling all work a hollow sham."[122] A hollow man in an Unreal City, Russell felt like a ghost himself. This feeling haunted him for most of his life.[123] "I shall never lose the sense of being a ghost," he wrote to Lady Ottoline from prison in 1918.[124] "I am haunted—some ghost, from some extra-mundane region, seems always trying to tell me something that I am to repeat to the world, but I cannot understand the message. But it is from listening to the ghost that one comes to feel oneself a ghost."[125] Fifty years later he laments that, unlike Spinoza, who was able to "attach" his "intellectual love" to a "somewhat abstract God," he himself has "loved a ghost, and in loving a ghost my inmost self has itself become spectral."[126] These painful confessions suggest that denying the reality of spectral objects such as God, the past, and Hamlet was part of a lifelong effort on Russell's part to *acquire* a robust sense of his *own* reality in order not to be haunted like Hamlet.

Perhaps because he failed to achieve this result by logical means alone, he eventually tried his hand at writing fiction. Not surprisingly, Hamlet played a leading role in his literary efforts. The main character of his short story "Satan in the Suburbs or Horrors Manufactured Here" (1953) is Dr. Murdoch Mallako, whose name (or rather pseudo-name!) is derived from Hamlet's characterization of the action in the dumb show as "miching mallecho" (3.2.137).[127]

Ray Monk regards "Satan in the Suburbs" as possibly "the most deeply reveal-ing piece of autobiographical writing that Russell ever produced."[128] The story begins with an unnamed narrator's discovery that Dr. Mallako has taken up residence in the London district of Mortlake. His advertised promise to manufacture horrors attracts several local clients whose lives are eventually destroyed when they act out crimes that he tempts them to commit. After failing to bring Mallako to justice, the narrator becomes misanthropic, invent-ing a device designed to destroy every living creature on Earth. Before setting it off, he visits Mallako to gloat at the doctor's imminent death, but when he tells Mallako how the device is supposed to work he learns that it won't actually work and that he has inadvertently shown Mallako how *he* can destroy humanity. Now it is Mallako's turn to gloat at the narrator's imminent death. Luckily, the narrator kills Mallako before he can destroy the world. But he is haunted thereafter by Mallako's ghost, who taunts him for a lack of genuine heroism and (evidently) true philanthropy. At the end of the story, the nar-rator's sole hope for a meaningful relationship with another human being lies in the person of the widowed Mrs. Ellerker, the only female client whom Dr. Mallako had tempted to commit a crime. She, like the narrator, is now a resident of an insane asylum.

D. H. Lawrence once accused Russell of harboring a repressed desire to annihilate humanity.[129] Mallako traces the roots of his misanthropy to "an emotionally deprived and repressed childhood" that Monk finds not unlike "Russell's own," but Mallako's description of childhood abuse goes well beyond anything reported by Russell.[130] A more telling parallel would seem to be that between Russell and the narrator, both of whom struggle with repressed misanthropy while yearning for genuine love.[131]

Another story that Russell wrote, "The Psychoanalyst's Nightmare," fea-tures a posthumous Hamlet. At the annual meeting of "the Limbo Rotary Club, presided over by a statue of Shakespeare," Macbeth, Lear, Othello, Antony, Romeo, and Hamlet take turns recounting the manner in which they were cured of neuroses by Dr. Bombasticus, a psychoanalyst said to be capable of "ministering to a mind diseased."[132] Thanks to timely intervention, each of them managed to become a well-adjusted member of society and so avoid the tragedy that Shakespeare assigned him. Their reports are interrupted, however, when a tape recorder inside the statue repeats lines from the play that indicate the cost of their respective "cures"—the sacrifice of the great passions that gave their Shakespearean lives and deaths such grandeur. These reminders trouble them, but they prefer cursing the statue to acknowledging their bad consciences. Hamlet is the last to speak. He proclaims that it is bet-ter to "smile and be a villain, than weep and be a good man"—but then the statue throws back at him his words to Gertrude: "You go not till I set you up a glass / Where you may see the inmost part of you" (3.4.19–20). Overcome with shame, Hamlet repeats his self-castigating words in the play, "O, what a rogue and peasant slave am I!" (2.3.550). Wishing Dr. Bombasticus to Hell (as he once wished Claudius), he collapses, evidently succumbing to a second death. Suddenly, the "anguished voice" of Dr. Bombasticus is heard repenting, too late, from Hell ("I call upon St. Freud … in vain"). Instead of coming to his assistance, Hamlet's friends destroy the statue. When nothing remains but its head, a final quotation is heard: Puck's "Lord, what fools these mortals be!" (*A Midsummer Night's Dream* 3.2.115). The story concludes: "The five remained in Limbo. Dr. Bombasticus remained in Hell. But Hamlet was wafted above by angels and ministers of grace." A footnote adds that "Hamlet's place on the Committee" was taken by Ophelia, who, thanks to Dr. Bombasticus, had previously become Hamlet's "submissive wife."[133]

Though not up to the satiric standards of Swift (another writer whom Russell greatly admired), "The Psychoanalyst's Nightmare" effectively lampoons ego psychologists who combat, rather than foster, true individualism. By celebrating Hamlet's resistance to a spiritually stultifying analysis, Russell seems to have been defending his own lifelong refusal to succumb to social pressures. Having been imprisoned for opposing the First World War (he would later be imprisoned again for campaigning for nuclear disarmament) and legally prevented from teaching in New York (on the grounds that his writings about human sexuality were "lecherous, libidinous, lustful, venerous, erotomaniac, aphrodisiac, irreverent, narrow-minded, untruthful, and bereft of moral fiber"),[134] he had long prided himself on his Hamletlike individualism. What disturbed him was the fact that his individualism went hand in hand with a sense of being both haunted and ghostlike.

Together, "Satan in the Suburbs" and "The Psychoanalyst's Nightmare" suggest that a refusal to conform to social expectations may derive from an unresolved misanthropy, or vice versa. The tension between these two positions is reflected in the sins of the two doctors. The crimes that Mallako suggests to his patients are enactments of their own repressed fantasies. All he does is undo their repression. Bombasticus, by contrast, makes his patients repress the very passions that are the underlying causes of their crimes in Shakespeare. Russell seems to have struggled to find a middle ground between these two extremes. The fact that his Hamlet dies a second death and is "wafted" to heaven instead of being reborn on Earth reflects his personal deadlock. His version of Hamlet's afterlife is quite different from that of Nicolas Abraham, in whose "Sixth Act" a fully revived Hamlet learns to live without being haunted at all. Russell's Hamlet is closer to Derrida's in being irremediably haunted.

Significantly, Russell objected not only to the ghostly character of Meinong's theory of *objects* but to what he took to be the no less ghostly character of his conception of thinking *subjects*. In "On Objects of Higher Order and Their

Relationship to Internal Perception" (1899), Meinong distinguished three features of thought: first, the act of thinking by which a particular thought is generated; second, a thought's mental or psychological content; third, the nonmental object that the thought represents.[135] In *The Analysis of Mind* (1921), Russell responded that just as there weren't any objects of thought besides existent objects, so there wasn't an act of thinking to be distinguished from the bare occurrence of an actual thought. From the surface grammar of "I think so-and-so," one is led to suppose that "I" refers to the agent of an act, but "Meinong's 'act' is the ghost of the subject, or what once was the full-blooded soul."[136] A ghostly subject was no less "intolerable" than a ghostly object.

Like Russell, Gilbert Ryle associated the "Ghost in the Machine" with Hamlet: "Psychological theories which made no mention of the deliverances of 'inner perception' were at first likened to 'Hamlet' without the Prince of Denmark. But the extruded hero soon came to seem so bloodless and spineless a being that even the opponents of these theories began to feel shy of imposing heavy theoretical burdens upon his spectral shoulders."[137] Borrowing a phrase from Hamlet, A. J. Ayer asked in "An Honest Ghost?" (1970) whether Ryle had succeeded in "exorcizing the ghost": "The movements of the ghost have been curtailed, but it still walks, and some of us are still haunted by it."[138] John Searle, reviving Ryle's castigated idiom, characterizes Daniel Dennett's bald denial of "the existence of inner mental states" as the equivalent of "a performance of *Hamlet* without the Prince of Denmark."[139] Colin McGinn, reflecting on Hamlet's remark that "there is something in this more than natural if philosophy could find it out," argues in *Shakespeare's Philosophy* that Shakespeare (like McGinn himself) was both a "naturalist" and a "mysterian"—someone who rejects supernatural explanations of mental phenomena while acknowledging that they are irreducibly mysterious.[140]

Two years after the publication of "On Denoting," Meinong noted an important difference between the *de re* statement "Nothing actual (or real) is a ghost" (*Kein Wirkliches ist Gespenst*) and the (seemingly) *de dicto* statement "Ghosts do not exist" (*Gespenster existieren nicht*).[141] The former says of every existing object that none of them is a ghost. The latter says that there are no ghosts, yet it too can be regarded as a *de re* claim about nonexistent objects since it says *of ghosts* that none of them has existence. Russell's theory of descriptions denies that it is possible to speak *of ghosts*—all one can do is say *of existing objects* that none is a ghost. Yet, as Meinong argues, someone who denies the reality of ghosts is most plausibly interpreted as believing that a certain kind of object about which one can speak doesn't exist. Perhaps Russell was afraid of conceding this much. Despite his repudiation of Meinong's doctrine, he couldn't shake the sense that he *was* a ghost. Unable to resolve this deadlock, he could only gesture toward the difference between Dr. Bombasticus and (not Dr. Mallako but) St. Freud—that is, the difference between an ego analyst who could help him "adjust" his thinking to reality at the cost of his true identity and an analytic "rebel" who could help him preserve his own spirit of independence without losing touch with reality.[142] Was it possible to say "No" to society but "Yes" to the world, including other people? Was it possible to embody Hamlet's negativity without becoming melancholy?

Russell's logical conception of negation resembles that of Frege. For Frege, there is no essential difference between affirmative and negative statements. Any proposition, or thought, can be construed as affirmative or negative depending on how it is couched in language. For this reason, Frege restricts the concept of negation to the logical function by which a true proposition is made false, and a false proposition true. The idea that there are primitive *acts* of negation is rejected as chimerical: "Perhaps the act of negating, which maintains a questionable existence as the polar opposite of judging, is a chimerical construction, formed by a fusion of the act of judging with the negation that I have acknowledged as a possible component of a thought, and to which there corresponds in language the word 'not' as part of the predicate."[143] What Frege bequeathed to analytic philosophy is a strictly logical conception of negation that acknowledges no existentialist dimension. The existentialist dimension of negation was developed by Sartre, who, conversely, made no distinctive contribution to logic. What Russell tried to do was to develop the two types of negation in tandem, but without reflecting on the hinge that connected them.

Freud distinguishes two types of logical negation: negative predications and negative existentials. A negative predication denies that a given object has a particular property; a negative existential denies that there is anything in reality corresponding to a given mental representation. Every negation expresses a desire to repress something. The capacity to deny that a given object possesses a particular property derives from the primitive function of spitting out objects that don't taste good. The capacity to deny that there is any object corresponding to a mental representation derives from the cognitively more sophisticated function of testing to see whether the memory traces of objects once perceived still correspond to existing objects. In the first case, we repudiate what doesn't give us pleasure; in the second, we repudiate what doesn't exist, whether doing so causes us pleasure or pain. Affirmation represents a way of uniting ourselves with the world, whereas negation is a way of rejecting the world. Primordial rejection or repudiation is the fundamental stance of psychotics. Freud conjectures that a psychotic's "passion for universal negation" derives from a withdrawal of libido.[144] Besides accounting for the logical structure of psychosis, Freud's analysis of negation distinguishes denials based on a robust sense of reality from denials based on hatred. It is possible to deny the existence of Hamlet, God, and ghosts simply because one's sense of reality is determined by the experience of empirical reality-testing. But it is also possible to issue such denials because one hates (or fears) the objects in question, or hates (or envies) those who believe in them. In "Satan in the Suburbs," Russell was asking himself if his own passion for negation was rooted in hatred. In "The Psychoanalyst's Nightmare," he wondered whether it would be worth sacrificing the great passions that begin in negation (some of which have a libidinal dimension) for the sake of the tepid affirmation of reality at which adjustment therapy aims. His answer was unequivocal: "No." Such a negation didn't have to derive from hatred. On the contrary, it could spring from great love. Hamlet's negative statement "Man delights not me—nor woman neither" (2.2.309) is the flip side of his affirmation "What a piece of work is a man" (2.2.303–304).[145]What makes an individual great is negativity, that tremendous power that Hegel takes to be the defining feature of subjectivity (and the defining feature of definition). Despite Russell's unstinting hostility toward Hegel, tarrying with the negative seems to be his own philosophical modus operandi. Seems? Nay, it is.[146]

DETERMINATE NEGATION
AND ITS OBJECTIVE CORRELATIVE

No! I am not Prince Hamlet, nor was meant to be.
T. S. Eliot, "The Love Song of J. Alfred Prufrock"

"Hamlet" to himself were Hamlet—
Had not Shakespeare wrote—
Emily Dickinson, Poem 776

The mind of the poet is the shred of platinum.
T. S. Eliot, "Tradition and the Individual Talent"

"Determinate negation" is Hegel's way of working out the Spinozistic principle *Omnis determinatio est negatio*: "Every determination is negation." As Hegel
interprets it, Spinoza's principle states that everything finite, or determinate,
is a negation of the one substance that is God or nature. Hegel supplements
it with the dialectical principle that negation is inherent in substance itself:
Every negation *of* substance is negated *by* substance. Determinate negation
is then to be conceived as both the movement of negation and the result of
negation. But what exactly is determinate negation? How does Hegel think
the "not to be" of "To be or not to be"?

According to Robert Brandom, determinate negation is *material exclusion*, or
the fact that something's being determinate in some way precludes its being
determinate in materially incompatible ways ("To be p and therefore not to
be q"). For Slavoj Žižek, determinate negation is *material incompleteness*, or the
impossibility of anything's being fully determinate ("Neither to be p nor not
to be p, but to be *non-p*"). Underlying these two conceptions are compet-
ing interpretations of Hegelian spirit. For Brandom, material exclusion is
associated with a certain type of social exclusion, whereas for Žižek material incompleteness is associated with a certain type of social incompleteness.

Brandom takes inferential practices of determinate negation to originate in the social institution of norms and the mutual policing of commitments, whereas Žižek takes symbolic practices of determinate negation to be rooted in fundamental social antagonisms that manifest themselves as struggles for hegemony.

To elucidate their respective conceptions of determinate negation, both Brandom and Žižek appeal to T. S. Eliot's description of the process by which poets transform the traditions to which they belong. Predictably, they interpret Eliot, as they do Hegel, differently. We can understand why by turning from "Tradition and the Individual Talent" to another of Eliot's essays from *The Sacred Wood*, namely, "Hamlet and His Problems." According to Eliot, Hamlet lacks an adequate "objective correlative" for the emotional outburst that his mother's infidelity occasions. Hamlet's problem is said to be symptomatic of the play's failure to provide an adequate objective correlative for the emotional state that Shakespeare was in when he was writing it. How we conceive determinate negation will depend on how we understand Hegel's response to the problem of the objective correlative in German idealism— that is, the problem that arises when the thing in itself is subtracted from Kant's transcendental idealism. Like Hamlet, Hegelian spirit is in excess of *its* objective correlative, an excess that attests to Hegel's own writerly struggle to find an adequate expression for his conception of the absolute. Just as, for Eliot, Shakespeare's problem "*precludes* objective equivalence," so Hegel's philosophical discourse is *objectively* problematic in a specifically Kantian sense.[1] Brandom and Žižek respond differently to Hegel's Hamletlike problematicity. Brandom *dissolves* Hegel's problems by representing absolute idealism as a merely semantic and pragmatic doctrine. Žižek *resolves* them by taking spirit's lack of an objective correlative to be its true objective correlative. Whether either of these interpretations *absolves* Hegel of his Hamletian problematicity is the question I would like to broach in this brief epilogue.

In *Tales of the Mighty Dead*, Brandom takes determinate negation to be a function of determinateness.[2] To possess some determinate property p is *not* to possess any property q the possession of which is incompatible with the possession of p. This conception of "material exclusion or incompatibility" is "modally robust" in the sense that being p necessitates not being q (i.e., in any possible world in which x exists and is p, x is not q).[3] Determinate negation is an objective relation that then grounds the equally objective relation of material *implication*. If everything determinately negated by x's being p is determinately negated by anything that is r, then x's being p entails that it is r.[4] Like material exclusion, material implication is a relation that holds among the contents of our concepts and thus among the objects that fall under these concepts. We cannot grasp the sense of material relations of exclusion and inference without understanding them as constraints on the kinds of inferential moves a rational subject who grasped them would be entitled or obliged to make. It is this doctrine that Brandom identifies as Hegel's objective idealism. Objective idealism, then, is the semantic thesis that objective relations of material exclusion and implication are "reciprocally sense dependent" on subjective practices of inference.[5]

Brandom bases this account on Gilbert Harman's distinction between *formal* logical inferential relations and the inferential practices we engage in when we consider such relations.[6] Brandom takes Hegel to apply this distinction to relations and practices of *material* exclusion and inference, and to argue that all logical relations are sense dependent on inferential practices. Corresponding to logically necessary exclusions and entailments are normative necessities of commitment: by taking something to be determinate in some way I oblige myself—and, if successful in this endeavor, am taken by others to be obliged—not to take it to be certain other ways (or, in the case of entailments, to acknowledge further commitments to which I have implicitly committed myself). Just as the sense of the relations presupposes that of the commitments, so the sense of the commitments presupposes that of the relations: such is the twofold character of Hegel's objective idealism. It doesn't follow that relations and commitments couldn't exist without each other, for the *semantic* dependence of relations on commitments doesn't entail a corresponding "*reference* dependence."[7] In other words, objective idealism doesn't imply that without actually existing rational subjects there could be no objective relations of material exclusion and inference. Although the sense of such relations presupposes the sense of what it *would be* for rational subjects to engage in inferential activity, such relations could hold in a determinate world without rational subjects in it. (Whether there could be inferential activity in an indeterminate world is a separate question.) If sense dependence entailed reference dependence, objective idealism would imply that there could be no world without rational subjects in it, a view that Brandom thinks Hegel never seriously entertained.[8]

What Brandom's Hegel is committed to is "semantic holism," the doctrine that semantic contents—that is, conceptually articulable ways of being—are individuated by the relations they stand in to one another. Semantic holism is opposed to the atomistic view that material exclusion or determinate negation is a secondary operation imposed on antecedently given semantic contents that can be grasped independently of one another. Hegel is a holist because he takes determinacy to *consist* in material exclusion. More precisely, he is committed to "*weak* individuational holism," or the thesis that relations of material exclusion are *necessary* for the determination of individual semantic contents. Despite indications to the contrary, Hegel is not committed to "*strong* individuational holism," or the view that relations of material exclusion are *sufficient* for the determination of individual contents.[9] By making each individual item's semantic content a function of *nothing but* its relations to other such items, a strong holism would do away with intrinsic content altogether. Brandom regards this as an incoherent position, since it amounts to letting some content *p* be nothing apart from its relation to *q* while at the same time letting *q* be nothing apart from its relation to *p*. By completely reducing relata to relations, the relations themselves disappear.[10]

Hegel seems to be committed to strong holism because he believes that the relative individuation of semantic contents is symmetric rather than asymmetric. An asymmetric account would fix the sense of some determinate content *p* with respect to which the content *not-p* could then be determined. Hegel's symmetric account invites us instead to think of positing as the act of differentiating an entire field of mutually excluding contents, so that to determine something as *p* is to determine it as *not-q*, *not-r*, *not-s*, and so on, where no one item in the field (*p*, *q*, *r*, *s*, etc.) is granted a privileged status.[11] Symmetric relative individuation seems to lead from weak to strong holism, but Hegel is said by Brandom to dig in his heels by distinguishing the elements of relational structures from the relations between such elements. At the level of sense certainty in the *Phenomenology of Spirit*, consciousness represents determinate aspects of the world *as if* they were immediate givens. This view is "unstable," giving way to the picture of reciprocal dependency relations that characterizes the point of view of perception.[12] At this stage of the dialectic, consciousness learns that objective determinacy consists not in an indifferent multiplicity of property instantiations, but in the material exclusions that make each determination something essentially mediated. This is the stage at which symmetric relative individuation runs the risk of collapsing into an ungrounded set of relations without relata. This risk is overcome, however, at the level of understanding, when consciousness reintroduces the determinate contents of the first stage, now represented not as immediate givens but as signs that express the exclusions and implications generated at the second stage.[13] By representing observables as signs of theoretically articulable relational complexes, Hegel is able to ground his semantic holism in semiotic atoms of experience. The "brute thereness" of observables is purely expressive.[14] As Socrates points out in the *Theaetetus*, it is one thing to recognize signs as signs, another to understand their meaning.[15]

From Hegel's *objective* idealism Brandom turns to his *conceptual* idealism, or the view that "the structure and unity of the *concept* is the same as the structure and unity of the *self*."[16] The basis of this view is Hegel's account of the social character of rational subjectivity or selfhood. We become members of rational communities by recognizing others who recognize us. Such mutual recognition consists in acknowledging our individual and joint abilities to undertake theoretical and practical commitments of specific sorts. The sorts in question are determined by the available stock of linguistically articulated

concepts whose content is regulated by instituting agreements, judicial policing, and traditions. To be a rational member of a community is to be a *particular*
self-consciousness who counts as an *individual* by being "subsumed" under
the community *qua universal*.[17] This threefold determination of the subject as
universal, particular, and individual is what Hegel means by "the Concept."
The "life" of the Concept, or of spirit, is the totality of practices by which
the members of a community undertake and assess one another's inferential
commitments.[18] Particular concepts are the guiding norms of such commitments and so can be modeled on the selves who undertake them.

Making sure that the determinacy of commitments is respected is the primary policing function of a community. A community polices itself by regu-
lating the inclusion and exclusion of potential members, by holding those
recognized as actual members to their commitments, and by maintaining the
traditions that give those commitments their content. As the sedimentations
of past commitments, traditions are conservative, but they are also inherently subject to challenge. To challenge a tradition, one must patiently work
through its past commitments. Challenging a tradition is not the same as
abstractly negating it. Abstract negation often leaves the past—and the present—fundamentally unaltered. Challenging, by contrast, is an act of determinate negation that carries with it a willingness to be challenged in turn.
By working through both the past's claims on the present and the present's
claims on the past, we can change both the present and the past. To illustrate
this point, Brandom turns to Eliot: "As Eliot says … : 'Tradition … cannot be
inherited. If you want it you must obtain it by great labour'":[19]

> No poet, no artist of any art, has his complete meaning alone. His signifi-
> cance, his appreciation is his appreciation of his relation to the dead poets
> and artists. You cannot value him alone; you must set him, for contrast and
> comparison, among the dead. … The existing monuments form an ideal
> order among themselves, which is modified by the introduction of the new
> (the really new) work of art among them. The existing order is complete
> before the new work arrives; for order to persist after the supervention of
> novelty, the *whole* existing order must be, if ever so slightly, altered; and so the
> relations, proportions, values of each work of art toward the whole are read-
> justed; and this is conformity between the old and the new.[20]

Brandom goes on to describe the specific process by which philosophical
traditions can be appropriated and transformed. First, one must let the dead
speak in their own terms—not just by reading them, but by elaborating their
ideas through *de dicto* ascriptions of philosophical commitment. Next, or rather
at the same time, one must restate those commitments in one's own terms
through *de re* ascriptions of commitment. By going back and forth between

these idioms, we establish a genuine conversation with the "mighty dead." Whatever inferences we end up making on the dead's behalf are subject to contestation by proxy, that is, by other living philosophers and by future philosophers for whom we ourselves will eventually count as dead philosophers (whether mighty or not). For Hegel, the mightiest of the dead philosophers, making sense of the history of philosophy and making philosophical sense are two aspects of a single process.[21] Brandom reactivates Hegel's project by situating Hegel himself within a broadly conceived rationalist tradition that extends from Spinoza and Leibniz to Sellars.

In *Less Than Nothing*, Žižek sets out to "repeat Hegel" in another way.[22] If to say of some object x that it has some property p is to say that it excludes all those properties that are incompatible with p, then to say of x that it is *incomplete* is to say that there is some pair of contradictorily opposed properties q and *not-q* neither of which pertains to x. All that can be said of x in such a case is that it is *non-q* (rather than *not-q*). This is the basic form of an "infinite judgment" in the Kantian sense. For Kant, as for the Aristotelian logical tradition he inherits, an infinite judgment is an "indeterminate negation," but Žižek represents the Hegelian infinite judgment as the "'truth' of negative judgment" in the sense that an infinite judgment *determines* the inherent negativity or lack that prevents some determinate content from being *completely* determinate.[23] For Hegel, though not for Kant, this lack is ontological rather than epistemic: it is inscribed in things themselves rather than pertaining exclusively to appearances.

In the *Critique of Pure Reason*, Kant claims that appearances are exempt from the "principle of thoroughgoing determination," the principle that every object is fully determinate in the sense that, for every possible pair of contradictorily opposed predicates, one and only one of the two must be predicable of it. This principle would hold for intelligible noumena if we were entitled to posit such objects. Phenomena are exempt because, as temporal appearances, they are never given all at once but are always on their way *toward* completion. The empirical concepts that phenomena fall under by virtue of being *partly* determined by us are subject to a weaker "principle of *determinability*" according to which one and only one of each pair of contradictorily opposed predicates can belong to each concept.[24] This principle is weaker than the principle of thoroughgoing determination not only because it pertains to concepts rather than to things, but because it can function only as a regulative ideal for the process of empirical concept specification.[25]

By doing away with the thing in itself, Hegel effectively jettisons the principle of thoroughgoing determination in favor of a principle of *nonthoroughgoing* determination. This alternative principle is implicit in his reinterpretation of infinite judgment as the "truth" of determinate negation. The paradigmatic form of an infinite judgment is no longer *x is non-p*, a judgment that, according to Kant, excludes the object *x* from the class of things *p* without thereby positively determining it in any way. Rather, for Hegel, an infinite judgment expresses the discrepancy between an object and its properties. This discrepancy is expressed in category mistakes—judgments such as "The being of Spirit is a bone," "Spirit is no elephant," or "A lion is no table"—as well as tautologies such as "A rose is a rose." Category mistakes affirm or deny that some logical subject has some incomparable predicate. Tautologies not only suspend the very act of predication by identifying the logical subject with itself but in so doing they disclose the inherent negativity by virtue of which an object can be *related* to itself. The effect in either case is to reveal the object's incompleteness.

Objective incompleteness is a function of the subjective negativity that Hegel equates with spirit. To use Brandom's terminology, the lack of determinate content on the side of the object is *semantically modeled* on the lack that Žižek, following Lacan, equates with subjectivity. Indeed, objective incompleteness would appear to be reciprocally *reference dependent* on subjectivity, so that Hegel's objective idealism would be more than just a semantic doctrine. There couldn't be a world (that is, an incomplete world) without subjects, but this doesn't tell us whether ontological incompleteness is a function of subjectivity or vice versa.[26] Žižek argues that material substance is an ontological presupposition of spirit, but he also emphasizes the Hegelian view that spirit has to posit its own presuppositions. This metaphysical loop suggests that there is nothing ontologically prior to what Heidegger calls *Geworfenheit*, or Dasein's condition of being thrown into a world not of its own making.[27] The only way to make sense of this paradox is to conclude that the past is incomplete. Kant drew this very conclusion to resolve the antinomy that arises when we ask whether the history of the world is finite or infinite. It cannot be finite, Kant reasons, for in that case there would have been no sufficient reason for the world's coming into existence just when it did; but neither can it be infinite, for then the present could never have been reached. Kant concludes that the past history of the world has no determinate magnitude: it is only our historically situated retrospective gaze that "posits" the past *as* a totality. The moral of transcendental idealism is that there can be no nonlooping narrative that would reconstruct the total history of the world.[28] Hegel generalizes this Kantian lesson.

Elegant though it is, this solution might seem to pertain primarily, if not exclusively, to the *sense relation* between substantial presuppositions and the positing acts of subjects, leaving undetermined the *reference relation* between them. Žižek acknowledges this gap by invoking Lacan's distinction between the symbolic construction of reality and the "hard kernel of the Real." The latter resists retroactive constitution, breaking the otherwise undecidable, chicken-and-egg relation between substance and spirit. Žižek argues that

Hegel is a materialist rather than an idealist insofar as he represents subjectivity as an irreducible "crack" in the cosmos rather than as a presubstantial ground from which substance itself would proceed. Thus, although there couldn't be a world—that is, again, an incomplete world—without subjects in it, it is the world itself that serves as the fixed point of an asymmetric grounding relation. If Hegel nevertheless remains an idealist, he does so insofar as what counts for him *as* the Real is a function of irreducible conceptual antinomies rather than a brute given that resists conceptual determination.[29]

The material incompleteness of the phenomenal world is therefore not an "epistemological obstacle" but a "positive ontological condition."[30] Hegel reaches this position by tarrying with Kant's mathematical antinomies. The theses of the mathematical antinomies represent both past world history and the present size of the world (in the great and small) as finite. The antitheses represent each of these magnitudes as infinite. In each case, we seem to be faced with an exclusive either/or: either the object is finite, or it is not-finite, that is, infinite. Kant argues that the predicates *finite* and *infinite* are not contradictorily opposed in the antinomies because the scope of the objects they purport to determine is not fully determin*ate* but only indefinitely determin*able*. Only through the successive synthesis of appearances—that is, their temporal unfolding—can magnitudes of any sort be given. There is no fixed limit to either the retrospective gaze of the cosmologist, the telescopic gaze of the astrophysicist, or the microscopic gaze of the particle physicist; but this absence of limits doesn't make the magnitudes they measure *determinately* infinite. This result holds only if appearances are distinguished from things in themselves. If appearances were things in themselves, then every cosmological magnitude would have to be fully determinate. The difference between appearances and things in themselves is underscored by Kant's solution to the dynamical antinomies, the theses of which affirm the necessary reality of ungrounded grounds of phenomenal objects. Since no such grounds can be found within nature, their reality is denied by the antitheses. Kant resolves these conflicts by positing hypothetical noumenal grounds.

Like Kant, Hegel takes the phenomenal world to be incomplete, but instead of distinguishing phenomena from noumena he identifies ultimate reality with the inherently incomplete phenomenal world. This leads him to privilege the form of the mathematical antinomies over that of the dynamical antinomies. As Žižek puts it, Hegel embraces Lacan's "feminine" logic of the "non-All," in contradistinction to Kant's "masculine" logic of the "constitutive exception." The antinomial logic of the "non-All" is twofold: first, there is nothing that is not subject to a given logical function; but second, not everything is subject to the function in question. Crucial to Žižek's interpretation of this formula (and to the Lacanian matrix on which it is based) is that the logical form of "not everything" is fundamentally different from the logical form of positing an exception. The forms of the theses and antitheses of Kant's dynamical antinomies are, respectively, $\forall xFx$ and $\exists x{\sim}Fx$ (Kant's constitutive exceptions being a first cause and a necessary being). By embracing the mathematical/feminine logic of the "non-All" as a general metaphysical principle, Hegel doesn't eliminate so much as "feminize" these dynamical/masculine constitutive exceptions. "Non-All" is the name of the inherent gap that marks every object as incompletely determined. Thus, the principle of nonthoroughgoing determination—Hegel's incompleteness theorem—divides in two: on the one hand, there is nothing that is not determinate; on the other, not everything—non-All—is determinate.

Just as Brandom takes material exclusion to be reciprocally sense dependent on the commitments rational subjects endorse and enforce, so Žižek takes the material incompleteness of the non-All to be reciprocally sense dependent on commitments that are themselves inherently incomplete. Thus, the fact that the world is incomplete has as its corollary the incompleteness of those rational subjects for whom it is incomplete. Every social group is structured around its own inherent negativity—a sign not only of its lack of complete determinacy, but, more fundamentally, of its incomplete power of *self*-determination. This gap is the site of a "fundamental antagonism" among those who vie for the power of collective self-determination. Such a struggle for hegemony is more fundamental than the policing of commitments—or, rather, there is no policing of commitments that doesn't have the form of an "ideological struggle." Žižek's version of Hegel's expansion of what Brandom calls the "Harman point" (according to which expansion inferential relations are reciprocally sense dependent on inferential practices) is that the incomplete determinacy of *things* can only be understood as a possible stake in a struggle for hegemony.[31] A further implication is the quasi-Gödelian thought that every attempt to *completely* determine the world gives rise to material "inconsistencies" such as performative contradictions.

It is to account for the incomplete nature of self-determination that Žižek turns to "Tradition and the Individual Talent." Žižek takes Eliot at his word when he says that "the existing order is complete before the new work arrives; for order to persist after the supervention of novelty, the *whole* existing order must be, if ever so slightly, altered." For the existing order to be truly complete, Žižek reasons, it must belong to a totalized past. But a truly new work changes the past. Since the actual past cannot be changed, Žižek concludes that what Eliot means by "tradition" must be a virtual past, or what Deleuze calls the "pure past."[32] Everything that exists in the pure past is both quasi-eternal and subject to revision (much as, in George Orwell's *1984*, new alliances are treated as having always already been in place).[33] What sustains the pure past is its symbolic character. The pure past is an essentially tenseless space of symbolic inscription. It is tenseless in the sense that although symbolic commitments are always inscribed at determinate moments of historical time, they become, temporarily, valid for all times. When Eliot's poet places himself among the dead, he subjects himself to this impersonal medium of symbolic inscription. Describing the process by which the traditional poet "must develop or procure the consciousness of the past," he writes:

> What happens is a continual surrender of himself as he is at the moment to something which is more valuable. The progress of an artist is a continual self-sacrifice, a continual extinction of personality.
>
> There remains to define this process of depersonalization and its relation to the sense of tradition. It is in this depersonalization that art may be said to approach the condition of science.[34]

Depersonalization involves freeing "the mind which creates" from the person who experiences "emotions and feelings" ("the man who suffers"). Such purification enables "the mind of the poet" to play the role of a catalyst: when "a bit of finely filiated platinum is introduced into a chamber containing oxygen and sulphur dioxide ... the two gases ... form sulphurous acid" without ("apparently") affecting the platinum. Analogously, the mind of the poet plays a catalytic role with respect to his or her emotions and feelings, facilitating a reaction that produces a new work of art. The new work doesn't *express* the poet's emotions and feelings; on the contrary, it is essentially nonexpressive. The reason we must place the poet "among the dead" to evaluate him (Eliot's language isn't gender-neutral) is that the poet himself must engage in an act of *self*-mortification to make a *vital* contribution to a tradition that is "immortal" or, better, "undead."[35]

By entering the society of dead poets, the living poet becomes the conduit of their voices. This involves letting them speak through him while letting himself speak through them. This division of poetic labor corresponds to Brandom's distinction between *de dicto* and *de re* ascriptions of commitment. But there is another dimension to this Elysian encounter, so like Dante's appropriation of—or by—Virgil's voice in *The Divine Comedy* (and Eliot had a similar relationship to Dante). Žižek observes that Lacan first took the aim of psychoanalysis to be the subjectivization, or personalization, of the analysand. To enable the analysand to discover his or her own authentic voice, the discourse of the analyst was supposed to function as "the medium of prosopopoeia." Eventually, Lacan came to believe that the true aim of analysis was *depersonalization*, or the transformation of "the words of the analysand into prosopopoeia."[36] In the first instance, the aim of analysis was to free the analysand from the voices of the dead (much as Henry Miller wanted to be free of Hamlet); in the second, it was *to set the analysand among the dead*. Far from simply "mortifying" the analysand—or, rather, by mortifying her—desubjectivization enabled the poet within her to play the role of a catalyst, reconfiguring the voices of the dead into something like a new "work of art."

It is this element of desubjectivization that is missing from Brandom's reading of Eliot. Robert Pippin has criticized Brandom for treating all discursive commitments as assertoric, and for making it seem as if recognitive communities arise out of an "original normless situation."[37] Žižek suggests that these criticisms don't go far enough. For Brandom and Pippin alike, human discourse is essentially normative in the sense that to speak is, first and foremost, to bind ourselves to norms. For Žižek, normative commitment is subordinate to something more fundamental, namely, symbolic identification, or what we have previously characterized as "election."[38] By taking on a symbolic identity, one comes to be recognized by others as entitled to make certain normative commitments. Such an entitlement consists in limited powers of determination, that is, portions of the general social power to predicate something of something. Symbolic identities make normative commitments possible while retaining their status as fundamental enigmas that cause us anxiety. This twofold character is evidenced in the kinds of ultimate justifications they ground, typically self-referential pronouncements of the sort "Because I said so," where the force of the "I" is split between the assumed social role and the anxious subject secretly wondering whether or why this is his or her role. Since self-binding normative commitments presuppose the underlying force of symbolic commitments over which we have limited control, they carry with them a secondary, reflexive, and "rationalizing" character. Like Hamlet, we may *resist* a symbolic identification (as occurs, in different ways, in hysteria and psychosis) or *overidentify* with one (as occurs, again in different ways, in obsessional neurosis and perversion), but such acts can never be fully reduced to (or *aufgehoben* into) normative commitments. On the contrary, normativity itself, like normality and abnormality, is a by-product of symbolic identification. According to Žižek, Brandom, like Pippin, overlooks this fact.[39]

It is because the symbolic order is virtual (or fictional) that the world it frames is incompletely determined. Determinate negation is the permanent possibility of radically transforming the symbolic order. One way to characterize the difference between Brandom and Žižek would be to say that Brandom is a semantic pluralist whose primary aim is to multiply texts and interpretations, whereas Žižek is a revolutionary committed to radical transformation.[40] Another way to put it would be to note that Brandom's world is Parmenidean in the sense that it is impervious to genuine becomings and Events. Becomings, in the strict Heraclitean sense, are situations in which *being p* does *not* materially exclude *being not-p*, whereas Events, in the Badiouian sense, are transformations that literally change which "possible world" we inhabit (rather than simply introducing a temporal change within a world fixedly privileged as actual). To accommodate becomings and Events, it is necessary to accept the incompleteness principle that Žižek attributes to Hegel. If becomings and Events are essentially virtual rather than actual, then a *merely* actual world is strictly impossible—again, on the assumption of material incompleteness.

For Kant, the idea of a materially *complete* world is problematic in the specific sense of lacking an objective correlative: "We can have no acquaintance with an object that corresponds to an idea, even though we can have a problematic concept of it."[41] By jettisoning the thing in itself, Hegel reconfigures Kant's conception of an idea. "Absolute idea" is his name for the idea of the idea itself, or for an idea that *is* its own objective correlative. Absolute knowing is spirit's representation of itself *as* the absolute idea.

In "Hamlet and His Problems," Eliot claims that not "Hamlet the character" but "*Hamlet* the play" is "the primary problem."[42] The play is problematic because the problem to which the play would be the solution doesn't admit of an adequate solution:

> Nothing that Shakespeare can do with the plot can express Hamlet for him. And it must be noticed that the very nature of the *donées* of the problem precludes objective equivalence. To have heightened the criminality of Gertrude would have been to provide the formula for a totally different emotion in Hamlet; it is just *because* her character is so negative and insignificant that she arouses in Hamlet the feeling which she is incapable of representing. … We must simply admit that here Shakespeare tackled a problem which proved too much for him. Why he attempted it at all is an insoluble puzzle; under compulsion of what experience he attempted to express the inexpressibly horrible, we cannot ever know. … We should have, finally, to know something which is by hypothesis unknowable, for we assume it to be an experience which, in the manner indicated, exceeded the facts. *We should have to understand things which Shakespeare did not understand himself.*[43]

This last remark is crucial: not only did Shakespeare try to solve a problem that had no solution, but he was led to this problem by something within his soul that was itself an insoluble problem both for him and for us.[44] Putting Eliot's two essays together, we can take him to be saying that while writing *Hamlet* Shakespeare was unable to perform the necessary act of depersonalization that he successfully performed when he wrote his genuine artistic masterpieces. *Hamlet* may not be a successful work of art, but it is Shakespeare's truest "problem play" and therefore his most philosophical. It is Shakespeare's testament to what happens when a poet's analysis comes up against its unfathomable X. When that unfathomable X is posited "in and for itself" as an empty form, we get what Hegel called the absolute idea. Eliot's *Hamlet* expresses the truth of absolute idealism—just as absolute idealism expresses the truth of *Hamlet*.

Brandom misses this Hamletian dimension of Hegel's thought because he takes absolute idealism to be equivalent to objective idealism, conceived in terms of the view that determinate negation is material exclusion, plus conceptual idealism, conceived as normative pragmatism.[45] Since his pragmatism doesn't entail metaphysical idealism, there can be no lack of an objective correlative for the "game of giving and asking for reasons." The only sorts of things that *could* go missing would be the moves necessary to constitute and play such a game. Wilfrid Sellars remarks that "A game without moves is *Hamlet* without the prince of Denmark indeed!"—but for both Sellars and Brandom, there could be a fully determinate world without a game.[46] Objects, facts, and laws are, essentially, the kinds of things that *could* be expressed by singular terms, assertions, and inferences, but there *could* be objects, facts, and laws in a world without rational subjects.[47] Spirit can be *abstractly* negated.

Žižek doesn't highlight the Hamletian dimension of Hegel's thought, but it is implicit in his notion that the absolute idea lacks an objective correlative. His additional twist is to take this very lack to *be* the absolute idea's true correlative. Hegel "succeeds" precisely where he fails. The same can be said of Shakespeare. Long before Eliot, *Hamlet* was regarded as a failure in comparison with the tragedies of antiquity ("O Hamlet, what a falling-off was there" [1.5.47]). But for Hegel, as for Freud, Hamlet's lack of an objective correlative epitomizes modern subjectivity. *Hamlet*'s failure is the very mark of its success.

Žižek reminds us that *Hamlet* derives from a myth that is older than the Oedipus myth. While accepting the psychoanalytic idea that *Hamlet* "repeats" *Oedipus Tyrannus*, Žižek asks why this repetition takes the form that it does. He conjectures that it has something to do with Hamlet's "secret":

> Instead of the linear/historicist reading of *Hamlet* as a secondary distortion of the Oedipal text, the Oedipus myth is (as Hegel had already claimed) the founding myth of Western Greek civilization … and it is in Hamlet's "distortion" of the Oedipus myth that its repressed content articulates itself. What, then, is the pre-Oedipal "secret" of Hamlet? One should *retain* the insight that Oedipus is a proper "myth," and that the Hamlet narrative is its "modernizing" dislocation/corruption; the lesson is that the Oedipus "myth"—and, perhaps, mythic "naivety" itself—serves to obfuscate some prohibited *knowledge*, ultimately the knowledge about the father's obscenity. … In contrast to tragedy, which is based on some misrecognition or ignorance, melodrama always involves some unexpected and excessive knowledge possessed not by the hero but by his or her other, the knowledge imparted to the hero at the very end, in the final melodramatic reversal.[48]

What secret knowledge would be imparted to Hamlet at the end of the play? That the door of the Law was intended for him alone and now Horatio will close it? Alas, the Ghost doesn't return to "tell the secrets of [his] prison-house" (1.5.14), and Hamlet dies before he can tell his:

> Had I but time—as this fell sergeant, Death,
> Is strict in his arrest—O, I could tell you—
> But let it be.
>
> (5.2.336–338)

The rest is silence. If *Hamlet* fails even as a melodrama, it does so in the same way that the *Phenomenology of Spirit* and the *Science of Logic* do, namely, as revelations of absolute knowing as absolute unknowing.

Eliot is right: the presence of platinum enables oxygen and sulfur dioxide to produce sulfuric acid. But platinum, as Wikipedia tells us, is an imperfect catalyst: "Platinum was formerly employed as a catalyst for the reaction, but as it is susceptible to poisoning by arsenic impurities in the sulfur feedstock, vanadium (V) oxide (V_2O_5) is now preferred."[49]

The objective correlative of determinate negation, Hamlet is the shred of vanadium oxide.

NOTES

PROLOGUE

1. Unless noted otherwise, all references to Shakespeare are to *The Riverside Shakespeare*, 2nd ed., ed. G. Blakemore Evans et al. (Boston: Houghton Mifflin, 1997).

2. Martin Heidegger, "Who Is Nietzsche's Zarathustra?," in Heidegger, *Nietzsche*, vol. 2: *The Eternal Recurrence of the Same*, trans. David Farrell Krell (New York: HarperCollins, 1991), 213.

3. Gilles Deleuze and Félix Guattari, *What Is Philosophy?*, trans. Hugh Tomlinson and Graham Burchell (New York: Columbia University Press, 1994), 64.

4. "Who is 'Zarathustra'? He is the thinker whose figure Nietzsche prophetically poetized—and had to poetize because he is the extreme, namely, what is uttermost in the history of metaphysics." Martin Heidegger, *Nietzsche*, vol. 3: *The Will to Power as Knowledge and as Metaphysics*, trans. David Farrell Krell (New York: HarperCollins, 1991), 135. "The conceptual persona is not the philosopher's representative but, rather, the reverse: the philosopher is rather the envelope of his principal conceptual persona and of all the other personae who are the intercessors … , the real subjects of his philosophy." Deleuze and Guattari, *What Is Philosophy?*, 64. Besides Zarathustra, Nietzsche plays many other conceptual characters, including Dionysus, the Antichrist, and Hamlet. Other conceptual characters mentioned by Deleuze and Guattari include the Platonic Socrates, Nicholas of Cusa's Idiot, and Kierkegaard's Don Juan (61–62, 64, 66).

5. Some conceptual characters are named for the philosophers who invented them: "the Cartesian," "the Kantian." Through the use of the indefinite singular, we distinguish such roles from those who play them ("a Cartesian," "a Kantian"). Scholastic honorifics such as "the Philosopher" (Aristotle), "the Commentator" (Averroes), "the Angelic Doctor" (Aquinas), and "the Subtle Doctor" (Duns Scotus) can be regarded as inimitable conceptual characters whom no other thinker has the right to play (in the same way that no other New York Yankee can wear Babe Ruth's number or be called "the Sultan of Swat").

6. Friedrich Nietzsche, *The Birth of Tragedy and Other Writings*, trans. Ronald Speirs, ed. Raymond Geuss and Ronald Speirs (New York: Cambridge University Press, 1999), 40; G. W. F. Hegel, *Hegel's Aesthetics: Lectures on Fine Art*, vol. 1, trans. T. M. Knox (New York: Oxford University Press, 1988), 231; Arthur Schopenhauer, *The World as Will and Representation*, vol. 1, trans. E. F. J. Payne (New York: Dover, 1969), 324.

7. "It is the split between 'I' and 'Hamlet the Dane,' between the vanishing point of the subject of the enunciation and his support in symbolic identification, which is primordial: the moment of 'passage to the act' is nothing but an illusory moment of decision when the subject's being seems to coincide without remainder with his symbolic mandate." Slavoj Žižek, *For They Know Not What They Do: Enjoyment as a Political Factor*, 2nd ed. (New York: Verso, 2002), 155–156. Cf. Žižek, *Tarrying with the Negative: Kant, Hegel, and the Critique of Ideology* (Durham, NC: Duke University Press, 1993), 276n38.

8. Margherita Pascucci, *Philosophical Readings of Shakespeare: "Thou Art the Thing Itself"* (New York: Palgrave Macmillan, 2013), 29. I will have more to say about Pascucci's book in a forthcoming review in *Renaissance Quarterly*.

9. "Descartes … seems to have realized … that … the validity of his argument depends essentially on existential presuppositions. For … he tried to formulate these presuppositions … by saying that 'we can conceive nothing except as existent (*nisi sub ratione existentis*). … This statement … prima facie contradicts what Descartes says in the *Third Meditation* about 'ideas … considered only in themselves, and not as referred to some other thing,' namely that 'they cannot, strictly speaking, be false.' It also contradicts the plain fact that we can think of (mentally consider) unicorns, or Prince Hamlet, without thereby committing ourselves to maintaining that they exist." Jaakko Hintikka, "Cogito, Ergo Sum: Inference or Performance?" *Philosophical Review* 71, no. 1 (January 1962), 3–32, at 9–10. Hintikka's Hamlet has been taken up by many other philosophers, including Kripke and Nozick. "'Hamlet soliloquizes' is of course true. … So does it follow that one can say that Hamlet soliloquizes, but Hamlet does not exist? And I am sure that according to the story Hamlet *thought* too, so maybe 'Hamlet thinks' does not imply 'Hamlet exists,' and this is an invalid form, as Hintikka says." Saul Kripke, *Reference and Existence: The John Locke Lectures* (New York: Oxford University Press, 2013), 58. "Suppose Shakespeare had written for Hamlet the line, 'I think, therefore I am,' or a fiction is written in which a character named Descartes says this, or suppose a character in a dream of mine says this; does it follow that they exist?" Robert Nozick, *Philosophical Explanations* (Cambridge, MA: Harvard University Press, 1981), 202n.

10. Hintikka, "Cogito, Ergo Sum," 17.

11. "For Jaques it would have been too deep; for Iago too habitual a communion with the heart that belongs, or ought to belong, to all mankind." R. A. Foakes, ed., *Coleridge's Criticism of Shakespeare: A Selection* (Detroit: Wayne State University Press, 1989), 85.

12. See, e.g., Herman Rapaport, *Between the Sign and the Gaze* (Ithaca: Cornell University Press, 1994), 78, and Colin McGinn, *Shakespeare's Philosophy: Discovering the Meaning behind the Plays* (New York: HarperCollins, 2006), 52–53.

13. Among those who attribute to Hamlet a Montaigne-inspired moderate skepticism are Graham Bradshaw, *Shakespeare's Scepticism* (Ithaca: Cornell University Press,

1987), 123; Millicent Bell, *Shakespeare's Tragic Skepticism* (New Haven: Yale University Press, 2002), 4; and McGinn, *Shakespeare's Philosophy*, 38.

14. René Descartes, "Meditations on First Philosophy," in *The Philosophical Writings of Descartes*, vol. 2, trans. John Cottingham, Robert Stoothoff, and Dugald Murdoch (New York: Cambridge University Press, 1984), 61–62, italics added.

15. Gilbert Ryle, *The Concept of Mind*, with an intro. by Daniel C. Dennett (Chicago: University of Chicago Press, 2000), 18.

16. Patricia Smith Churchland, *Brain-Wise: Studies in Neurophilosophy* (Cambridge, MA: MIT Press, 2002), 2. For a canonical discussion of the question about whether it is possible to think without phantasms, see Pietro Pomponazzi, "On the Immortality of the Soul," trans. W. H. Hay II, in *The Renaissance Philosophy of Man*, ed. Ernst Cassirer, P. O. Kristeller, and J. H. Randall, Jr. (Chicago: University of Chicago Press, 1948), 280–381.

17. Descartes, *Meditations on First Philosophy*, 21.

18. Simon Williams, *Shakespeare on the German Stage*, vol. 1: 1586–1914 (New York: Cambridge University Press, 1990), 38.

19. John R. Cole, *The Olympian Dreams and Youthful Rebellion of René Descartes* (Urbana: University of Illinois Press, 1992), 33, 53.

20. Ibid., 34.

21. Ibid., 38.

22. Ibid., 35–36, 55.

23. Ibid., 37, 56. Desmond Clarke renders the Latin phrase as "It is, and it is not"—to be and not to be? Desmond M. Clarke, *Descartes: A Biography* (New York: Cambridge University Press, 2006), 60.

24. Cole, *The Olympian Dreams and Youthful Rebellion of René Descartes*, 36.

25. Ibid., 37.

26. Sigmund Freud, "Some Dreams of Descartes: A Letter to Maxime Leroy," in *The Standard Edition of the Complete Psychological Works of Sigmund Freud*, volume 21: 1927–1931, ed. James Strachey (London: Vintage, 2001), 204.

27. For a summary, see Alan Gabbey and Robert E. Hall, "The Melon and the Dictionary: Reflections on Descartes's Dreams," *Journal of the History of Ideas* 59, no. 4 (Oct. 1998), 651–668.

28. Among Kant's papers for his unfinished *Opus Postumum* is a note that says, "N.B. The melon must be eaten today—with Prof. Gensichen—and, at this opportunity … the income from the university." Immanuel Kant, *Opus Postumum*, ed. Eckart Förster, trans. Eckart Förster and Michael Rosen (New York: Cambridge University Press, 1995), 247.

29. René Descartes, "Discourse on the Method of Rightly Conducting One's Reason and Seeking the Truth in the Sciences," in *The Philosophical Writings of Descartes*, vol. 2, 113, 115.

30. Max Horkheimer, *Eclipse of Reason* (New York: Continuum, 1974), 137.

31. "Thus the chasm that has opened up between consciousness and action has to do with the philosophy of history and it is connected with the gulf between inner and outer that must have come as a great shock at around this period, a shock that we can scarcely imagine and that has been reflected in philosophy in the writings of Descartes, Shakespeare's near contemporary." Theodor W. Adorno, *History and Freedom: Lectures 1964–1965*, ed. Rolf Tiedemann, trans. Rodney Livingtsone (Malden, MA: Polity, 2006), 231–232. "It is at the outset of the self-emancipating modern subject's self-reflection, in *Hamlet*, that we find the divergence of insight and action paradigmatically laid down. The more the subject turns into a being-for-itself, the greater the distance it places between itself and the unbroken accord with a given order, the less will its action and consciousness be one." Theodor W. Adorno, *Negative Dialectics*, trans. E. B. Ashton (New York: Continuum, 1973), 228.

32. "In the unreconciled condition, nonidentity is experienced as negativity. From the negative, the subject withdraws to itself, and to the abundance of its ways to react." Adorno, *Negative Dialectics*, 31.

33. G. W. F. Hegel, *Phenomenology of Spirit*, trans. A. V. Miller (New York: Oxford University Press, 1977), 18–19.

34. Adorno calls this division between consciousness and action "the Hamlet Syndrome." Adorno, *History and Freedom*, 237.

35. "His whole being is nothing but language, text, printed pages, stories that have already been written down. He is made up of interwoven words; he is writing itself, wandering through the world among the resemblances of things." Michel Foucault, *The Order of Things: An Archaeology of the Human Sciences* (New York: Vintage, 1994), 46.

36. Ivan Turgeniev, "*Hamlet and Don Quixote*," trans. Josef Jiri Kral and Pavel Durdik, in *Critical Responses to* Hamlet *1600–1900*, vol. 4: *1850–1900*, ed. David Farley-Hills, John Manning, and Johanna Procter (New York: AMS Press, 2006), 726.

37. Plato, *Plato's Sophist: Part II of The Being of the Beautiful*, trans. Seth Benardete (Chicago: University of Chicago Press, 1986), II.21–22 (231d–e).

38. "It will be necessary for us, in defending ourselves, to put the speech of our father Parmenides to the torture and force it to say that 'that which is not' is in some respect, and again, in turn, 'that which is' is not in some point." Ibid., II.33 (241d).

39. Goethe, *Faust Part I*, line 1338, as translated in Eva Brann, *The Ways of Naysaying: No, Not, Nothing, and Nonbeing* (Lanham: Rowman & Littlefield, 2001), 36.

40. "And for this reason unless one perceived things one would not learn or understand anything, and when one contemplates one must simultaneously contemplate an image; for images are like sense-perceptions (*aisthēmata*), except that they are without matter." Aristotle, *Aristotle's De Anima Books II and III*, trans. D. W. Hamlyn (Oxford: Oxford University Press, 1968), 65–66 (432^a).

41. Saint Augustine, *Confessions*, trans. Henry Chadwick (New York: Oxford University Press, 1998), 43, 114.

42. Dermot Moran, *The Philosophy of John Scottus Eriugena: A Study of Idealism in the Middle Ages* (New York: Cambridge University Press, 2004), 230.

43. Rosalie Colie, *Paradoxia Epidemica: The Renaissance Tradition of Paradox* (Princeton: Princeton University Press, 1966), 222.

44. "Although there were Italian and Latin antecedents, the first English tract of this trifling sort was *The Prayse of Nothing* (1585), doubtfully attributed to Sir Edward Dyer. This prose treatise not only claims for Nothing the distinction of being the origin and end of everything, but speculates upon how much better most things would be if Nothing had caused or influenced them." Paul A. Jorgensen, *Redeeming Shakespeare's Words* (Berkeley: University of California Press, 1962), 26–27.

45. Maire Jaanus Kurrik suggests that Shakespeare's Timon of Athens should be regarded as "the greatest figure of pure negation produced in the Renaissance": "Timon's misanthropy … can only culminate in self-negation and in the preference of nothingness over any form of being." Kurrik, *Literature and Negation* (New York: Columbia University Press, 1979), 15–16. Simon Critchley and Jamieson Webster argue that "negativity in desire is what Hamlet must assume, but cannot." Critchley and Webster, *Stay, Illusion! The Hamlet Doctrine* (New York: Pantheon, 2013), 179.

46. Kurrik, *Literature and Negation*, 35.

47. "For it is the same thing to think and to be." Parmenides of Elea in Kathleen Freeman, *Ancilla to the Pre-Socratic Philosophers: A Complete Translation of the Fragments in Diels*, Fragmente der Vorsokratiker (Cambridge, MA: Harvard University Press, 1957), 42.

48. G. W. F. Hegel, *Hegel's Lectures on the History of Philosophy*, vol. 3, trans. E. S. Haldane and Frances H. Simson (Atlantic City: Humanities Press, 1983), 241.

49. "He has looked within, as Hume did later, and found not a coherent, substantial self but a mysterious chasm, a gap where the simple self ought to be—a kind of throbbing nothingness." McGinn, *Shakespeare's Philosophy*, 43. Horkheimer and Adorno make a similar point: "The unity of the personality has been recognized as illusory since Shakespeare's Hamlet." Max Horkheimer and Theodor W. Adorno, *Dialectic of Enlightenment: Philosophical Fragments*, ed. Gunzelin Schmid Noerr, trans. Edmund Jephcott (Stanford: Stanford University Press, 2002), 126. For Hume's general disdain of Shakespeare, see Stanley Stewart, *Shakespeare and Philosophy* (New York: Routledge, 2010), chapter 3 ("Hume's Shakespeare").

50. McGinn cites Sartre on page 47 of *Shakespeare's Philosophy*. Sartre himself appeals to the example of an actor playing Hamlet to illustrate the nature of the kind of role-playing that Hamlet frets about. See Jean-Paul Sartre, *Search for a Method*, trans. Hazel E. Barnes (New York: Alfred A. Knopf, 1963), 45–46.

51. Immanuel Kant, *Critique of Pure Reason*, trans. Paul Guyer and Allen W. Wood (New York: Cambridge University Press, 1998), 259–260 (B157–159).

52. "An oak tree planted in a precious pot which should only have held delicate flowers. The roots spread out, the vessel is shattered." Johann Wolfgang von Goethe, *Goethe's Collected Works*, vol. 9: *Wilhelm Meister's Apprenticeship*, ed. and trans. Eric A. Blackall in cooperation with Victor Lange (Princeton: Princeton University Press, 1995), 146. In *2 Henry IV* Doll Tearsheet asks, "Can a weak vessel bear such a huge full hogshead?" (2.4.62–63).

53. "Shakespeare wished to impress upon us the truth that action is the great end of existence—that no faculties of intellect, however brilliant, can be considered valuable, or otherwise than as misfortunes, if they withdraw us from, or render us repugnant to action—and lead us to think and think of doing, until the time has escaped when we ought to have acted." Coleridge, *Coleridge's Criticism of Shakespeare*, 72.

54. Samuel Taylor Coleridge, *Biographia Literaria*, vol. 2, ed. James Engell and W. Jackson Bate (Princeton: Princeton University Press, 1984), 6, 134.

55. "At once it struck me, what quality went to form a Man of Achievement, especially in Literature and which Shakespeare possessed so enormously—I mean *Negative Capability*, that is when man is capable of being in uncertainties, Mysteries, doubts, without any irritable reaching after fact & reason. Coleridge, for instance, would let go by a fine isolated verisimilitude caught from the Penetralium of mystery, from being incapable of remaining content with half-knowledge." John Keats, Letter to George and Tom Keats, December 21, 27 (?), 1817, in *Selected Letters of John Keats*, rev. ed., ed. Grant F. Scott (Cambridge, MA: Harvard University Press, 2002), 60. "Hamlet's final stance personifies Shakespeare's Negative Capability." Harold Bloom, *Shakespeare: The Invention of the Human* (New York: Riverhead Books, 1998), 12.

56. For Keats's influence on Eliot, see the references cited in Li Ou, *Keats and Negative Capability* (New York: Continuum, 2009), 193–194n5.

57. T. S. Eliot, "Hamlet and His Problems," in *The Sacred Wood and Major Early Essays* (Mineola, NY: Dover, 1998), 55, 58.

58. "If the vase may be filled, it is because in the first place in its essence it is empty." Jacques Lacan, *The Seminar of Jacques Lacan Seminar VII: The Ethics of Psychoanalysis 1959–1960*, ed. Jacques-Alain Miller, trans. Dennis Porter (New York: W. W. Norton, 1992), 120.

59. James L. Calderwood, *To Be and Not To Be: Negation and Metadrama in* Hamlet (New York: Columbia University Press, 1983), 67.

60. Jonathan Hope distinguishes four basic types of negation in Shakespeare: adverbial, morphological, grammatical, and double negatives. Jonathan Hope, *Shakespeare's Grammar* (London: Arden Shakespeare, 2003), 169–171. All four appear in Hamlet's brief soliloquy as he prepares to visit Gertrude (counting "not unnatural" as a double negative):

> O heart, lose *not* thy nature! let *not* ever
> The soul of Nero enter this firm bosom,
> Let me be cruel, *not* unnatural;
> I will speak daggers to her, but use *none*.
> My tongue and soul in this be hypocrites—
> How in my words somever she be shent,
> To give them seals *never* my soul consent!
>
> (3.2.393–399, italics added)

61. "Thus the subject-matter of a repressed image or thought can make its way into consciousness on condition that it is *denied*." Sigmund Freud, "Negation," in *General Psychological Theory: Papers on Metapsychology* (New York: Simon & Schuster, 1991), 213–214.

62. "In place of Hamlet's implied and Aristotle's explicit law of the excluded middle (a thing is either A or not-A) we have Shakespeare's law of the included middle (a thing may be both A and not-A)." Calderwood, *To Be and Not To Be*, xiv.

63. Graham Priest, *Doubt Truth to Be a Liar* (New York: Oxford University Press, 2008), 208.

64. Ibid., 209.

65. Freud's equivalent thought is that Hamlet both loves and hates Ophelia. Commenting on the doubt of obsessional neurotics he writes, "The doubt corresponds to the patient's internal perception of his own indecision, which, in consequence of the inhibition of his love by his hatred, takes possession of him in the face of every intended action. The doubt is in reality a doubt of his own love—which ought to be the most certain thing in his whole mind. … A man who doubts his own love may, or rather *must*, doubt every lesser thing." To this last sentence Freud appends a footnote citing Hamlet's letter to Ophelia. Sigmund Freud, "Notes Upon a Case of Obsessional Neurosis, in *Three Case Studies*, ed. Philip Rieff (New York: Collier, 1993), 75.

66. Deleuze characterizes Bartleby's "negative preference" thus: "I would prefer nothing rather than something: not a will to nothingness, but the growth of a nothingness of the will … a negativism beyond all negation." Gilles Deleuze, "Bartleby; or, The Formula," in *Essays Critical and Clinical*, trans. Daniel W. Smith and Michael A. Greco (New York: Verso, 1998), 71. Colie argues that "Where Macbeth discovers that death is oblivion, Hamlet discovers that it is not. … In the end, Hamlet knows for himself the relation between 'to be' and 'not to be' by which even his own death can affirm life." Colie, *Paradoxia Epidemica*, 240.

67. Eliot, "Hamlet and His Problems," 55.

68. "Hamlet's dispossession has been ignored, so, too, Hamlet's investment in land." Margreta de Grazia, *Hamlet without Hamlet* (New York: Cambridge University Press, 2007), 3.

69. As is, Bradley conjectures that Hamlet "must have seen Marcellus often." A. C. Bradley, *Shakespearean Tragedy*, 4th ed. (New York: Palgrave Macmillan, 2007), 311.

70. See L. C. Knights, *How Many Children Had Lady Macbeth? An Essay in the Theory and Practice of Shakespeare Criticism* (Cambridge: Minority Press, 1933).

71. See Stanley Edgar Hyman, *Iago: Some Approaches to the Illusion of His Motivation: A Study in Pluralist Criticism* (New York: Atheneum, 1970).

72. G. Wilson Knight, *The Wheel of Fire*, 2nd ed. (New York: Routledge, 2001), 288. Harold Jenkins makes a similar point with regard to Hamlet's invocation of hell (3.2.389) just before he visits his mother in her chamber: "In this mood the hero comes closest to the villain he would damn … , even resembles the evil figures of other plays: Iago, scheming against Othello, says 'Hell and night Must bring this monstrous birth to the world's light.'" Jenkins, "Longer Notes," in William Shakespeare, *Hamlet*, ed. Harold Jenkins (London: Arden, 1982), 512.

73. In *A Vindication of the Rights of Women* Mary Wollstonecraft appropriates both Hamlet's and Iago's misogynistic remarks: "And this desire making mere animals of them,

when they marry they act as such children may be expected to act:—they dress; they paint, and nickname God's creatures." "But what have women to do in society? I may be asked, but to loiter with easy grace; surely you would not condemn them all to suckle fools and chronicle small beer!" She also gives a feminist spin to Hamlet's retort to Gertrude that *he* has that within which passes show: "Women are always to *seem* to be this and that—yet virtue might apostrophize them, in the words of Hamlet—Seems! I know not seems!—Have that within that passeth show!" Mary Wollstonecraft, *A Vindication of the Rights of Men and A Vindication of the Rights of Women*, ed. Sylvana Tomaselli (New York: Cambridge University Press, 1995), 77, 181, 238.

74. Søren Kierkegaard, *Concluding Unscientific Postscript*, ed. and trans. Alastair Hannay (New York: Cambridge University Press, 2009), 111. Kierkegaard also recognized a potentially diabolical side to Hamlet: "If Hamlet is kept in purely esthetic categories, then what one wants to see is that he has the demonic power to carry out such a resolution." Søren Kierkegaard, *Stages on Life's Way*, ed. and trans. Howard V. Hong and Edna H. Hong (Princeton: Princeton University Press, 1988), 453.

75. Cf. Coleridge's comparison of Hamlet and Edmund: "Edmund is what, under certain circumstances, any man of powerful intellect might be, if some other qualities and feelings were cut off. Hamlet is, inclusively, an Edmund, but different from him as a whole, on account of the controlling agency of other principles which Edmund had not." Coleridge, *Coleridge's Criticism of Shakespeare*, 103.

76. "Skepticism's 'doubt' is motivated not by (not even where it is expressed as) a (misguided) intellectual scrupulousness but by a (displaced) denial, by a self-consuming disappointment that seeks world-consuming revenge." Stanley Cavell, *Disowning Knowledge in Seven Plays of Shakespeare*, updated ed. (New York: Cambridge University Press, 2003), 6. For Cavell, Othello's doubts about Desdemona's fidelity represent a "cover story for a deeper conviction" that he is trying to disavow (138). Cf. Cavell's representation of "the skeptic as nihilist" in his discussion of Leontes on page 208.

77. Michael Allen Gillespie, *Nihilism before Nietzsche* (Chicago: University of Chicago Press, 1996), chapters 1 and 2.

78. Describing Russell's abandonment of the ancient metaphysical conceptions of being and nonbeing for the modern logical conceptions of existence and nonexistence, Brann remarks, "One of the consequences … of such hard-edged logicistic views is that they call forth as their complement softly sophisticated gropings into human existence, such as existentialism." Brann, *The Ways of Naysaying*, 80. It is in this precise sense that there is an existentialist side to Russell's own nonlogical philosophical writings.

CHAPTER 1

1. Friedrich Nietzsche, *The Birth of Tragedy and Other Writings*, ed. Raymond Geuss and Ronald Speirs, trans. Ronald Speirs (New York: Cambridge University Press, 1999), 40.

2. Sophocles, "Oedipus at Colonus," in *Sophocles I*, 3rd ed., ed. and trans. Mark Griffith, Glenn W. Most, David Grene, and Richmond Lattimore (Chicago: University of Chicago Press, 2013), 202.

3. Nietzsche, *The Birth of Tragedy*, 27.

4. Ibid., 24.

5. "'Socrates,' it said, 'make music and work at it!'" Plato, *Phaedo*, trans. Eva Brann, Peter Kalkavage, and Eric Salem (Newburyport, MA: Focus, 1998), 31 (60e). Just before reporting his dream, Socrates reflects that Aesop should have written a fable to illustrate the fact that pain and pleasure cannot be experienced simultaneously but seem always to be given in succession. Such a fable would illustrate Nietzsche's description of the oscillation between tragic ecstasy and disgust with everyday life. Set to music, would it represent a rebirth of tragedy or a philosophical metatragedy?

6. Nietzsche, *The Birth of Tragedy*, 82.

7. Ibid., 67, 75.

8. "*Shakespeare der Dichter der Erfüllung, er vollendet Sophocles, er ist der musiktreibende Sokrates*" ("Shakespeare the poet of fulfillment, he completed Sophocles, he is the music-driving [or music-making] Socrates"). Friedrich Nietzsche, *Sämtliche Werke: Kritische Gesamtausgabe*, vol. 7, ed. Giorgio Colli and Mazzino Montinari (Berlin: de Gruyter, 1967–), 201. Cf. Raymond Geuss's introduction to Nietzsche, *The Birth of Tragedy*, xxviin., and Duncan Large, "Nietzsche's Shakespearean Figures," in *Why Nietzsche Still? Reflections on Drama, Culture, and Politics*, ed. Alan Schrift (Berkeley: University of California Press, 2000), 49.

9. Nietzsche, *The Birth of Tragedy*, 81.

10. Ibid., 40.

11. "It came to be from an improvisatory beginning (both it and comedy, one from those who took the lead in the dithyramb and the other from those in the phallic songs, which even now in many cities continue by customary practice)." Aristotle, *On Poetics*, trans. Seth Benardete and Michael Davis (South Bend: St. Augustine's Press, 2002), 13 (1449^a).

12. "When we turn away blinded after a strenuous attempt to look directly at the sun, we have dark, coloured patches before our eyes, as if their purpose were to heal them; conversely, those appearances of the Sophoclean hero in images of light, in other words, the Apolline quality of the mask, are the necessary result of gazing into the inner, terrible depths of nature—radiant patches, as it were, to heal a gaze seared by gruesome night." Nietzsche, *The Birth of Tragedy*, 46.

13. This way of distinguishing opera from tragedy and Wagnerian music drama can be related to Freud's distinction between neurosis and psychosis. Opera would be a neurotic (specifically "hysterical") form of art insofar it fundamentally accepts, and then seeks to avoid, reality. Tragedy and music drama would be psychotic forms of art insofar as they reject ordinary reality in favor of a direct affective presentation of the drives. The Apollonian images they then offer by way of compensation can be likened to secondary efforts to recreate the lost buffer of everyday reality.

14. The sheet music for "To Bee or Not to Bee &c." can be found in Macdonald Emslie, "Pepys' Shakespeare Song," *Shakespeare Quarterly* 6, no. 2 (spring 1955), 164–170.

15. Alison Latham, *Oxford Dictionary of Musical Works* (New York: Oxford University Press, 2004), 69.

16. Julie Sanders, *Shakespeare and Music: Afterlives and Borrowings* (Malden, MA: Polity, 2007), 16, 35, 56n20, 61. Elaine Sisman observes that "Haydn was the first composer to be mentioned in conjunction with the great flourishing of Shakespeare on the German stage" and that "contemporary reports assert that Haydn wrote orchestral music for *Hamlet* in 1774." Elaine Sisman, "Haydn, Shakespeare, and the Rules of Originality," in *Haydn and His World*, ed. E. Sisman (Princeton: Princeton University Press, 1997), 26.

17. Eugene Helm, "The 'Hamlet' Fantasy and the Literary Element in C. P. E. Bach's Music," *Musical Quarterly* 58, no. 2 (April 1972), 277–296. Commenting on Gerstenberg's extreme poetic license, Helm notes that "Hamlet's suicidal thoughts lack a dimension of the Shakespeare version, that of 'the dread of something after death … '; and … Socrates's words are a bit like what the dying Tristan might have sung" (286).

18. Friedrich Nietzsche, *Selected Letters of Friedrich Nietzsche*, ed. and trans. Christopher Middleton (Indianapolis: Hackett, 1996), 273.

19. David Bevington notes that "An operatic *Hamlet* at the Haymarket in 1712 took its inspiration chiefly from Saxo Grammaticus's *Historia Danica*." Closer to home, Bevington calls attention to rock operas, including Cliff Jones's *Rockabye Hamlet* and Janek Ledecký's *Musikal Hamlet*; rap versions, including Moe Moskowitz's *Hamlet Rap* and Rob Krakovski's *The Trage-D of Prince Hammy-T* (attributed to "Chill Will"); and the musical sequel staged at the end of Andrew Fleming's 2008 film *Hamlet 2*. David Bevington, *Murder Most Foul: Hamlet through the Ages* (New York: Oxford University Press, 2011), 92, 193–195. Bevington also mentions musical settings of Hamlet's letter to Ophelia (91).

20. Richard Wagner, *My Life*, vol. 1 (New York: Dodd, Mead & Co., 1911), 29.

21. "In the same relation as stood the car of Thespis, in the brief time span of the flowering of Athenian art, to the stage of Aeschylus and Sophocles, so stands the stage of Shakespeare … to the theatre of the future. The deed of the one and only Shakespeare … is yet but the kindred deed of the solitary Beethoven …: only where these twain Prometheuses—Shakespeare and Beethoven—shall reach out hands to one another—there … will the poet also find redemption." Richard Wagner, *Wagner on Music and Drama*, ed. Albert Goldman and Evert Sprinchorn (New York: Da Capo, 1964), 80.

22. Friedrich Nietzsche, *Untimely Meditations*, ed. Daniel Breazeale, trans. R. J. Hollingdale (New York: Cambridge University Press, 1997), 199.

23. "*Vor allem ist es ein mißratenes Werk.*" Nietzsche, *Sämtliche Werke*, vol. 10, ed. Alfred Baeumler (Leipzig: Alfred Kroener, 1930), 184.

24. Nietzsche, *The Gay Science: With a Prelude in German Rhymes and an Appendix of Songs*, ed. Bernard Williams, trans. Josefine Nauckhoff (New York: Cambridge University Press, 2001), 94.

25. Ibid., 93.

26. Friedrich Nietzsche, *Ecce Homo*, trans. Duncan Large (New York: Oxford University Press, 2007), 26.

27. Friedrich Nietzsche, *Beyond Good and Evil: Prelude to a Philosophy of the Future*, trans. R. J. Hollingdale (New York: Penguin, 2003), 153. Hamlet characteristically shifts between undermining and affirming such class distinctions.

28. Ibid., 209. The *abbé* Ferdinando Galiani, an eighteenth-century economist, was another of Nietzsche's favorite authors.

29. As a schoolboy Nietzsche once played the role of Hotspur. In this sequence of roles—Hotspur, Hamlet, Brutus—we can recognize a kind of dialectical progression from spontaneous activity to reflective thought to deliberate action—as well as a political shift from armed rebellion to regicide to revolution, and a humoral shift from choler to (what he later perceived as) false melancholy to profound melancholy.

30. Nietzsche, *The Birth of Tragedy*, 5.

31. Nietzsche, *Ecce Homo*, 10, 26, 94; Nietzsche's ellipses. Duncan Large call attention to the first two passages in "Nietzsche's Shakespearean Figures," 58. Commenting on the same passages, Critchley and Webster ask: "Might we not ponder whether the Dionysian Nietzsche identifies himself with Hamlet in his opposition to the crucified Christ? Might not the melancholy and misanthropy that he finds in Hamlet be that abyss that he recognizes in himself? Might it not be the irresistible oceanic undertow of negation that pulls against Nietzsche's otherwise relentless assertion of affirmation and that threatens to submerge and drown him?" Simon Critchley and Jamieson Webster, *Stay, Illusion! The Hamlet Doctrine* (New York: Pantheon, 2013), 204.

32. Nietzsche, *The Gay Science*, 94.

33. Friedrich Nietzsche, *On the Genealogy of Morals and Ecce Homo*, trans. Walter Kaufmann (New York: Vintage, 1989), 246.

34. "Ultimately it is because Bacon-Shakespeare is revealed as a lover of masks that Nietzsche, the lover of masks, can use Bacon-Shakespeare himself as … a mask, another 'metaphor' for 'Nietzsche.'" Large, "Nietzsche's Shakespearean Figures," 59.

35. Jean Starobinski summarizes: "The frequent citations from *Hamlet* found in Freud's correspondence are, I think, not simply the mark of a cultivated man with an admirable knowledge of the classics but evidence of Freud's profound fascination with the Shakespearean character." Jean Starobinski, "Hamlet and Oedipus," in *The Living Eye*, trans. Arthur Goldhammer (Cambridge, MA: Harvard University Press, 1989), 154.

36. Sigmund Freud, letter to Fliess dated September 21, 1897, in *The Complete Letters of Sigmund Freud to Wilhelm Fliess, 1887–1904*, ed. Jeffrey Moussaieff Masson (Cambridge, MA: Harvard University Press, 1985), 265.

37. Sigmund Freud, letter to Fliess dated October 15, 1897, in *The Complete Letters*, 272.

38. Sigmund Freud, *The Interpretation of Dreams*, trans. James Strachey (New York: Avon, 1998), 299.

39. Cited in Peter Gay, "Freud and the Man from Stratford," in *Reading Freud: Explorations and Entertainments* (New Haven: Yale University Press, 1990), 7.

40. Sigmund Freud, "Mourning and Melancholia," in *General Psychological Theory: Papers on Metapsychology* (New York: Simon & Schuster, 1991), 165.

41. Ibid., 168, and footnote.

42. In his study of the Rat Man Freud writes, "The language of an obsessional neurosis—the means by which it expresses its secret thoughts—is, as it were, only a dialect of the language of hysteria." Sigmund Freud, "Notes Upon a Case of Obsessional Neurosis," in *Three Case Studies* (New York: Simon & Schuster, 1996), 2. On the nature of moral masochism, see Freud, "The Economic Problem in Masochism," in *General Psychological Theory*, 199.

43. "From understanding this tragedy of destiny [*Oedipus Tyrannus*] it was only a step further to understanding a tragedy of character—*Hamlet*, which had been admired for three hundred years without its meaning being discovered or its author's motives guessed." Sigmund Freud, *An Autobiographical Study*, trans. James Strachey (New York: W. W. Norton, 1989), 72. "Again it was pointed out from psychoanalytic quarters how easily the riddle of another dramatic hero, Shakespeare's procrastinator, Hamlet, can be solved by reference to the Oedipus complex." Sigmund Freud, *An Outline of Psychoanalysis*, trans. James Strachey (New York: W. W. Norton, 1989), 74–75.

44. Sigmund Freud, "On Psychotherapy," in *The Standard Edition of the Complete Psychological Works of Sigmund Freud*, vol. 7: 1901–1905 (London: Hogarth Press, 1953), 262.

45. Sigmund Freud, *The Question of Lay Analysis*, trans. James Strachey (New York: W. W. Norton, 1989), 6.

46. Sigmund Freud, "Negation," in *General Psychological Theory*, 213.

47. "Incidentally, I have in the meantime ceased to believe that the author of Shakespeare's works was the man from Stratford." Freud, *The Interpretation of Dreams*, 300n. This passage was added to the 1930 edition of the text.

48. Gay, "Freud and the Man from Stratford," 37.

49. Masson, *The Complete Letters*, 272.

50. "As long as Hamlet remained the work of the Stratford actor whose father died in 1601, *Hamlet* and psychoanalytic theory were united by a kind of twinship, for both were born in similar circumstances. Now this twinship is denied or, rather, established on another basis. Did Freud hope thereby to cover his own tracks?" Starobinski, "Hamlet and Oedipus," 170. Linking Freud's interpretation of *Hamlet* to his speculations about the historical Moses, Lyotard argues that Freud's Hamlet is a "Jewish Oedipus" whose repression incorporates a prohibition against graven images: "Just as Hamlet by killing Polonius on the other stage will fail to recognize his parricidal desire and remain seized by the task intimated by the voice, in the same way the Hebrew people—by killing Moses in an *acting-out*—foregoes recognizing itself as the father's murderer and cuts off the path of reconciliation, the one traced by the desire to see: the Christian path that announces at its end the vision of the father." Jean-François Lyotard, "Jewish Oedipus," trans. Susan Hanson, in *Driftworks*, ed. Roger McKeon (New York: Semiotext(e), 1984), 52.

51. Nietzsche, *The Gay Science*, 93.

52. Sigmund Freud, "On the Mechanism of Paranoia," in *General Psychological Theory*, 20–21.

53. Slavoj Žižek, *For They Know Not What They Do: Enjoyment as a Political Factor* (New York: Verso, 1991), 202. Elsewhere Žižek gives the example of the way in which a similar inner shift enabled "the Renaissance" to allow "antiquity" to "begin to exert its influence." Here he focuses on the self-reflective twist by which "the new zeitgeist had to constitute itself by literally *presupposing itself in its exteriority, in its external conditions* (in antiquity)." Slavoj Žižek, *Tarrying with the Negative: Kant, Hegel, and the Critique of Ideology* (Durham, NC: Duke University Press, 1993), 147. Although he doesn't explicitly refer to Shakespeare in this context, his analysis could easily be applied to many of Shakespeare's works.

54. Giorgio Agamben argues that every example has the structure of "an *exclusive inclusion*": "What the example shows is its belonging to a class, but for this very reason the example steps out of its class in the very moment in which it exhibits and delimits it." Giorgio Agamben, *Homo Sacer: Sovereign Power and Bare Life*, trans. Daniel Heller-Roazen (Palo Alto: Stanford University Press, 1998), 22–23. The converse of an example is an exception, which Agamben characterizes as "an *inclusive exclusion*" (22). An exemplary example would be, as it were, an *exceptional* example: something that stands out as having special significance even if it has acquired its special status only by being arbitrarily singled out. An exemplary example of an exemplary example is the tourist attraction of "the most photographed barn in America" in Don DeLillo's novel *White Noise*. Agamben agrees with Carl Schmitt that the sovereign is he who can decide the state of exception. In *1 Henry VI* King Henry—a weak sovereign—unwittingly sets in motion his own deposition when he treats his decision to wear a red rose rather than a white as an arbitrary choice with no special significance: "I see no reason, if I wear this rose, / That any one should therefore be suspicious / I more incline to Somerset than York" (4.1.152–154). See chapter 5.

55. Harold Bloom, *The Western Canon: The Books and School of the Ages* (New York: Macmillan, 1995), 350.

56. "In Goethe's *Faust*, the 'Spirit of the Ages' refers only to the past ages, with the skeptical comment that it is the gentlemen's (they are historians) own spirit in which the ages are reflected. From the same period as Goethe's outline for *Faust* comes Herder's essay on Shakespeare, at the conclusion of which Goethe is named as the friend whose duty it is to translate the genius of Shakespeare, whose world has already passed, into our language and the spirit of the present." Karl Löwith, *From Hegel to Nietzsche: The Revolution in Nineteenth-Century Thought* (New York: Columbia University Press, 1991), 201.

57. Johann Gottfried Herder, *Kritische Wälder, oder Betrachtungen, die Wissenschaft und Kunst des Schönen*, vol. 3 (Riga: J. F. Hartknoch, 1769), 96.

58. Macbeth expresses the dark flip side of this thought: "To know my deed, 'twere best not know myself" (2.2.70).

59. Cited in William Shakespeare, *Hamlet*, ed. Ann Thompson and Neil Taylor (London: Arden, 2006), 1.

60. "You said nothing about my interpretation of *Oedipus Rex* and *Hamlet*. Since I have not told it to anyone else, because I can well imagine in advance the bewildered rejection, I should like to have a short comment on it from you." Sigmund Freud, letter to Fliess dated November 5 1897, in *The Complete Letters*, 277.

61. "Hamlet's playing of a great variety of stereotyped melancholy parts ... is itself symptomatic of a character who refuses to be identified entirely with any of the roles that he plays, and whose real melancholy is made evident through the evasiveness and aggressive wit with which he manipulates such roles." Bridget Gellert Lyons, *Voices of Melancholy* (New York: W. W. Norton, 1975), 78.

62. Descartes says something similar: "But one who spends too much time travelling eventually becomes a stranger in his own country; and one who is too curious about the practices of past ages usually remains quite ignorant about those of the present." René Descartes, "Discourse on the Method of Rightly Conducting One's Reason and Seeking the Truth in the Sciences," in *The Philosophical Writings of Descartes*, vol. 1, trans. John Cottingham, Robert Stoothoff, Dugald Murdoch (New York: Cambridge University Press, 1985), 114.

63. Jaques's voluntary exile from the circle of couples may be contrasted with the complementary ways in which Shylock and Antonio are respectively excluded and included at the end of *The Merchant of Venice*.

64. G. Wilson Knight speaks of Iago's desire to untune "the *Othello* music": "Cynicism is his philosophy, his very life, his 'motive' in working Othello's ruin." Knight, *The Wheel of Fire* (New York: Routledge, 1989), 127.

65. "Why is it that all those who have become eminent in philosophy or politics or poetry or the arts are clearly of an atrabilious temperament, and some of them to such an extent as to be affected by diseases caused by black bile, as is said to have happened to Heracles among the heroes?" (Pseudo-)Aristotle, *Problems*, Book 30, chapter 1, trans. E. S. Forster, in *The Complete Works of Aristotle*, ed. Jonathan Barnes, vol. 2 (Princeton: Princeton University Press, 1984), 1498–1499.

66. Marsilio Ficino, *Three Books on Life: A Critical Edition and Translation*, with introduction and notes by Carol V. Kaske and John R. Clark (Tempe: Arizona Center for Medieval and Renaissance Studies, 2002), 113, 115.

67. Ibid., 115.

68. Ibid., 117.

69. Frances Yates, *The Occult Philosophy in the Elizabethan Age* (New York: Routledge, 2001), 188. For a contrasting view of Dee, see William H. Sherman, *John Dee: The Politics of Reading and Writing in the English Renaissance* (Amherst: University of Massachusetts Press, 1995).

70. Winfried Schleiner, *Melancholy, Genius, and Utopia in the Renaissance* (Wiesbaden: Harrassowitz, 1991), 29. Cf. Raymond Klibansky, Erwin Panofsky, and Fritz Saxl, *Saturn and Melancholy: Studies in the History of Natural Philosophy, Religion, and Art* (London: Nelson, 1964).

71. René Descartes, *Meditations on First Philosophy* in *The Philosophical Writings of Descartes*, vol. 2, trans. John Cottingham, Robert Stoothoff, and Dugald Murdoch (New York: Cambridge University Press, 1984), 13.

72. "Assuredly, says Descartes, 'such people are insane, and I would be thought equally mad if I took anything from them as a model for myself. '… One cannot suppose that one is mad, even in thought, for madness is precisely a condition of impossibility for thought." Michel Foucault, *History of Madness*, ed. Jean Khalfa, trans. Jonathan Murphy and Jean Khalfa (New York: Routledge, 2006), 45.

73. Ibid., 24, 45–46.

74. "A specific decision has been taken since the *Essays* of Montaigne. When the latter went to meet Tasso, there was nothing to assure him that all thought was not haunted by the ghost of unreason. … Descartes by contrast has now acquired that certainty, and he grasps it firmly: madness, quite simply, is no longer his concern." Ibid., 45–46.

75. Ibid., 27.

76. Ibid., 38.

77. Ibid., 38.

78. Ibid., xxix.

79. "It matters little exactly what day in the autumn of 1888 Nietzsche went definitively mad, and from which point his texts were suddenly more the concern of psychiatry than of philosophy; all those texts, including the postcard to Strindberg, belong to Nietzsche, and all are connected in a common parentage to *The Birth of Tragedy*." Ibid., 537.

80. Jacques Derrida, "Cogito and the History of Madness," in *Writing and Difference*, trans. Alan Bass (Chicago: University of Chicago Press, 1978), 50.

81. Descartes, *Meditations on First Philosophy*, 62, translation modified.

82. Michel Foucault, "My Body, This Paper, This Fire," in *History of Madness*, 559.

83. Michel Foucault, "Reply to Derrida," in *History of Madness*, 582.

84. Ibid., 589.

85. Max Stirner, *The Ego and Its Own*, ed. David Leopold, trans. Steven Tracy Byington (revised by Leopold) (New York: Cambridge University Press, 1995), 43.

86. Ibid., 77.

87. Jacques Derrida, *Specters of Marx: The State of the Debt, the Work of Mourning, and the New International* (New York: Routledge, 1994), 133.

88. Jacques Derrida, "'To Do Justice to Freud': The History of Madness in the Age of Psychoanalysis," in *Resistances—Of Psychoanalysis*, trans. Peggy Kamuf, Pascale-Anne Brault, and Michael Naas (Stanford: Stanford University Press, 1998), 86.

89. "I am trying, since this is, unfortunately, the only recourse left us in the solitude of questioning, to imagine the principle of the reply. It would perhaps be something like this: what one must stop believing in is principality or principleness." Ibid., 117.

90. Foucault, *History of Madness*, 340; Derrida, "'To Do Justice to Freud,'" 104.

91. Derrida, *Specters of Marx*, 6.

92. "The souls in Dante's *Inferno*, or the supernatural apparitions in Shakespeare's *Hamlet*, *Macbeth* or *Julius Caesar*, may be gloomy and terrible enough, but they are no more really uncanny than Homer's jovial world of gods." Sigmund Freud, "The Uncanny," in *Writings on Art and Literature and Art* (Stanford: Stanford University Press, 1997), 227.

93. "The writer of the present contribution, indeed, must himself plead guilty to a special obtuseness in the matter. … It is long since he has experienced or heard of anything which had given him an uncanny impression." Ibid., 194.

94. Nicolas Abraham, "The Phantom of Hamlet, or The Sixth Act preceded by the Intermission of 'Truth,'" in Nicolas Abraham and Maria Torok, *The Shell and the Kernel*, vol. 1, ed. and trans. Nicholas T. Rand (Chicago: University of Chicago Press, 1994), 187.

95. Ibid., 190.

96. Derrida, *Specters of Marx*, 29.

97. Of a manically anti-Marxist discourse, Derrida writes: "This dominating discourse often has the manic, jubilatory, and incantatory form that Freud assigned to the so-called triumphant phase of mourning work. … It proclaims: Marx is dead, communism is dead, very dead, and along with it its hopes, its discourse, its theories, and its practices." Ibid., 51–52. Of the attacks on Stirner: "'The Leipzig Council—Saint Max' [Stirner] also organizes … an *irresistible* but *interminable* hunt for ghosts [*Gespenst*] and for *revenants* or spooks [*Spuk*]. *Irresistible* like an effective critique, but also like a compulsion; *interminable* as one says of an analysis." Ibid., 47.

98. Henry Miller, *Henry Miller's Hamlet Letters*, ed. Michael Hargraves (Santa Barbara: Capra Press, 1988), 19.

99. Ibid., 17, 19.

100. Ibid., 18.

101. Ibid., 56.

102. Ibid., 93.

103. Ibid., 102, 110, 140.

104. Karl Marx, "The Eighteenth Brumaire of Louis Bonaparte," in *Later Political Writings*, ed. Terrell Carver (New York: Cambridge University Press, 1996), 32, 34.

105. Ibid., 115.

106. Walter Benjamin, "On Some Motifs in Baudelaire," in *Selected Writings*, vol. 4: 1938–1940, ed. Howard Eiland and Michael W. Jennings (Cambridge, MA: Harvard University Press, 2003), 335. It is not clear whether Benjamin is thinking of the historical Timon or Shakespeare's Timon.

107. "Only Shakespeare was capable of striking Christian sparks from the baroque rigidity of the melancholic. … If the profound insight with which Rochus von Liliencron recognized the ascendancy of Saturn and marks of *acedia* in Hamlet, is not to

be deprived of its finest object, then this drama will also be recognized as the unique spectacle in which these things are overcome in the spirit of Christianity. It is only in this prince that melancholy self-absorption attains to Christianity." Walter Benjamin, *The Origin of German Tragic Drama*, trans. John Osborne (New York: Verso, 1998), 158.

108. "Historical time is infinite in every direction and unfulfilled at every moment. … A process that is perfect in historical terms … is in fact an idea. This idea of fulfilled time is the dominant historical idea in the Bible: it is the idea of messianic time. Moreover, the idea of a fulfilled historical time is never identical with the idea of an individual time. This feature naturally changes the meaning of fulfillment completely, and it is this that distinguishes tragic time from messianic time." Walter Benjamin, "Trauerspiel and Tragedy," in *Selected Writings*, vol. 1: 1913–1926, ed. Marcus Bullock and Michael W. Jennings (Cambridge, MA: Harvard University Press, 1996), 55–56. Cf. Walter Benjamin, "On the Concept of History," in *Selected Writings*, vol. 4, 395–396. Just as Nietzsche took the death of Socrates to mark the birth of philosophical thought out of the demise of tragedy, so Julia Reinhard Lupton and Kenneth Reinhard take the death of Hamlet to anticipate the birth of psychoanalysis ("not-quite-philosophy") out of *Trauerspiel*. Julia Reinhard Lupton and Kenneth Reinhard, *After Oedipus: Shakespeare in Psychoanalysis* (Ithaca: Cornell University Press, 1993), 52. They further suggest that "Socrates and Hamlet are not opposites," as Nietzsche implies, "but rather two moments of *Trauerspiel*, or even two aspects of the same moment: the simultaneous disappearance and restoration of the tragic in philosophy" (53).

109. Serge Leclaire argues that uncertainty as to whether one is dead or alive is a distinctive feature of obsessional neurosis. Serge Leclaire, "Jerome, or Death in the Life of the Obsessional," in *Returning to Freud: Clinical Psychoanalysis in the School of Lacan*, ed. and trans. Stuart Schneiderman (New Haven: Yale University Press, 1987).

110. "Hamlet is a beautiful and noble heart; not inwardly weak at all, but, without a powerful feeling for life, in the feebleness of his melancholy he strays distressed into error He persists in the inactivity of a beautiful inner soul which cannot make itself actual or engage in the relationships of his present world." G. W. F. Hegel, *Hegel's Aesthetics: Lectures on Fine Art*, vol. 1, trans. T. M. Knox (Oxford: Oxford University Press, 1975), 583–584.

111. Agnes Heller makes a similar point: "One of Hamlet's selves is alienated from the other, and all his lonely attempts to put them together, to mend the self thus torn, are in vain." Agnes Heller, *The Time Is Out of Joint: Shakespeare as Philosopher of History* (Lanham: Rowman & Littlefield, 2002), 45.

112. Jennifer Ann Bates, *Hegel and Shakespeare on Moral Imagination* (Albany: SUNY Press, 2010), 72.

113. Ibid., 73.

114. Ibid., 72.

115. Hegel, *Phenomenology of Spirit*, trans. A. V. Miller (New York: Oxford University Press, 1977), 208.

116. Ibid., 19.

117. Bates, *Hegel and Shakespeare on Moral Imagination*, 55–56.

118. Ibid., 73.

119. Ibid., 75.

120. Ibid., 70–71.

121. Ibid., 56, 71, 74.

122. Hegel, *Phenomenology of Spirit*, 10.

123. Bates, *Hegel and Shakespeare on Moral Imagination*, 82.

124. Ibid., 74.

125. Ibid., 357n84.

126. Ibid., 247.

127. Ibid., 357n84.

128. Northrop Frye, *A Natural Perspective: The Development of Shakespearean Comedy and Romance* (New York: Columbia University Press, 1995), 7; cited in Bates, 250.

129. Knight, *The Wheel of Fire*, 14.

130. Nor is it essentially different from the still darker self-exclusions of Richard III and Iago, as Auden implicitly surmises in "The Sea and the Mirror": "*I am I, Antonio, / By choice myself alone.*" W. H. Auden, *The Sea and the Mirror: A Poem* (Princeton: Princeton University Press, 2003), 14.

131. As Leonato says to Don Pedro of Beatrice in *Much Ado About Nothing*: "There's little of the melancholy element in her, my lord. She is never sad but when she sleeps, and not ever sad then, for I have heard my daughter say, she hath often dreamt of unhappiness, and wak'd herself with laughing" (2.2.342–346). This lovely image bears comparison with Caliban's even lovelier image of awakening from a beautiful dream only to cry "to dream again" (*The Tempest* 3.2.135–143).

132. "For you, most wicked sir, whom to call brother / Would even infect my mouth, I do forgive / Thy rankest fault—all of them" (*The Tempest* 5.1.130–132). Bates shows how forgiveness can cure infection. Here I am highlighting the manner in which forgiveness cannot entirely free itself from the beautiful soul's claim to purity. Bates, *Hegel and Shakespeare on Moral Imagination*, 290.

133. On this theme in Hegel, see Rebecca Comay, *Mourning Sickness: Hegel and the French Revolution* (Stanford: Stanford University Press, 2010).

134. Stanley Cavell, *Pursuits of Happiness: The Hollywood Comedy of Remarriage* (Cambridge, MA: Harvard University Press, 1981), 19.

135. This is true of Beatrice and Benedick, either insofar as they are effectively wedded from the very beginning of the play, or else insofar as they are symbolically married when they confess their mutual love in church.

136. Cavell, *Disowning Knowledge in Seven Plays of Shakespeare*, updated ed. (New York: Cambridge University Press, 2003), 55.

137. To which, going from the sublime to the ridiculous, we may compare Hostess Quickly's "Alas, alas, put up your naked weapons, put up your naked weapons" (2 Henry IV 2.4.206–207).

138. "After a series of tragedies which mark the lowest point of despair (Hamlet, King Lear, etc.), the tone of Shakespeare's plays unexpectedly changes and we enter the realm of a fairy-tale harmony where life is governed by a benevolent Fate which brings to a happy conclusion all conflicts (The Tempest, Cymbeline, etc.)." Žižek, Tarrying with the Negative, 115.

139. Bates, Hegel and Shakespeare on Moral Imagination, 63.

140. Hegel, Phenomenology of Spirit, 49.

141. Lawrence Rhu, "On Cavell on Shakespeare: Losing Mamillius, Finding Perdita," presented at a symposium at the Newberry Library entitled "Shakespeare and the History of Philosophy," March 2009.

142. Auden, The Sea and the Mirror, 14.

143. Compare Caesar's warning about Cassius: "He loves no plays, / As thou dost, Antony; he hears no music. … Such men as he be never at heart's ease / Whiles they behold a greater than themselves, / And therefore are they very dangerous" (1.2.203–204, 208–210).

CHAPTER 2

1. Michael Dobson, The Making of the National Poet: Shakespeare, Adaptation, and Authorship, 1660–1769 (New York: Oxford University Press, 1995), 203.

2. Good overviews of the eighteenth century reception of Shakespeare in Germany can be found in Roy Pascal, Shakespeare in Germany 1740–1815 (New York: Octagon Books, 1971), 1–36, and Simon Williams, Shakespeare on the German Stage, vol. 1: 1586–1914 (New York: Cambridge University Press, 1990), chapter 1.

3. Alexander Pope, "Preface to the Works of Shakespeare," in The Major Works, ed. Pat Rogers (New York: Oxford University Press, 2006), 185.

4. Roger Paulin, The Critical Reception of Shakespeare in Germany 1682–1914: Native Literature and Foreign Genius (New York: Georg Olms Verlag, 2003), 14; John Pemble, Shakespeare Goes to Paris: How the Bard Conquered France (New York: Palgrave, 2005), 5.

5. "Our Shakespeare! Thus we may call him, even if he happened to be born in England by mistake. Thus we may call him by right of spiritual conquest. And should we succeed in vanquishing England in the field, we should, I think, insert a clause into the peace treaty stipulating the formal surrender of William Shakespeare to Germany." Ludwig Fulda, cited in Wilhelm Hortmann, Shakespeare on the German Stage: The Twentieth Century (New York: Cambridge University Press, 1998), 4.

6. Williams, Shakespeare on the German Stage, vol. 1, 7, 51; Paulin, The Critical Reception of Shakespeare in Germany, 39. My thanks to Colin McQuillan for alerting me to Gottsched's earlier remarks about Julius Caesar, which can be found in Johann Christoph Gottsched, Versuch einer Critischen Dichtkunst (Leipzig: Breitkopf, 1751), 221, 614.

7. Gotthold Ephraim Lessing, "The Seventeenth Letter Concerning the Newest Literature," in *Essays on German Theater*, ed. Margaret Herzfeld-Sander (New York: Continuum, 1985), 1.

8. Ibid., 2. Cf. A. W. Ward and A. R. Waller, *The Cambridge History of English Literature*, vol. 5: *The Drama to 1642*, 295; Paulin, *The Critical Reception of Shakespeare in Germany*, 86–90.

9. Lessing, "The Seventeenth Letter," 3.

10. Coleridge, A. W. Schlegel, and Heine all credited Lessing with introducing Shakespeare to Germany. See F. W. Meisnest, "Lessing and Shakespeare," *PMLA* 1904 (234–249), 234–235.

11. Performances of unrevised versions of the plays were slow in coming. Early productions were made to conform to the Aristotelian unities of time, place, and action, and the plays were modified to present starker contrasts between good and evil characters. Williams, *Shakespeare on the German Stage*, 49–50, 86–87.

12. "The first page I read made me a slave to Shakespeare for life. And when I had finished reading the first drama, I stood there like a man blind from birth whom a magic hand has all at once given light." Johann Wolfgang von Goethe, "Shakespeare: A Tribute," in Goethe, *The Collected Works*, vol. 3: *Essays on Art and Literature*, ed. John Gearey, trans. Ellen von Nardroff and Ernest H. von Nardroff (New York: Suhrkamp, 1986), 163.

13. "But even if we admit that they do keep to these rules, French drama is still not the same thing as Greek drama. Why? Because nothing in their inner essence is the same—not action, manners, language, purpose, nothing." Johann Gottfried Herder, *Shakespeare*, ed. and trans. Gregory Moore (Princeton: Princeton University Press, 2008), 17–18.

14. In 1772, Herder objected to the overly Shakespearean character of Goethe's *Götz von Berlichingen*. See Paulin, *The Critical Reception of Shakespeare in Germany*, 156–157, 160.

15. "Hamann was able to draw out of Kant's powerful orbit one of his best students, Johann Herder, in the course of the early 1760s, and he communicated many impulses to Herder which Kant found extremely dangerous." John Zammito, *The Genesis of Kant's Critique of Judgment* (Chicago: University of Chicago Press, 1992), 34.

16. Paulin, *The Critical Reception of Shakespeare in Germany*, 137; Ioannis D. Evrigenis and Daniel Pellerin, introduction to Johann Gottfried Herder, *Another Philosophy of History and Selected Political Writings*, trans. Evrigenis and Pellerin (Indianapolis: Hackett, 2004), xix.

17. Herder, *Shakespeare*, 46, translation slightly modified. In his 1778 essay on sculpture Herder advises his readers to approach a statue as Hamlet proposes to remember the Ghost: "Like Hamlet we must remove from our minds all trivial copies and all scribbled letters and characters." Johann Gottfried Herder, *Sculpture: Some Observations on Shape and Form from Pygmalion's Creative Dream*, ed. and trans. Jason Gaiger (Chicago: University of Chicago Press, 2002), 66. Connecting the name "Hamlet" to the German word for "mutton" (*Hammel*), he goes on to comment on the aptness of the Ghost's assurance that the tale he could unfold would make Hamlet's "knotted and combined locks to part, / And each particular hair to stand an end, / Like quills upon the fretful pro-

pentine" (1.5.18–20). Ibid., 68. In *Adrastea* (1801), he writes: "What an influence the academic enthusiasm [*Begeisterung*] for metaphysics has upon young men of Hamlet's character is well known. The Queen thinks he has become melancholy in Wittenberg, and entreats him not to return thither. In this mood he belongs now most assuredly more to the *speculative* than the *active* portion of mankind,—happy idea which the poet takes from our Wittenberg, from the German fondness for metaphysics!" Cited in Horace Howard Furness, ed., *A New Variorum Edition of Shakespeare: Hamlet*, vol. 2: *Appendix* (Philadelphia: J. B. Lippincott, 1877), 277; Johann Gottfried Herder, *Werke Band 10: Adrastea*, ed. Günter Arnold (Frankfurt: Deutscher Klassiker Verlag, 2000), 334. In 1796, Christian Garve, coauthor of the first review of the *Critique of Pure Reason*, argued in *Ueber die Rollen der Wahnwitzigen in Shakespeares Schauspielen* that whereas Ophelia goes genuinely mad, Hamlet only feigns madness. A summary of Garve's argument can be found in Furness, *A New Variorum Edition*, 275–276.

18. Sanford Budick, *Kant and Milton* (Cambridge, MA: Harvard University Press, 2010), 12.

19. "Both Milton and Shakespeare are Kant's usual modern examples of genius, but Milton is far more important to him than Shakespeare." "Kant's aesthetic formation is both strongly Miltonic and largely (though not totally) pre-Shakespearean." Ibid., 12, 17n9.

20. Immanuel Kant, *Anthropology from a Pragmatic Point of View*, ed. and trans. Robert Louden (Cambridge: Cambridge University Press), 73; Immanuel Kant, *Die Vorlesung des Wintersemesters 1772/73 aufgrund der Nachschriften* (Parow), in *Kants Gesammelte Schriften*, vol. 25, book 2 (Berlin: Walter de Gruyter, 1997), 336.

21. Sabina Laetitia Kowalewski and Werner Stark, eds., *Königsberger Kantiana* [*Immanuel Kant: Werke: Volksausgabe, Bd. 1, hrsg. von Arnold Kowalewski*] (Hamburg: Felix Meiner, 2000), 210. For the hearsay conjecture, see Otto Schlapp, *Kants Lehre vom Genie und die Entstehung der "Kritik der Urteilskraft"* (Göttingen: Vandenhoeck and Ruprecht, 1901), 246.

22. Kant, *Die Vorlesung des Wintersemesters 1772/73 aufgrund der Nachschriften* (Collins), in *Kants Gesammelte Schriften*, vol. 25, book 2, 175.

23. Kant, *Critique of the Power of Judgment*, ed. Paul Guyer, trans. Paul Guyer and Eric Matthews (New York: Cambridge University Press, 2000), 188, 191.

24. "Taste, like the power of judgment in general, is the discipline (or corrective) of genius, clipping its wings and making it well behaved or polished." Ibid., 197.

25. Ibid., 192.

26. "We leave it to critics of the elegant [*schönen*] style in philosophy, or to the author's ultimate revision of his work, to consider whether it would not, for example, be better to say 'not only day and night and the changes of the season alter the climate' than … 'not only day and night and the roundelay [*Reihentanz*] of the changing seasons alter the climate'; whether the following image—no doubt admirably suited to a dithyrambic ode—can appropriately be used in conjunction with a description of such changes in terms of natural history. … 'Round Jupiter's throne its (i.e. the earth's) *Horae* dance a roundelay, and although what takes shape beneath their feet is only an imperfect perfection … the child of nature—physical regularity and beauty—is everywhere born of an inner love and marital union." Immanuel Kant, "Reviews of Herder's *Ideas on*

the *Philosophy of the History of Mankind*," in Kant, *Political Writings*, 2nd ed., ed. Hans Reiss, trans. H. B. Nisbet (New York: Cambridge University Press, 1991), 216.

27. Plato, "Ion," in *Complete Works*, ed. John M. Cooper (Indianapolis: Hackett, 1997).

28. Herder, *Shakespeare*, 28, 31.

29. John H. Zammito, *Kant, Herder, and the Birth of Anthropology* (Chicago: University of Chicago Press, 2002), 344.

30. Gilles Deleuze, "On Four Poetic Formulas That Might Summarize the Kantian Philosophy," in *Essays Critical and Clinical*, trans. Daniel W. Smith and Michael A. Greco (Minneapolis: University of Minnesota Press, 1997), 28.

31. Ibid., 187n1.

32. Henry Somers-Hall notes that the traditional model goes back to Plato's *Timaeus*. On Deleuze's reading, he adds, it is not Hamlet and Kant but Hamlet and Nietzsche's Zarathustra who succeed in willing the eternal return of the same. Henry Somers-Hall, "Time Out of Joint: Hamlet and the Pure Form of Time," *Deleuze Studies* 5 (December 2011), 56–76.

33. Deleuze, "On Four Poetic Formulas," 28.

34. Immanuel Kant, *Gesammelte Schriften*, ed. Katharina Peters-Holger, Dieter Krallman (Berlin: Reimer, 1902–), vol. 15, part 2, 875. My thanks to Mira Kraft for helping me translate this passage.

35. Moses Mendelssohn, "On the Sublime and Naive in the Fine Sciences," in Mendelssohn, *Philosophical Writings*, ed. and trans. Daniel O. Dahlstrom (New York: Cambridge University Press, 1997), 206, 213–214. "Mendelssohn composed two translations of 'To be or not to be' into iambic pentameters, Lessing a translation into prose." Pascal, *Shakespeare in Germany*, 7n2. "By roughly 1760," there were "at least four different translations of Hamlet's famous soliloquy." Paulin, *The Critical Reception of Shakespeare in Germany*, 55.

36. Jean-Paul Sartre, *Being and Nothingness: A Phenomenological Essay on Ontology*, trans. Hazel E. Barnes (New York: Washington Square Press, 1984), 347, 349.

37. Immanuel Kant, *Critique of Pure Reason*, trans. Paul Guyer and Allen W. Wood (New York: Cambridge University Press, 1998), 246 (B131). Sartre develops this theme at greater length in *The Transcendence of the Ego: An Existentialist Theory of Consciousness*, trans. Forrest Williams and Robert Kirkpatrick (New York: Farrar, Straus & Giroux, 1959).

38. "I can not be he, I can only play *at being* him; that is, imagine to myself that I am he. And thereby I affect him with nothingness. In vain do I fulfill the functions of a café waiter. I can be he only in the neutralized mode, as the actor is Hamlet, by mechanically making the *typical gestures* of my state and by aiming at myself as an imaginary café waiter through those gestures taken as an 'analogue.'" Sartre, *Being and Nothingness*, 103. Simon Critchley and Jamieson Webster suggest that *Hamlet* is fundamentally about spying and shame: "Hamlet's world is a globe defined by the omnipresence of espionage. *Hamlet* is arguably the drama of surveillance in a police state." "For us, at its deepest, this is a play about shame, the nothing that is the experience of shame ... the affect of the veil contra Nietzsche for whom it is disgust. ... The

political world of *Hamlet* and our own time … are stuffed full of sham shame … *sham-letization*. But true shame is … a moment of seeing oneself from the outside in the manner of Hamlet's endless soliloquies." Simon Critchley and Jamieson Webster, *Stay, Illusion! The Hamlet Doctrine* (New York: Pantheon, 2013), 48, 228–231.

39. Deleuze, "On Four Poetic Formulas," 30.

40. On the uncertain but probable date of this letter, see Arnulf Zweig's discussion in Immanuel Kant, *Correspondence*, ed. and trans. Arnulf Zweig (New York: Cambridge University Press, 1999), 75n2.

41. Immanuel Kant, "Dreams of a Spirit-Seer Elucidated by Dreams of Metaphysics," in *Theoretical Philosophy 1755–1770*, ed. and trans. David Walford in collaboration with Ralf Meerbote (New York: Cambridge University Press, 1992), 342.

42. Kant, letter to Charlotte von Knobloch dated August 10, 1763, in *Correspondence*, 71–72.

43. Ibid., 74.

44. "Departed souls and pure spirits can never, it is true, be present to our outer senses, nor can they in any fashion whatever stand in community with matter, though they may indeed act upon the spirit of man, who belongs, with them, to one great republic. And they can exercise this influence in such a way that the representations, which they awaken in him, clothe themselves, according to the law of his imagination, in images which are akin to them, and create the vision of objects corresponding to them, so that they present the appearance of existing externally to him." Immanuel Kant, "Dreams of a Spirit-Seer," 328. This was a traditional hypothesis that Albert the Great (among others) professed and that Dante invokes in Canto 17 of *Purgatorio*: "O imagination, that sometimes so steals us from the world outside that we do not hear though a thousand trumpets sound around us, / who moves you, if sense offers you nothing? A light moves you that is formed in the heavens, by itself or by a will that guides it downward [*O imaginativa, che ne rube / talvolta sì di fuor ch'om non s'accorge / perché dintorno suonin mille tube, // che move te, se 'l senso non ti porge? / Moveti lume che nel ciel s'informa, /per sé o per voler che giù lo scorge*]." Dante Alighieri, *The Divine Comedy of Dante Alighieri*, vol. 2: *Purgatorio*, ed. and trans. Robert M. Durling (New York: Oxford University Press, 2004), 276–277. On Albert the Great, see the note by Durling and Ronald L. Martinez on 284.

45. Stephen Greenblatt highlights the paradoxical character of this address: "Once again he questions whether what he is seeing is real—'Art thou any thing?'—but the mode of direct address (as opposed, that is, to asking, 'Is it any thing?') belies the very attempt to challenge its reality." Greenblatt, *Hamlet in Purgatory* (Princeton: Princeton University Press, 2001), 182. Greenblatt also notes that the authoritative character of tradition could lend attenuated testimony greater epistemic force than first-hand testimony: "*Saint Patrick's Purgatory* … surrounds the vision with a network of names … that serve to authenticate the eyewitness account and set it in the context of a larger community among whom the narrative has been circulating. Here, as in other early visionary accounts of the afterlife, direct testimony is evidently less prized than an authorizing medium of transmission" (74). Locke was one of the first

philosophers to resist this line of reasoning: "Any Testimony, the farther off it is from the original Truth, the less force and proof it has. The Being and Existence of the thing it self, is what I call the original Truth. A credible Man vouching his Knowledge of it, is a good proof: But if another equally credible, do witness it from his Report, the Testimony is weaker; and a third that attests the Hear-say of an Hear-say, is yet less considerable." John Locke, *An Essay Concerning Human Understanding*, ed. Peter H. Nidditch (New York: Oxford University Press, 1975), 663–664.

46. Gertrude could be suffering from a negative hallucination, seeming to see nothing where in fact there is something.

47. Immanuel Kant, *Observations on the Feeling of the Beautiful and Sublime*, trans. John T. Goldthwait (Berkeley: University of California Press, 2003), 63, 66.

48. Paul Kottman highlights Horatio's role as a corroborating witness, from confirming that the appearance of the Ghost is "more than fantasy" (1.1.54) to making sure that Hamlet's "imaginations" are not "foul" (3.2.83) to being charged by Hamlet to "Report [him] and [his] cause aright / To the unsatisfied" (5.2.339–40). Paul A. Kottman, *A Politics of the Scene* (Stanford: Stanford University Press, 2008), chapter 7. Agnes Heller observes that our view of Hamlet is mediated from the beginning through Horatio's eyes: "We assume Horatio's perspective, the vision of the best friend. ... And since we see Hamlet through Horatio's eyes, he is charismatic for us." Agnes Heller, *The Time Is Out of Joint: Shakespeare as Philosopher of History* (Lanham: Rowman & Littlefield, 2002), 49. On the possibility that indirect evidence might be more reliable than direct evidence, Ernest Jones (playing Horatio to Freud's Hamlet) writes in defense of Freud's interpretation of the play: "This may prove to be less hypothetical than it sounds, even if we have to rely more on internal than external evidence; circumstantial evidence is notoriously more often trustworthy than direct evidence." Ernest Jones, *Hamlet and Oedipus* (New York: W. W. Norton, 1976), 114.

49. "Hypotheses are ... allowed in the field of pure reason only as weapons of war, not for grounding a right but for defending it. ... If, therefore, you come up against the difficulty for the immaterial nature of the soul which is not subjected to any corporeal transformation ... that experience seems to prove that both the elevation as well as the derangement of our mental powers are merely different modifications of our organs, you can weaken the power of this proof by assuming that our body is nothing but the fundamental appearance to which the entire faculty of sensibility and therewith all thinking are related, as their condition, in our present state (in life)." Kant, *Critique of Pure Reason*, 663 (A778/B806).

50. Besides accounting for hallucinations of external objects, Kant's theory of projection also explains the genesis of hypochondria—imagined sensations that converge in (or "migrate to") bodily organs other than the brain. See Immanuel Kant, "Essay on the Maladies of the Head," trans. Holly Wilson, in *Anthropology, History, and Education* (New York: Cambridge University Press, 2007), 72.

51. Kant, "Dreams of a Spirit-Seer," 345.

52. Sigmund Freud, "Fetishism," in *The Standard Edition of the Complete Psychological Works of Sigmund Freud*, vol. 21: 1927–1931 (London: Vintage, 2001), 152–153.

53. Kant, "Dreams of a Spirit-Seer," 345–346.

54. Kant, *Correspondence*, 70. "Women are particularly prone to lend credence to stories of prophecy, interpretations of dreams, and all kinds of other wondrous things." Kant, "Dreams of a Spirit-Seer," 342.

55. Kant, "Dreams of a Spirit-Seer," 354.

56. "A philosopher however looks at poets, lovers, and visionaries the way a man looks at a monkey, with amusement and pity." Kant, *Correspondence*, 53. In the same letter Hamann remarks, "I must almost laugh at the choice of a *philosopher* to change my mind. I look upon the finest logical demonstration the way a sensible girl regards a love letter" (52).

57. Kant, *Anthropology from a Pragmatic Point of View*, 74.

58. Frederick S. Frank, "Publication History of *The Castle of Otranto* and *The Mysterious Mother*," in Henry Walpole, *The Castle of Otranto and The Mysterious Mother*, ed. Frederick S. Frank (Peterborough: Broadview Press, 2003), 45.

59. Voltaire, *The Works of Voltaire: A Contemporary Version: Essays on Literature, Philosophy, Art, History*, vol. 19, part 1, trans. William F. Fleming (New York: The St. Hubert Guild, 1901), 137–138.

60. Gotthold Ephraim Lessing, *Hamburgische Dramaturgie* 11, cited in Furness, *A New Variorum Edition*, 267.

61. Ibid., 268.

62. Ibid., 269.

63. Herder makes this point about Shakespeare in *Sculpture*, 95.

64. Lessing, *Hamburgische Dramaturgie*.

65. See p. 170n92. Marjorie Garber argues that when Freud turns his attention to Hoffmann, he is still looking awry at Shakespeare: "The central literary work that provides Freud with his chief enabling example of uncanniness, Hoffmann's story 'The Sand-Man,' is described in terms that closely resemble the plot of *Hamlet*. ... Thus in not talking about *Hamlet* Freud is in a sense talking about *Hamlet*." Marjorie Garber, *Shakespeare's Ghost Writers: Literature as Uncanny Causality* (New York: Routledge, 1987), 127–128.

66. Hegel, who disliked Hoffmann, represents the Ghost "as just an objective form of Hamlet's inner presentiment." G. W. F. Hegel, *Hegel's Aesthetics: Lectures on Fine Art*, vol. 1, trans. T. M. Knox (New York: Oxford University Press, 1988), 231.

67. Immanuel Kant, *Prolegomena to Any Future Metaphysics with Selections from the Critique of Pure Reason*, rev. ed., ed. Gary Hatfield (New York: Cambridge University Press, 2004), 10, 90.

68. "If the vital force were not always kept active in sleep by dreams, it would be extinguished and the deepest sleep would have to bring death along with it." Immanuel Kant, *Anthropology from a Pragmatic Point of View*, 68.

69. "This intuiting of himself that is required of the philosopher, in performing the act whereby the self arises for him, I refer to as *intellectual intuition*." J. G. Fichte, *The Science of Knowledge*, ed. and trans. Peter Heath and John Lachs (New York: Cambridge University Press, 1982), 38.

70. "I hereby declare that I regard *Fichte's Wissenschaftslehre* as a totally indefensible system. For pure theory of science is nothing more or less than mere *logic*, and the principles of logic cannot lead to any material knowledge, since logic, that is to say, *pure logic*, abstracts from the content of knowledge." Kant, *Correspondence*, 559.

71. Kant, *Critique of Pure Reason*, 417 (A350).

72. Analogously, Fichte acknowledged that the I of transcendental apperception was an empty "nothing"—he simply denied that this nothing was unproductive. Ned Lukacher and Slavoj Žižek have pointed out that there is an ambiguity in Bushy's suggestion that by looking "awry" we both "distinguish form" and see "nought but shadows." Ned Lukacher, *Time-Fetishes:The Secret History of Eternal Recurrence* (Durham, NC: Duke University Press, 1998), 73; Slavoj Žižek, *Looking Awry: An Introduction to Jacques Lacan through Popular Culture* (Cambridge, MA: MIT Press, 1991), 10–12. Bushy's ambiguity has an analogue in Kant, for whom the noumenal realm is both intelligible "form" and "nought but shadows."

73. Compare the mood swings of Socrates's friends in the *Phaedo* as they find themselves buffeted between hope and fear about the prospects for the soul's immortality. Only Socrates retains his equanimity throughout.

74. "Melancholia offers the paradox of an intention to mourn that precedes and anticipates the loss of the object." Giorgio Agamben, *Stanzas:Word and Phantasm in Western Culture*, trans. Ronald L. Martinez (Minneapolis: University of Minnesota Press, 1993), 20.

75. See G. Wilson Knight, *The Wheel of Fire: Interpretations of Shakespearian Tragedy* (New York: Routledge, 2001), 50.

76. Kant, *Critique of Pure Reason*, 671 (A794/B822).

77. Immanuel Kant, "Anthropology Mrongovius," in *Lectures on Anthropology*, ed. Allen W. Wood and Robert B. Louden (New York: Cambridge University Press, 2012), 423.

78. In *Cymbeline*, Posthumus Leonatus reasons as Troilus initially does, deriving the infidelity of all mothers from his (mis-)perception of Imogen's infidelity: "We are all bastards" (2.5.2).

79. Cf. Cicero's identification of Hecuba and Niobe in his *Tusculan Disputations*, cited in Yves Peyré, "Niobe and the Nemean Lion: Reading *Hamlet* in the Light of Ovid's *Metamorphoses*," in *Shakespeare's Ovid:The Metamorphoses in the Plays and Poems*, ed. A. B. Taylor (New York: Cambridge University Press, 2000), 130.

80. This anamorphic division of their gazes is anticipated in the two portraits upon which they both gaze: "Look here upon this picture, and on this, / The counterfeit presentment of two brothers" (3.4.53–54).

81. Kant, *Critique of Pure Reason*, 100 (Aix).

82. Kant, *Prolegomena*, 7.

83. Zammito, *Kant, Herder, and the Birth of Anthropology*, 124.

84. The parallel between Troilus's response to Pandarus's question about the contents of Cressida's last letter—"Words, words, mere words" (5.3.108)—and Hamlet's response to Polonius's question about what he is reading—"Words, words, words" (2.2.92)—invites us to take Hamlet to be reading a letter from Ophelia, despite the First Folio's stage direction, "Enter Hamlet reading on a Booke."

85. Immanuel Kant, "On a Recently Prominent Tone of Superiority in Philosophy," in *Theoretical Philosophy after 1781*, ed. Henry Allison and Peter Heath (New York: Cambridge University Press, 2002), 444. Cf. Kant, *Critique of the Power of Judgment*, 194n.

86. Kant, *Groundwork of the Metaphysics of Morals*, in *Practical Philosophy*, ed. Mary J. Gregor (New York: Cambridge University Press, 1996), 50; *Critique of Practical Reason*, in *Practical Philosophy*, 257. Cf. Slavoj Žižek, *The Ticklish Subject: The Absent Centre of Political Ontology* (New York: Verso, 2008), 40–44.

87. "The feeling of the sublime is thus a feeling of displeasure from the inadequacy of the imagination in the aesthetic estimation of magnitude for the estimation by means of reason, and a pleasure that is thereby aroused at the same time from the correspondence of this very judgment of the inadequacy of the greatest sensible faculty in comparison with ideas of reason, insofar as striving for them is nevertheless a law for us." Kant, *Critique of the Power of Judgment*, 141.

88. Ibid., 50.

89. Samuel Taylor Coleridge, *The Collected Works of Samuel Taylor Coleridge*, 7: *Biographia Literaria: Or, Biographical Sketches of My Literary Life and Opinions*, ed. James Engell and W. Jackson Bate (Princeton: Princeton University Press, 1985), vol. 2, 133–134.

90. See the first epigraph to this chapter. Samuel Taylor Coleridge, *Coleridge's Criticism of Shakespeare: A Selection*, ed. R. A. Foakes (Detroit: Wayne State University Press, 1989), 81.

91. Coleridge, *Biographia Literaria*, vol. 2, 6, 134. "As Coleridge allowed, it was *Hamlet* which drove him to 'philosophical criticism'; only after reading Kant's account of the primacy of mind in the *Critique of Pure Reason* did he recognize 'Shakespeare's deep and accurate science in mental philosophy'—what he termed his 'psychological genius.'" Margreta de Grazia, *Hamlet without Hamlet* (New York: Cambridge University Press, 2007), 16. "Hamlet was the Play, or rather Hamlet himself was the Character, in the intuition and exposition of which I first made my turn for philosophical criticism, and especially for insight into the genius of Shakespear." Samuel Taylor Coleridge, *A Book I Value: Selected Marginalia*, ed. H. J. Jackson (Princeton: Princeton University Press, 2003), 95.

92. Coleridge, *Coleridge's Criticism of Shakespeare*, 142.

93. Rodolphe Gasché, *The Idea of Form: Rethinking Kant's Aesthetics* (Stanford: Stanford University Press, 2003), 206; cf. Martha B. Helfer, *The Retreat of Representation: The Concept of Darstellung in German Critical Discourse* (Albany: State University of New York Press, 1996), 22.

94. Stephen Greenblatt, *Hamlet in Purgatory*, 312n65. In 1583, John Foxe used the term "hypotyposis" as a synonym for "poesy." George Puttenham, in *The Arte of English Poesy* (1589), defined "hypotyposis" as "the counterfeit, otherwise called the figure of representation."

95. Kant, *Critique of the Power of Judgment*, 225.

96. Ibid., 226.

97. Ibid., 227.

98. Ibid., 301n.

99. Kant, *Religion within the Boundaries of Mere Reason*, in *Religion and Rational Theology*, ed. and trans. Allen W. Wood and George di Giovanni (New York: Cambridge University Press, 1996), 82; Immanuel Kant, *Opus Postumum*, trans. Eckart Förster and Michael Rosen (New York: Cambridge University Press, 1993), 204–205.

100. In his anthropology lectures, Kant praises *Paradise Lost* for its lofty representations of "the world of spirits [*Geister*]." Cited in Budick, *Kant and Milton*, 13, translation slightly modified. (Budick renders *Geister* as "invisible beings.")

101. Kant, *Critique of Practical Reason*, in *Practical Philosophy*, 166.

102. "The reader who looks unwillingly at Iago gazes at Lady Macbeth in awe, because though she is dreadful she is also sublime. The whole tragedy is sublime." A. C. Bradley, *Shakespearean Tragedy*, 4th ed. (New York: Palgrave Macmillan, 2007), 252.

103. Ibid., 273.

104. William Chauncey Fowler, *English Grammar: The English Language in Its Elements and Forms, with a History of Its Origin and Development* (New York: Harper & Brothers, 1858), 329.

105. "The lecturer alluded to the prejudiced idea of Lady Macbeth as a monster, as a being out of nature and without conscience. On the contrary, her constant effort throughout the play was … to bully conscience." Coleridge, *Coleridge's Criticism of Shakespeare*, 105. On the crisscrossing of Macbeth's and Lady Macbeth's experience of conscience, see Bradley, *Shakespearean Tragedy*, 286–287.

106. In the *Critique of Judgment*, Kant observes that "a person may desire something in the most lively and persistent way even though he is convinced that he cannot accomplish it or even that it is absolutely impossible: *e.g., to wish that which has been done to be undone*, to yearn for the more rapid passage of a burdensome time, etc." Kant, *Critique of the Power of Judgment*, 32, my italics. Lady Macbeth's categorical statements about the past—"what's done, is done" (3.2.12) and "what's done cannot be undone" (5.1.68)—suggest that she has lost the ability to desire the impossible, while Macbeth's counterfactual wishes—"Wake Duncan with thy knocking! I would thou coulds't!" (2.2.71); And to our dear friend Banquo, whom we miss; / Would he were here!" (3.4.89–90)—show that he has not. The first of these two wishes is clearly heartfelt; the second is less so, but there is dramatic irony in the fact that on some level Macbeth genuinely desires the thing he professes to desire. For an excellent discussion of counterfactuals in the play, see Iolanda Plescia, "Il discorso del futuro in *Macbeth*," *Memoria di Shakespeare* 7 (2009), 135–150.

107. Kant, *Critique of Pure Reason*, 338–339, 354 (A235–236/B294–295). Kristina Grob suggested this comparison between Kant's island and Prospero's.

108. Kant, *Opus Postumum*, 10–11.

109. "The first act of the faculty of representation is the consciousness of myself which is a merely logical act underlying all further representation, through which the subject makes itself into an object." Ibid., 186.

110. "The Northern Prince says 'time is out of joint.' Can it be that the Northern philosopher says the same thing: that he should be Hamletian because he is Oedipal?" Gilles Deleuze, *Difference and Repetition*, trans. Paul Patton (New York: Columbia University Press, 1994), 88.

111. Friedrich Schiller, *On the Aesthetic Education of Man in a Series of Letters*, ed. and trans. Elizabeth M. Wilkinson and L. A. Willoughby (New York: Oxford University Press, 1982).

112. Jürgen Habermas, "Modernity: An Unfinished Project," in *Habermas and the Unfinished Project of Modernity: Critical Essays on* The Philosophical Discourse of Modernity, ed. Maurizio Passerin d'Entrèves and Seyla Benhabib (Cambridge, MA: MIT Press, 1997), 37–55.

CHAPTER 3

1. "Truly, my dear Fichte, I would not be vexed if you, or anyone else, were to call *Chimerism* the view I oppose to the Idealism that I chide for *Nihilism*." Friedrich Heinrich Jacobi, "Jacobi to Fichte," in *The Main Philosophical Writings and the Novel Allwill*, trans. George di Giovanni (Montreal: McGill-Queen's University Press, 1994), 519.

2. Translated as "the all-quashing Kant" in Moses Mendelssohn, *Morning Hours: Lectures on God's Existence*, trans. Daniel O. Dahlstrom and Corey Dyck (New York: Springer, 2011), xix.

3. Friedrich Heinrich Jacobi, "David Hume on Faith, or Idealism and Realism, A Dialogue," in *The Main Philosophical Writings*, 297. Žižek contends that in his very effort to defend a "naive realism" against "delirious ghost-seeing," Kant showed that "*they are both on the same side.*" Žižek, *Tarrying with the Negative: Kant, Hegel, and the Critique of Ideology* (Durham: Duke University Press, 1993), 90, his italics.

4. Friedrich Heinrich Jacobi, "Concerning the Doctrine of Spinoza in Letters to Herr Moses Mendelssohn," in *The Main Philosophical Writings*, 181.

5. In Jacobi's formulation: "*Gigni de nihilo nihil, in nihilum nil potest reverti.*" Ibid., 205.

6. Immanuel Kant, "What Does It Mean to Orient Oneself in Thinking?," in *Religion and Rational Theology*, ed. and trans. Allen W. Wood and George di Giovanni (New York: Cambridge University Press, 1996), 7–18.

7. Arthur Schopenhauer, *The World as Will and Representation*, vol. 1, trans. E. F. J. Payne (New York: Dover, 1966), 324.

8. Arthur Schopenhauer, *The World as Will and Representation*, vol. 2, trans. E. F. J. Payne (New York: Dover, 1966), 583.

9. Kant distinguishes his "critical" idealism from Berkeley's "visionary" idealism in Immanuel Kant, *Prolegomena to Any Future Metaphysics with Selections from the Critique of Pure Reason*, rev. ed., ed. Gary Hatfield (New York: Cambridge University Press, 2004), 45.

10. Schopenhauer, *The World as Will and Representation*, vol. 1, 3. Schopenhauer claims that space and time are creations of our brains. Presumably he means to distinguish the transcendental brain that plays the functional role of *natura naturans*, nature in its active role, from the empirical brain that is part of *natura naturata*, nature as passive product.

11. "All previous explanations of spirit phenomena have been *spiritualistic*; precisely as such, they are the subject of Kant's criticism in the first part of his *Träume eines Geistersehers*. Here I am attempting an *idealistic* explanation." Arthur Schopenhauer, "Essay on Spirit-Seeing and Everything Connected Therewith," in *Parerga and Paralipomena*, vol. 1, trans. E. F. J. Payne (New York: Oxford University Press, 1974), 229.

12. Ibid., 227, 263.

13. Freud suggests that the periodic deployment and withdrawal of our perceptual "feelers [*Fühlern*]" might explain the origin of our representations of time and space and so justify Kant's characterization of them as "necessary forms of thought." Sigmund Freud, *Beyond the Pleasure Principle*, ed. and trans. James Strachey (New York: W. W. Norton, 1989), 31.

14. Kant conjectures that our clearest and most distinct representations might occur during dreamless sleep. Immanuel Kant, "Dreams of a Spirit-Seer Elucidated by Dreams of Metaphysics," in *Theoretical Philosophy 1755–1770*, ed. and trans. David Walford in collaboration with Ralf Meerbote (New York: Cambridge University Press, 1992), 263.

15. Schopenhauer, "Essay on Spirit-Seeing," 231.

16. Arthur Schopenhauer, *Parerga and Paralipomena*, vol. 2, trans. E. F. J. Payne (New York: Oxford University Press, 1974), 456.

17. Schopenhauer, *The World as Will and Representation* vol. 1, xxi, translation slightly modified.

18. Samuel Taylor Coleridge, *Coleridge's Criticism of Shakespeare: A Selection*, ed. R. A. Foakes (Detroit: Wayne State University Press, 1989), 167.

19. Schopenhauer, *The World as Will and Representation*, vol. 1, 17. Cf. Immanuel Kant, *Critique of Pure Reason*, ed. and trans. Paul Guyer and Allen W. Wood (New York: Cambridge University Press, 1998), 339 (A235/B295).

20. By this point he had long since given up his own academic post, having failed to attract students when he deliberately scheduled his lectures to compete with those of Hegel. See David E. Cartwright, *Schopenhauer: A Biography* (New York: Cambridge University Press, 2010), 365.

21. Arthur Schopenhauer, "On Philosophy at the Universities," in *Parerga and Paralipomena*, vol. 1, trans. E. F. J. Payne (New York: Oxford University Press, 2000), 178. Given his hostility toward his own mother, Schopenhauer's characterization of Gertrude as Hamlet's *nichtswürdigen Mutter* (literally, "worthless mother") suggests that a deeper identification is at work in this passage. In a letter to Anthime Grégoire de Blésimaire

he characterized Johanna Schopenhauer as a "good novelist" but a "bad mother" (*mauvaise mère*). Arthur Schopenhauer, *Gesammelte Briefe*, ed. Arthur Hübscher (Bonn: Bouvier, 1978), 159; cited in Cartwright, *Schopenhauer: A Biography*, 13.

22. "The top of his performance was the Ghost in his own *Hamlet*." Nicholas Rowe, "Some Account of the Life and Writings of William Shakspere," in *The Dramatick Works of William Shakespeare with Dr. Samuel Johnson's Preface and Notes*, vol. 1, 2nd ed. (Boston: Munroe & Francis, 1807), 8.

23. Schopenhauer, "On Philosophy at the Universities," 182.

24. Arthur Schopenhauer, *On the Basis of Morality*, trans. E. F. J. Payne (Indianapolis: Hackett, 1995), 43.

25. Immanuel Kant, "Groundwork of the Metaphysics of Morals," in *Practical Philosophy*, ed. and trans. Mary J. Gregor (New York: Cambridge University Press, 1996), 67.

26. Schopenhauer, *On the Basis of Morality*, 126.

27. Gilles Deleuze, "On Four Poetic Formulas That Might Summarize the Kantian Philosophy," in *Essays Critical and Clinical*, trans. Daniel W. Smith and Michael A. Greco (New York: Verso, 1998), 35.

28. Or Schelling, though he generally gets off a bit more lightly.

29. "Cordelia, Coriolanus, hardly more." Schopenhauer, *The World as Will and Representation*, vol. 2, 437.

30. Cartwright, *Schopenhauer: A Biography*, 514.

31. Arthur Schopenhauer, *On the Fourfold Root of the Principle of Sufficient Reason and On the Will in Nature*, rev. ed., trans. Mme. Karl Hillebrand (London: George Bell and Sons, 1891), 222.

32. Schopenhauer traces the roots of Hegel's conception of spirit to the three sophists' collective failure to heed Kant's refutation of the ontological argument. Arthur Schopenhauer, *On the Fourfold Root of the Principle of Sufficient Reason*, trans. E. F. J. Payne (La Salle, IL: Open Court, 1974), 16. Elsewhere he chides Kant for including "the dear little angels"—spirits—in the class of thinkable rational beings. Schopenhauer, *On the Basis of Morality*, 64.

33. Leo Rauch, *Hegel and the Human Spirit: A Translation of the Jena Lectures on the Philosophy of Spirit (1805–6) with commentary* (Detroit: Wayne State University Press, 1983), 87.

34. G. W. F. Hegel, *Phenomenology of Spirit*, trans. A. V. Miller (New York: Oxford University Press, 1977), 19; my italics.

35. Ibid., 9.

36. Ibid., 60.

37. G. W. F. Hegel, *Hegel's Lectures on the History of Philosophy*, vol. 3, trans. E. S. Haldane and Frances H. Simson (Atlantic Highlands: Humanities Press, 1974), 546–547.

38. Hegel, *Phenomenology of Spirit*, 201, 208. If "*the being of Spirit is a bone*" is Hegel's speculative equivalent to Hamlet's "Alas, poor Yorick!" (5.1.184), "the soul is non-mortal" would be Kant's equivalent to Hamlet's "Alas, poor Ghost!" (1.5.4). In passing

from spirit-seeing to grave-digging, Hamlet foreshadows Hegel's overcoming of Kantian metaphysics. Spirit as Kant conceives it is essentially unlocatable ("'Tis here!" … "'Tis gone!" [1.1.142–144]), whereas spirit as Hegel conceives it locates itself in the remainder of what it negates. "Absolute knowing" involves "the inwardizing and the Calvary [Schädelstätte] of absolute spirit," a frame of mind not unlike Hamlet's contemplation of the skulls of Alexander, Caesar, and "my Lord Such-a-one, that prais'd my Lord Such-a-one's horse" (5.1.84–85). Ibid., 493. Hegel compares the infinite judgment that spirit is a bone to Nature's identification of "the organ of generation … with the organ of urination [Pissen]." Ibid., 210. This speculative identity is elaborated upon by the Porter in Macbeth, who observes that drink has the dialectical ("equivocating") power of promoting the male organ's twofold ends of "lechery" and "urine." Drink occasions a deflating passage from the higher end to the lower ("Lechery, sir, it provokes, and unprovokes" [2.3.29]). Unprovoking would seem to run counter to the uplifting character of the Hegelian Aufhebung, but Hegel himself emphasizes the humorous aspect of the identity. Note too that for both Hegel and the Porter, the equivocating dialectic culminates in drunken sleep: "The True is thus the Bacchanalian revel in which no member is not drunk; yet because each member collapses as soon as he drops out, the revel is just as much transparent and simple repose" (ibid., 27). "The being of Spirit is a bone" reminds us that procreating thought culminates not just in "death's counterfeit" (2.3.76) but in death itself.

39. "Yet nowadays they make even Shakespeare's characters ghostly [gespenstig], and suppose that we must find interesting, precisely on their own account, nullity [Nichtigkeit] and indecision in changing and hesitating and trash of this sort [Quatschlichkeit]." Hegel, Aesthetics: Lectures on Fine Art, vol. 1, trans. T. M. Knox (New York: Oxford University Press, 1975), 244. On Hamlet as a beautiful soul, see 231.

40. Ibid., 243.

41. Schelling, cited in Sigmund Freud, The Uncanny, trans. David McLintock (New York: Penguin, 2003), 132.

42. F. W. J. Schelling, in Sämmtliche Werke (Stuttgart, 1857), 649, cited in Davide Stimille, The Face of Immortality: Physiognomy and Criticism (Albany: SUNY Press, 2004), 186.

43. Hegel, Aesthetics: Lectures on Fine Art, vol. 1, 242–243.

44. Ibid., 153.

45. Schopenhauer characterizes Kant's infinite judgment as "a blind window," which is more than he could say on behalf of Hegel's infinite judgments. Schopenhauer, The World as Will and Representation, vol. 1, 456.

46. Ludwig Börne, "Hamlet, von Shakespeare," in Gesammelte Schriften Erster Theil (Hamburg: Hoffmann and Campe, 1835), 197. A critic of Hegel, Börne had converted from Judaism to Christianity.

47. Søren Kierkegaard, Stages on Life's Way, ed. and trans. Howard V. Hong and Edna H. Hong (Princeton: Princeton University Press, 1988), 452–453.

48. Leonardo Lisi suggests that the oscillation between the aesthetic and religious dimensions has to do with whether Hamlet can give his conflict with Claudius

religious significance. See Leonardo F. Lisi, "Hamlet: The Impossibility of Tragedy/The Tragedy of Impossibility," in *Kierkegaard's Figures and Literary Motifs: Kierkegaard Research: Sources, Reception, and Resources*, vol. 16, ed. Jon Stewart (Hampshire: Ashgate, forthcoming).

49. This, I take it, is what Taciturnus is getting at when he concludes "that Shakespeare stands unrivaled, despite the progress the world will make, that one can always learn from him, and the more one reads him, the more one learns." Kierkegaard, *Stages on Life's Way*, 454. Jennifer Bates points out that *Hamlet* represents, for Kierkegaard, an exemplary instance of indirect communication. The difference between the "rub" of Hamlet's "dread of something after death" and the "'Offense' of Christianity" is that between "self-annihilation before the negative" and "a leap of faith before the paradox." See Jennifer Ann Bates, "Hamlet and Kierkegaard on Outwitting Recollection," in *Shakespeare and Continental Philosophy*, ed. Jennifer Ann Bates and Richard Wilson (Edinburgh: Edinburgh University Press, forthcoming).

50. Søren Kierkegaard, *Concluding Unscientific Postscript to* Philosophical Fragments, vol. 1, ed. and trans. Howard V. Hong and Edna H. Hong (Princeton: Princeton University Press, 1992), 163.

51. Ibid., 15.

52. "Both Kierkegaard and Hamlet were shut-up soliloquizers." Richard Kearney, "Kierkegaard on Hamlet: Between Art and Religion" in *The New Kierkegaard*, ed. Elsebet Jegstrup (Bloomington: Indiana University Press, 2004), 225. The suggestion that Kierkegaard identified with Hamlet is longstanding: "The Danish philosopher Harald Høffding (1843–1931) characterized him as a 'descendant' of Shakespeare's Hamlet, and the Scottish theologian Peter Taylor Forsyth (1848–1921) called him 'the great and melancholy Dane in whom Hamlet was mastered by Christ.'" Eric Ziolkowski, *The Literary Kierkegaard* (Evanston: Northwestern University Press, 2011), 183.

53. Søren Kierkegaard, *Søren Kierkegaard's Journals and Papers*, vol. 5, *Autobiographical Part One: 1829–1848*, ed. and trans. Howard V. Hong and Edna H. Hong assisted by Gregor Malantschuk (Bloomington: Indiana University Press,1978), 328. Kierkegaard seems to be thinking of Hamlet's lines, "Had I but time—as this fell sergeant, Death, / Is strict in his arrest—O, I could tell you— / But let it be" (5.2.336–338). In an entry from 1839 he writes: "Personality will for all eternity protest against the idea that absolute contrasts can be mediated (and this protest is incommensurable with the assertion of mediation); for all eternity it will repeat its immortal dilemma: to be or not to be— that is the question (Hamlet)." Søren Kierkegaard, *Søren Kierkegaard's Journals and Papers*, vol. 2, F-K, ed. and trans. Howard V. Hong and Edna H. Hong assisted by Gregor Malantschuk (Bloomington: Indiana University Press, 1970), 210. In the first volume of *Either/Or*, author A suggests that Hamlet's unutterable secret is his suspicion of his mother's complicity in the murder of her husband: "Hamlet is such a tragic figure because he suspects his mother's crime." Søren Kierkegaard, *Either/Or*, part 1, ed. and trans. Howard V. Hong and Edna H. Hong (Princeton: Princeton University Press, 1987), 155.

54. Søren Kierkegaard, *The Concept of Anxiety: A Simply Psychologically Orienting Deliberation on the Dogmatic Issue of Hereditary Sin*, ed. and trans. Reidar Thomte in collaboration with Albert B. Anderson (Princeton: Princeton University Press, 1980), 128.

55. Richard Wagner, *Richard Wagner's Tristan und Isolde: Complete Text with Original Stage Directions*, trans. Peter Bassett (Kent Town: Wakefield Press, 2006), 107. Like Tristan, Juliet longs to flee the tedious day to enjoy a night of bliss ("Come, night; come, Romeo, come, thou day in night" [3.2.17]), and she too dies before she can be united with her beloved. In both cases, the union of the lovers in death is as erotic as it is tragic.

56. Wagner, *Richard Wagner's* Tristan und Isolde, 107.

57. Friedrich Nietzsche, *The Birth of Tragedy and Other Writings*, trans. Ronald Speirs (New York: Cambridge University Press, 1999), 100.

58. Elisabeth Kuhn, *Friedrich Nietzsches Philosophie des Europäischen Nihilismus* (Berlin: Walter de Gruyter, 1992), 20.

59. Friedrich Nietzsche, *Untimely Meditations*, ed. Daniel Breazeale, trans. R. J. Hollingdale (New York: Cambridge University Press, 1997), 141.

60. Friedrich Nietzsche, *Beyond Good and Evil: Prelude to a Philosophy of the Future*, trans. R. J. Hollingdale (New York: Penguin, 2003), 136.

61. Friedrich Nietzsche, *Writings from the Late Notebooks*, ed. Rüdiger Bittner, trans. Kate Sturge (New York: Cambridge University Press, 2003), 146.

62. "Man still prefers to will *nothingness*, than *not* will." Friedrich Nietzsche, *On the Genealogy of Morals*, rev. student ed., ed. Keith Ansell-Pearson, trans. Carol Diethe (New York: Cambridge University Press, 2007), 120.

63. "The Christian moral hypothesis ... endowed man with an absolute *value*. ... It shielded man from despising himself. ... In sum, morality was the great *antidote* to practical and theoretical nihilism." Nietzsche, *Writings from the Late Notebooks*, 116.

64. "Nihilism is standing at the gate: from where does this uncanniest of guests come to us?" Ibid., 83.

65. Friedrich Nietzsche, *The Gay Science: With a Prelude in German Rhymes and an Appendix of Songs*, ed. Bernard Williams, trans. Adrian del Caro (New York: Cambridge University Press, 2001), 120.

66. Friedrich Nietzsche, *Twilight of the Idols*, in *The Anti-Christ, Ecce Homo, Twilight of the Idols, and Other Writings*, ed. Aaron Ridley, trans. Judith Norman (New York: Cambridge University Press, 2005), 171.

67. Friedrich Nietzsche, *Thus Spoke Zarathustra*, ed. Robert Pippin, trans. Adrian del Caro (New York: Cambridge University Press, 2006), 105.

68. Martin Heidegger, "The Word of Nietzsche: 'God is Dead,'" in *The Question Concerning Technology and Other Essays*, trans. William Lovitt (New York: Harper Torchbooks, 1977), 104; my italics.

69. Friedrich Gundolf, *Shakespeare und der deutsche Geist* (Berlin: Bondi, 1911).

70. "Where Fichte had opposed German primordialness to the dead spirit of the Romanized culture of the French, that contrast seemed no longer appropriate. In the new geopolitical picture, the role of opponent fell instead to the Anglo-Saxons and the Russians. ... The German character was in every respect the exact opposite of the English character, [Max] Scheler said." Hans Sluga, *Heidegger's Crisis: Philosophy and Politics in Nazi Germany* (Cambridge, MA: Harvard University Press, 1993), 79.

71. Martin Heidegger, *Introduction to Metaphysics*, trans. Gregory Fried and Richard Polt (New Haven: Yale University Press, 2000), 40–41.

72. Ibid., 213.

73. Jürgen Habermas, "Martin Heidegger: On the Publication of Lectures from the Year 1935," trans. Dale Ponikvar, in *Graduate Faculty Philosophy Journal* 6, no. 2 (fall 1977), 155–180.

74. Karl Reinhardt, *Sophocles*, trans. Hazel Harvey and David Harvey (Oxford: Blackwell, 1979), 6. A trace of the philosophical Seneca can be found in Hamlet's neo-Stoic assertion that "there is nothing either good or bad, but thinking makes it so" (2.2.249–250).

75. Reinhardt, *Sophocles*, 28.

76. Martin Heidegger, *Parmenides*, trans. André Schuwer and Richard Rojcewicz (Bloomington: Indiana University Press, 1992), 73. The idea that Shakespeare and Aeschylus-Sophocles belong to "incomparable worlds" goes back to Herder's conception of a *Zeitgeist*, but Heidegger is pursuing a different line of thought.

77. Martin Heidegger, "The Age of the World Picture," in *The Question Concerning Technology and Other Essays*, 117; translation slightly modified.

78. "The tragic heroes of the ancients show resolute and stoical subjection under the unavoidable blows of fate; the Christian tragedy, on the other hand, shows the giving up of the whole will-to-live, cheerful abandonment of the world in the consciousness of its worthlessness and vanity. But I am fully of opinion that the tragedy of the moderns is at a higher level than that of the ancients. Shakespeare is much greater than Sophocles; compared with Goethe's *Iphigenia*, that of Euripides might be found almost crude and vulgar. ... The ancients displayed little of the spirit of resignation." Schopenhauer, *World as Will and Representation*, vol. 2, 434–435.

79. "Neither the various descriptions of the human heart and personal character nor particular complications and intrigues can find their place completely in Greek drama; nor does the interest turn on the fates of individuals. ... In modern, or romantic, poetry, on the other hand, the principal topic is provided by an individual's passion, which is satisfied in the pursuit of a purely subjective end, and, in general, by the fate of a single individual and his character in special circumstances." Hegel, *Hegel's Aesthetics: Lectures on Fine Art*, vol. 2, trans. T. M. Knox (Oxford: Oxford University Press, 1975), 1206. "In ancient tragedy, the action itself has an epic element; it is just as much event as action. This, of course, is because the ancient world did not have subjectivity reflected in itself." Kierkegaard, *Either/Or*, 143.

80. Heidegger, *Introduction to Metaphysics*, 1. Schlegel had translated "To be, or not to be, that is the question" as "*Sein oder Nichtsein, das ist hier die Frage.*"

81. Martin Heidegger, *Gesamtausgabe Band 55: Der Anfang des abendländischen Denkens Logik: Heraklits Lehre vom Logos* (Frankfurt: Vittorio Klostermann, 1979), 276; my translation.

82. Heidegger, *Introduction to Metaphysics*, 89, 117.

83. Ibid., 113; Reinhardt, *Sophocles*, 116; cf. 98.

84. Hegel, *Phenomenology of Spirit*, 283.

85. Heidegger, *Introduction to Metaphysics*, 113–114.

86. Ibid., 112.

87. Nietzsche, *The Birth of Tragedy*, 39–40.

88. Nietzsche, *Twilight of the Idols*, 170.

89. Nietzsche, cited in Heidegger, *Introduction to Metaphysics*, 38.

90. Heidegger, *Introduction to Metaphysics*, 15.

91. Ibid., 213.

92. Sluga, *Heidegger's Crisis*, 93, 129–131.

93. Martin Heidegger, *Nietzsche*, vol. 4: Nihilism, trans. David Farrell Krell (New York: HarperSanFrancisco, 1987), 21.

94. Ibid., 22.

95. Ibid.

96. Heidegger, *Introduction to Metaphysics*, 111.

97. Ibid., 189.

98. Ibid. Reinhardt attributes a kind of "pessimism" to the ancient Greeks (Reinhardt, *Sophocles*, 3). This may be the basis for Heidegger's reproof of his "modern subjectivisms and psychologisms." Heidegger, *Introduction to Metaphysics*, 113. Yet Heidegger concedes that "the Greeks were ... more pessimistic than a pessimist can ever be" (189). Schopenhauer illustrates the doctrine of pessimism by reflecting on the life cycle of a blind mole whose sole purpose is to reproduce the conditions of its existence in "permanent night." Schopenhauer, *The World as Will and Representation*, vol. 2, 353.

99. Heidegger, *Introduction to Metaphysics*, 190.

100. Ibid., 159; Nietzsche, *Writings from the Late Notebooks*, 83.

101. Heidegger, *Introduction to Metaphysics*, 188.

102. Ibid., 159–160.

103. "Anxiety reveals the nothing"; "Da-sein means: being held out into the nothing"; "Only because the nothing is manifest in the ground of Dasein can the total strangeness of beings overwhelm us." Martin Heidegger, "What Is Metaphysics?," trans. David Farrell Krell, in Heidegger, *Basic Writings*, rev. and exp. ed. (New York: HarperSanFrancisco, 1993), 26, 101, 103, 109.

104. Heidegger, *Introduction to Metaphysics*, 116.

105. Martin Heidegger, "Hölderlin and the Essence of Poetry," in *Elucidations of Hölderlin's Poetry*, trans. Keith Hoeller (New York: Humanity Books, 2000), 52.

106. Ibid., 55.

107. Ibid., 64; cf. *Introduction to Metaphysics*, 112–113.

108. David Pacini picks up on this connection in his foreword to Dieter Heinrich, *Between Kant and Hegel: Lectures on German Idealism*, ed. David S. Pacini (Cambridge, MA: Harvard University Press, 2003), xxxiii: "Hölderlin's is a gaze akin to Shakespeare's admonition in *King Lear*: 'Look with thine ears.'"

109. Heidegger, "Hölderlin and the Essence of Poetry," 61. ("Und alle trinken jetzt ohne Gefahr / Das himmlische Feuer, doch uns, ihr Dichter uns gebührt / Mit entblößtem Haupt, unter / Gottes Gewittern, zu stehen, und des / Vaters Strahlen, sie selbst, sie selbst, / Zu fassen, und eingehüllet, und gemildert, / im Liede den Menschen, die wir lieben, die himmlische / Gabe zu reichen.")

110. Martin Heidegger, "Spiegel Interview with Martin Heidegger," trans. Lisa Harries, in *Martin Heidegger and National Socialism: Questions and Answers*, ed. Günther Neske and Emil Kettering (New York: Paragon House, 1990), 57, translation slightly modified. Ned Lukacher, *Daemonic Figures: Shakespeare and the Question of Conscience* (Ithaca: Cornell University Press, 1994), 147–149.

111. Heidegger develops his conception of *Gelassenheit* in a second reading of *Antigone* in his 1942 lecture course on Hölderlin's "The Ister." Martin Heidegger, *Hölderlin's Hymn "The Ister,"* trans. William McNeill and Julia Davis (Bloomington: Indiana University Press, 1996). Harold Jenkins rejects the idea that "Let be" is a further expression of Hamlet's readiness: "Many eds. wrongly take this to be part of Hamlet's reflection, expressing his resignation to the course of events. A misplaced ingenuity has even tried to make it answer 'To be or not to be.' But it merely recognizes an interruption which requires their dialogue to break off." Harold Jenkins, editor's note in William Shakespeare, *Hamlet*, ed. Harold Jenkins (London: Arden, 1982), 407.

112. *Dikē* is also rendered as *Fug* in Heidegger's *Introduction to Metaphysics*, but without reference to *adikia* (171).

113. Jacques Derrida, *Specters of Marx: The State of the Debt, the Work of Mourning, and the New International*, trans. Peggy Kamuf (New York: Routledge, 1994), 23–29, 161.

114. Emmanuel Levinas, *Time and the Other and Additional Essays*, trans. Richard A. Cohen (Pittsburgh: Duquesne University Press, 1987), 72.

115. Jacques Lacan, *The Seminar of Jacques Lacan Seminar VII: The Ethics of Psychoanalysis 1959–1960*, ed. Jacques-Alain Miller, trans. Dennis Porter (New York: W. W. Norton, 1992), 320.

116. Ibid., 50.

117. Ibid., 51, 70n.

118. Emmanuel Levinas, *Existence and Existents*, trans. Alphonso Lingis (Pittsburgh: Duquesne University Press, 2001), 51–60. "The *there is* fills the void left by the negation of Being." Emmanuel Levinas, *Otherwise Than Being or Beyond Essence*, trans. Alphonso Lingis (Pittsburgh: Duquesne University Press, 1998), 4.

119. Levinas, *Existence and Existents*, 58.

120. Ibid., 57.

121. Emmanuel Levinas, *Totality and Infinity: An Essay on Exteriority*, trans. Alphonso Lingis (Pittsburgh: Duquesne University Press, 1998), 231.

122. Levinas, *Time and the Other*, 73.

123. Ibid., 50.

124. Levinas, *Existence and Existents*, 57.

125. "Everything that is not simply nothing, *is*—and for us, even Nothing 'belongs' to 'Being.'" Heidegger, *Introduction to Metaphysics*, 89.

126. Emmanuel Levinas, "Ethics as First Philosophy," in *The Levinas Reader*, ed. Seán Hand (New York: Wiley-Blackwell, 2001), 86.

127. Lukacher, *Daemonic Figures*, 97.

CHAPTER 4

1. Karl Werder, *The Heart of Hamlet's Mystery*, trans. Elizabeth Wilder (New York: G. P. Putnam's Sons, 1907), 74. The passage in quotation marks is from Carl Hebler's *Aufsätze über Shakespeare* (Bern: J. Dalp'schen, 1865), 114: "*Aber er verweilt in diesem Stadium zu lang.*" Werder and Hebler are discussing Hamlet's first soliloquy rather than the one in 3.3.

2. Ned Lukacher, *Daemonic Figures: Shakespeare and the Question of Conscience* (Ithaca: Cornell University Press, 1994), 134–135.

3. The three senses that David and Ben Crystal give for "tarry" are "1 stay, remain, linger," "2 stay for, wait for, allow time for," and "3 await, expect anticipate." They gloss Ulysses's use of "tarrying" in "There is no tarrying here, the hart Achilles / Keeps thicket" (2.3.258–259) as "waiting, delaying, lingering," but I see no justification for "delaying" in this context. David Crystal and Ben Crystal, *Shakespeare's Words: A Glossary and Language Companion* (New York: Penguin, 2002), 444.

4. This is to take "the whips and scorns of time" to be the genus of subsequently mentioned species, or else as a Hegelian "concrete universal": a genus that *is* one of its own species.

5. Patience involves tarrying, as Pandarus reminds Troilus when he says that he who "will have a cake" must "tarry the grinding" of the wheat (*Troilus and Cressida* 1.1.15).

6. Cf. Jacques Derrida, "The Time Is Out of Joint," trans. Peggy Kamuf, in *Deconstruction is/in America: A New Sense of the Political*, ed. Anselm Haverkamp (New York: NYU Press, 1995), 14–38.

7. Timothy Chappell, *Reading Plato's* Theaetetus (Indianapolis: Hackett, 2005), 121–122 (172d–e).

8. Franz Kafka, *The Trial*, trans. Breon Mitchell (New York: Schocken Books, 1998), 91.

9. In fact, Socrates anticipates Hamlet: "For I've heard too that one should meet one's end in propitious silence." Plato, *Plato's Phaedo*, trans. Eva Brann, Peter Kalkavage, Eric Salem (Newburyport, MA: Focus, 1998), 101 (118a).

10. My thanks to Paul Kottman for prompting me to think more carefully about this passage.

11. For Richard Wilson, *Measure for Measure* registers the ongoing historical transition from a regime based on terror to a biopolitical state: "The scaffold and the gibbet are consigned to history, 'like unscoured armour' [1,2,165], in this therapeutic society, but in its fresh benevolent guise the confessional state has arrogated to itself an unprecedented observation of its subjects' lives. ... It is 'the quality of mercy' that its power is written not on its subjects' skin and bones, but scored into their hearts." Richard Wilson, *Shakespeare in French Theory: King of Shadows* (New York: Routledge, 2007), 113.

12. Portia is trying to gain time, while Bassanio is trying to gain surplus-time. The fact that his selection of the lead casket is successful suggests that it is by submitting to the "law of the father" that he acquires the very surplus-time that I here take to exceed the order of the law. His choice of the lead casket, "which rather threaten'st than dost promise aught" (3.2.105), involves another kind of suspension of the law—not of the decree of Portia's father, but of the economic legalism that the play associates with Shylock. Submitting to the authority of the play's absent father, Bassanio contributes to the passage from the religion of the Father to the religion of the Son. Something similar could be said about Hamlet, whose surplus-time is associated with the memory of his father.

13. Friar Laurence advises Romeo not to "stand on sudden haste," but to go "wisely and slow; they stumble that run fast" (*Romeo and Juliet* 2.3.93–94). Romeo and Juliet are constantly torn between the imperative to hasten and the wish to tarry. Sir Thomas Browne glosses the maxim as "celerity should always be contempered with cunctation." Sir Thomas Browne, "Pseudoxia Epidemica," in *The Works of Sir Thomas Browne*, vol. 2, ed. Geoffrey Keynes (Chicago: University of Chicago Press, 1964), 341.

14. Cf. Emilia's exchange with Desdemona in 4.3 of *Othello*: "*Desdemona:* Wouldst thou do such a deed for all the world? *Emilia:* The world's a huge thing; it is a great price for a small vice. ... Who would not make her husband a cuckold to make him a monarch?" (4.3.67–69, 75–77).

15. I thank my wife, Dianne Rothleder, for helping me complete this thought.

16. Although it doesn't contradict my reading, I hesitate to appeal to Tamora's suggestion that Demetrius and Chiron "tarry" with Titus Andronicus while she returns to the emperor to tell him how she has "govern'd [her] determin'd jest" (5.2.139, 141). A happier usage is the Shepherd's "I'll tarry till my son come" in *The Winter's Tale* (3.3.77). Perhaps "tarry" comes close to signifying "delay" in two of Dr. Caius's three uses of the term in *The Merry Wives of Windsor*: "By my trot, I tarry too long" (1.4.62) and "You may be gone; it is not good you tarry here" (1.4.110–111). But Dr. Caius isn't blaming either Simple or himself for delaying so much as for loitering. Besides, even the misplacing Mistress Quickly accuses him of "abusing ... the King's English" (1.4.5–6).

17. Michel Foucault, "Nietzsche, Genealogy, History," trans. Donald F. Brouchard and Sherry Simon, in *Aesthetics, Method, and Epistemology*, ed. James D. Faubion (New York: New Press, 1999), 36–391.

18. Jacques Derrida, *Given Time: I. Counterfeit Money*, trans. Peggy Kamuf (Chicago: University of Chicago Press, 1992), 1–5.

19. Since Hamlet kills Claudius before the king learns of Rosencrantz's and Guildenstern's deaths, the interim turns out to be perpetual.

20. Samuel Johnson, "Notes on *Hamlet*," in William Shakespeare, *Hamlet*, ed. Robert S. Miola (New York: W.W. Norton, 2011), 239.

21. Immanuel Kant, *Critique of Pure Reason*, trans. Paul Guyer and Allen W. Wood (New York: Cambridge University Press, 1998), 383 (A292/B348).

22. Ibid., 382 (A290–291/B347–348).

23. Samuel Taylor Coleridge, *Coleridge's Criticism of Shakespeare: A Selection*, ed. R. A. Foakes (Detroit: Wayne State University Press, 1989), 71. Likewise, Schlegel speaks of Hamlet's "pretexts to cover his want of determination." August Wilhelm Schlegel, *Lectures on Dramatic Art and Literature*, trans. John Black (London: George Bell & Sons, 1894), 405.

24. Coleridge observes that prescribing maxims suits the old Polonius, since maxims are "retrospective" rather than "prospective." Ibid., 89.

25. Cf. Slavoj Žižek, *The Sublime Object of Ideology* (New York: Verso, 1989), 60.

26. Ella Freeman Sharpe, "The Impatience of Hamlet," in *Collected Papers on Psycho-Analysis*, ed. Marjorie Brierley (London: Hogarth Press, 1950), 207.

27. Ibid., 208.

28. Lacan picks up on this: "Procrastination is … one of the essential dimensions of the tragedy. [¶] When, on the contrary, he does act, it is always too soon." Jacques Lacan, "Desire and the Interpretation of Desire in *Hamlet*," in *Literature and Psychoanalysis: The Question of Reading: Otherwise*, ed. Shoshana Felman (Baltimore: The Johns Hopkins University Press, 1982), 24.

29. Samuel Taylor Coleridge, *The Collected Works of Samuel Taylor Coleridge*, 7: *Biographia Literaria: Or, Biographical Sketches of My Literary Life and Opinions*, ed. James Engell and W. Jackson Bate (Princeton: Princeton University Press, 1985), vol. 1, 304–305.

30. "The first factor that I indicated to you in Hamlet's structure was his situation of dependence with respect to the desire of the Other, the desire of his mother. Here now is the second factor that I ask you to recognize: Hamlet is constantly suspended in the time of the Other, throughout the entire story until the very end." Lacan, "Desire and the Interpretation of Desire in *Hamlet*," 17.

31. Ibid., 15. Cf. Dominiek Hoens, "*Hamlet* and the Letter *a*," *Journal of Culture and the Unconscious* 2, no. 2 (fall 2002), 99.

32. Coleridge, *Coleridge's Criticism of Shakespeare*, 67.

33. André Gide, cited in Wilson, *Shakespeare in French Theory*, 52.

34. Gilles Deleuze, *Difference and Repetition*, trans. Paul Patton (New York: Continuum, 2004), 112.

35. Cf. Eva Brann, *The Ways of Naysaying: No, Not, Nothing, and Nonbeing* (Lanham: Rowman & Littlefield, 2001), 161.

36. Deleuze, *Difference and Repetition*, 112.

37. Cf. Jacques Lacan, *The Seminar of Jacques Lacan*, book 11: *The Four Fundamental Concepts of Psychoanalysis*, trans. Alan Sheridan (New York: W. W. Norton, 1998), 179.

38. G. W. F. Hegel, *Hegel's Lectures on the History of Philosophy*, vol. 3, trans. E. S. Haldane and Frances H. Simson (Atlantic Highlands: Humanities Press, 1974), 546–547.

39. Karl Marx, "The Eighteenth Brumaire of Louis Bonaparte," in *Later Political Writings*, ed. and trans. Terrell Carver (New York: Cambridge University Press, 1996), 115.

40. "The mouth as organ of speech in Shakespeare becomes the mouth as organ of eating in Marx." Peter Stallybrass, "'Well grubbed, old mole': Marx, *Hamlet*, and the (un)fixing of representation," in *Marxist Shakespeares*, ed. Jean E. Howard and Scott Cutler Shershow (New York: Routledge, 2001), 28. De Grazia makes a similar point: "hunger," not "longing for spiritual sustenance," is the motor of history. Margreta De Grazia, Hamlet *without* Hamlet (New York: Cambridge University Press, 2007), 24. Hamlet's identification of the Ghost with the mole can be regarded as yet another variation on the Hegelian infinite judgment that the being of spirit is a bone. De Grazia notes that Hegel implicitly identifies the mole with Hamlet himself rather than with the Ghost (28). Bataille contrasts Marx's materialist mole with Hegel's spiritual eagle in Georges Bataille, "The 'Old Mole' and the Prefix *Sur* in the Words *Surhomme* [Superman] and *Surrealist*," in *Visions of Excess: Selected Writings, 1927–1939*, ed. Allan Stoekl, trans. Allan Stoekl with Carl R. Lovitt and Donald M. Leslie, Jr. (Minneapolis: University of Minnesota Press, 1985), 34. As Derrida observes at the beginning of *Glas*, "Hegel" and "*aigle*" (eagle) are near homonyms in French. Jacques Derrida, *Glas*, trans. John P. Leavey, Jr., and Richard Rand (Lincoln: University of Nebraska Press, 1986), 1.

41. Karl Marx, "Critique of Hegel's Philosophy of Right: Introduction," in *Early Writings*, trans. Rodney Livingstone and Gregor Benton (New York: Penguin, 1992), 249. Cf. the Scholastic distinction between "formal" and "objective" reality that Descartes invokes in purporting to demonstrate the existence of God in his Third Meditation. The idea that there must be at least as much *formal* reality in the cause of an idea as there is objective reality in the idea is effectively recast by Marx in materialist terms.

42. Karl Marx, "Critique of Hegel's Doctrine of the State," in *Early Writings*, 86.

43. Karl Marx, "Speech at the Anniversary of the *People's Paper*," in *The Marx-Engels Reader*, 2nd ed. ed. Robert C. Tucker, ed. (New York: W. W. Norton, 1978), 578.

44. Wilson, *Shakespeare in French Theory*, 5.

45. Franz Mehring, cited in Stallybrass, "'Well grubbed, old mole,'" 20.

46. R. S. White, "Marx and Shakespeare," *Shakespeare Survey 45*: Hamlet *and Its Afterlife* (New York: Cambridge University Press, 1993), 90.

47. Cited in S. S. Prawer, *Karl Marx and World Literature* (New York: Verso, 2011), 210. Cf. White, "Marx and Shakespeare," 90.

48. Karl Marx, cited in Prawer, *Karl Marx and World Literature*, 215.

49. Other Hamlet-inspired remarks of Marx's include "There must be something rotten in the very core of a social system which increases its wealth without diminishing

its misery" and "Hamlet thought it disquieting that the dust of Alexander might have been used to stop a bunghole. What would Hamlet have said if he had seen the disintegrated head of Napoleon on the shoulders of the Plon-Plon?" Cited in White, "Marx and Shakespeare," 92–93.

50. Stallybrass, "Well grubbed, old mole," 25.

51. Marx, "The Eighteenth Brumaire of Louis Bonaparte," 32.

52. Hannah Arendt, "Karl Jaspers: Citizen of the World?" in *Men in Dark Times* (New York: Harcourt Brace, 1995), 91. In attributing this line of the Player King to Hamlet, Arendt implies that it is among the "dozen or sixteen" (2.2.541) that Hamlet adds to the play within the play. He expresses the same thought when he refers to "the divinity that shapes our ends, / Rough-hew them how we will" (5.2.10–11). In *The Origins of Totalitarianism*, Arendt cites Proust's "the question is not as for Hamlet, to be or not to be, but to belong or not to belong" (from *Sodom and Gomorrah*), noting the historical importance of assimilation to Jews and homosexuals. Hannah Arendt, *The Origins of Totalitarianism* (New York: Harcourt, 1976), 84.

53. Hannah Arendt, *On Revolution* (New York: Pelican, 1977), 52–53. Arendt is thinking primarily of the psychological effect of teleological conceptions of history, but a similar point would apply to a fatalistic (but nonteleological) conception according to which what will happen in the future is already determined and therefore outside our control. In the teleological case that concerns her, one represents oneself as a means to historically driven ends; in the fatalistic case, one represents one's future as if it already belonged to the past.

54. Hannah Arendt, "Personal Responsibility under Dictatorship," in *Responsibility and Judgment*, ed. Jerome Kohn (New York: Schocken Books, 2003), 26–27. Arendt repeats this theme in *The Promise of Politics*, ed. Jerome Kohn (New York: Schocken Books, 2005), 203.

55. When Macbeth says that he "will try the last," he does so in defiance of the fatalistic view that would force him to represent himself as already dead now that history has almost completed its idiotic tale. Macbeth is still busy being born.

56. Leon Trotsky, *History of the Russian Revolution*, trans. Max Eastman (Chicago: Haymarket Books, 2008), 343, 845. Cf. 396: "The men at the head of Centrobalt were not at all of the Hamlet type." Victor Serge, whom Trotsky regarded as similarly weak-willed, writes: "Weak Prince Hamlet, you faltered in that fog of crimes, but you put the question well. 'To be or not to be,' for the men of our age, means free will or servitude, and they have only to choose." Victor Serge, *Memoirs of a Revolutionary*, trans. Peter Sedgwick and George Paizis (New York: New York Review of Books, 2012), 78.

57. Roger Paulin, *The Critical Reception of Shakespeare in Germany 1682–1914: Native Literature and Foreign Genius* (Hildesheim: Georg Olms Verlag, 2003), 442–444.

58. Adolf Hitler, *Mein Kampf*, trans. Ralph Manheim (Boston: Houghton Mifflin, 1943), 177. "Hitler would certainly have heard or read … the Kaiser's speech of 6 August 1914. The phrase *Sein oder Nichtsein* … occurs twice—at the beginning of consecutive sentences." Felicity Rash, *The Language of Violence: Hitler's Mein Kampf* (New York: Peter Lang, 2006), 39.

59. Wilhelm Hortmann, *Shakespeare on the German Stage: The Twentieth Century* (New York: Cambridge University Press, 1998), 157. A more active Hamlet seems to have appeared as well in Gerhart Hauptmann's *Hamlet in Wittenberg* (1935) and *Im Wirbel der Berufung* (1936). See Paul S. Conklin, *A History of Hamlet Criticism 1601–1821* (New York: Humanities Press, 1968), 109–110n49.

60. Hermann Burte, "Intellectuals Must Belong to the People," in *Nazi Culture: Intellectual, Cultural, and Social Life in the Third Reich* (Madison: University of Wisconsin Press, 1981), ed. George L. Mosse, 145; cf. Michael Dobson, "Short Cuts," *London Review of Books* 31, no. 15 (August 2009), 22.

61. Wilson, *Shakespeare in French Theory*, 54.

62. Heiner Müller, "Hamletmachine," in *Hamletmachine and Other Texts for the Stage*, ed. and trans. Carl Weber (New York: Performing Arts Journal Publications, 1984). Critchley and Webster seem to be after something similar when they characterize Ophelia as "the Antigone within *Hamlet*." Simon Critchley and Jamieson Webster, *Stay, Illusion! The Hamlet Doctrine* (New York: Pantheon, 2013), 152.

63. Michelangelo Antonioni, *The Passenger*, cited in Murray Pomerance, *Michelangelo Red Antonioni Blue: Eight Reflections on Cinema* (Berkeley: University of California Press, 2011), 218. There are several reasons for regarding *The Passenger* (known in Italian as *Professione: Reporter*) as a *Trauerspiel*. First, critics complained that it is itself boring. Second, the reporter David Locke's desultory involvement in the brutal civil war in postcolonial Chad resembles the acedia that Benjamin takes to be a typical feature of *Trauerspiel*. Third, like Hamlet, Locke (Jack Nicholson) wants to "die by some accident" and be a witness of his own death. Finally, the famous seven-minute tracking shot, in which the camera slowly transcends the interior frame of Locke's hotel room while he is killed before circling back to become an exterior shot, strikes messianic sparks of precisely the sort that Benjamin identifies in the death of Hamlet.

64. Walter Benjamin, *The Origin of German Tragic Drama*, trans. John Osborne (New York: Verso, 1998), 137, 158.

65. Carl Schmitt, *Hamlet or Hecuba: The Intrusion of the Time into the Play*, trans. David Pan and Jennifer Rust (New York: Telos Press Publishing, 2009).

66. Besides Lilian Winstanley's *Hamlet and the Scottish Succession, Being an Examination of the Relations of the Play of Hamlet to the Scottish Succession and the Essex Conspiracy* (Cambridge: Cambridge University Press, 1921), Schmitt's construal of *Hamlet* as a thinly veiled commentary on contemporary politics is foreshadowed in James Plumptre's 1796 *Observations on Hamlet*. Cf. Paul S. Conklin, *A History of Hamlet Criticism 1601–1821* (New York: Humanities Press, 1968), 77n40.

67. Schmitt, *Hamlet or Hecuba*, 44.

68. Ibid., 22–23.

69. Ibid., 7.

70. Carl Schmitt, *Political Theology: Four Chapters on the Concept of Sovereignty*, trans. George Schwab (Chicago: University of Chicago Press, 1985), 5.

71. Walter Benjamin, "Paralipomena to 'On the Concept of World History,'" in *Selected Writings*, vol. 4: 1938–1940, ed. Howard Eiland and Michael W. Jennings (Cambridge, MA: Harvard University Press, 2003), 402. Cf. "History, Stephen said, is a nightmare from which I am trying to awake. … The bloodboltered shambles in act five is a forecast of the concentration camp sung by Mr Swinburne." James Joyce, *Ulysses: The 1922 Text* (New York: Oxford University Press, 2008), 34, 180.

72. Alain Badiou, *Theory of the Subject*, trans. Bruno Bosteels (New York: Continuum, 2009), 94. Oliver Feltham translates Mallarmé's phrase as "sour Prince of pitfalls." Alain Badiou, *Being and Event*, trans. Oliver Feltham (New York: Continuum, 2007), 194. A similar Schmittian inflection informs Massimo Cacciari's assessment: "In *Hamlet* the subject is powerless to establish himself as a substratum of the decision and, while gesturing toward the possibility of new 'orders,' without ever being able to name it, is forced to obey the logic of facts." Massimo Cacciari, *Hamletica*, 2nd ed. (Milan: Adelphi Edizioni, 2009), 41, my translation.

73. Alain Badiou, *Briefings on Existence: A Short Treatise on Transitory Ontology*, trans. Norman Madarasz (Albany: SUNY Press, 2006), 24; cf. Alain Badiou, *Ethics: An Essay on the Understanding of Evil*, trans. Peter Hallward (New York: Verso, 2001), 49: "Nothing in the world could arouse the intensity of existence more than this actor who lets me encounter Hamlet, this perception in thought of what it means to be two, this problem in algebraic geometry whose innumerable ramifications I suddenly discover, or this open-air meeting, by the doors of a factory, which confirms that my political statement does indeed bring people together and transform them."

74. Badiou, *Theory of the Subject*, 166.

75. Friedrich Nietzsche, *Thus Spoke Zarathustra*, ed. Robert Pippin, trans. Adrian del Caro (New York: Cambridge University Press, 2006), 16–17.

76. Slavoj Žižek, *For They Know Not What They Do: Enjoyment as a Political Factor*, 2nd. ed. (New York: Routledge, 2002), lxxxiii.

77. Aristotle, *On Poetics*, trans. Seth Benardete and Michael Davis (South Bend: St. Augustine's Press, 2002), 14 (1449^a).

78. "When Creon and Antigone confront each other, we should fail to appreciate fully the heroine's attitude but for the presence of Isemene." Milton W. Humphreys, introduction, in *The Antigone of Sophocles* (New York: Harper, 1891), xxii.

79. Aeschylus, *Aeschylus I: Oresteia*, trans. Richmond Lattimore (Chicago: University of Chicago Press, 1953), 125.

80. Slavoj Žižek, *Looking Awry: An Introduction to Jacques Lacan through Popular Culture* (Cambridge, MA: MIT Press, 1991), 23.

81. "It is important to see Hamlet as Antigone's tragic counterpart. Where he ends, she begins." Critchley and Webster, *Stay, Illusion!*, 98.

82. G. W. F. Hegel, *Natural Law: The Scientific Ways of Treating Natural Law, Its Place in Moral Philosophy, and Its Relation to the Positive Sciences of Law*, trans. T. M. Knox (Philadelphia: University of Pennsylvania Press, 1975), 105.

83. "If man is ever to solve that problem of politics in practice he will have to approach it through the problem of the aesthetic, because it is only through Beauty that man makes his way to Freedom." Friedrich Schiller, *On the Aesthetic Education of Man in a Series of Letters*, ed. and trans. Elizabeth M. Wilkinson and L. A. Willoughby (New York: Oxford University Press, 1982), 9.

84. "But for our Antigone it is different. I assume that Oedipus is dead. Even when he was alive, Antigone knew this secret but did not have the courage to confide in her father. By her father's death she is deprived of the only means of being liberated from her secret. To confide in any other living being now would be to dishonor her father; her life acquires meaning for her in its devotion to showing him the last honors daily, almost hourly, by her unbroken silence." Søren Kierkegaard, *Either/Or Part One*, ed. and trans. Howard V. Hong and Edna H. Hong (Princeton: Princeton University Press, 1987), 161.

85. "The substitution of Oedipus for Orestes made for an unlikely comparison. Until Freud hypothesized that all men desired to sleep with their mothers and kill their fathers, what did Oedipus and Hamlet have in common? The parallel depended on the postulation of a new region of character. And Freud here does Hegel one better: what differentiates the ancient from the modern is not just inwardness but subinwardness." De Grazia, Hamlet without Hamlet, 20.

86. Nicholas Rowe, excerpt from *Some Account of the Life, &c of Mr. William Shakespeare*, in *William Shakespeare: The Critical Heritage*, vol. 2: 1693–1733, ed. Brian Vickers (New York: Routledge, 1974), 201. He goes on to praise Shakespeare for "distinguish[ing] rightly between *Horror* and *Terror*," suggesting that Orestes provokes our horror, Hamlet our terror.

87. For details, see de Grazia, Hamlet without Hamlet, 12, 207–208n38.

88. Horace Howard Furness, ed., *A New Variorum Edition of Shakespeare: Hamlet*, vol. 2: *Appendix* (Philadelphia: J. B. Lippincott, 1877), 277; cited in de Grazia, Hamlet without Hamlet, 20.

89. "In order to exhibit in more detail the difference … between Greek and modern tragedy, I will direct attention only to Hamlet. His character is rooted in a collision similar to that treated by Aeschylus in the *Choephori* and Sophocles in the *Electra*. … But whereas in the Greek poets the King's death does have an ethical justification, in Shakespeare it is simply and solely an atrocious crime and Hamlet's mother is guiltless of it. Consequently the son has to wreak his revenge only on the fratricide King in whom he sees nothing really worthy of respect. Therefore the collision turns strictly here not on a son's pursuing an ethically justified revenge and being forced in the process to violate the ethical order, but on Hamlet's personal character. His noble soul is not made for this kind of energetic activity; and, full of disgust with the world and life, what with decision, proof, arrangements for carrying out his resolve, and being bandied from pillar to post, he eventually perishes owing to his own hesitation and a complication of external circumstances." G. W. F. Hegel, *Hegel's Aesthetics: Lectures on Fine Art*, vol. 2, trans. T. M. Knox (Oxford: Oxford University Press, 1975), 1225–1226.

90. Hegel, *Hegel's Aesthetics: Lectures on Fine Art*, vol. 1, 231.

91. Hegel, *Phenomenology of Spirit*, 446.

92. Coleridge speaks of Hamlet's "temporary mania." Coleridge, *Coleridge's Criticism of Shakespeare*, 75.

93. Chappell, *Reading Plato's* Theaetetus, 27 (144b).

94. Despite representing conscience as an auto-affective "appeal" by which Dasein calls itself "to its ownmost potentiality-for-Being-its-Self," Heidegger seems to associate it with "the voice of the friend whom every Dasein carries with it." Martin Heidegger, *Being and Time*, trans. John Macquarrie and Edward Robinson (New York: Harper & Row, 1962), 206, 314. Whether he understands the nature of the voice of the friend on the Hamlet–Horatio model or on the Orestes–Pylades model remains, I think, an open question. Lukacher maintains that hearkening to the inaudible source of an audible summons is central to both Shakespeare's and Heidegger's construals of conscience. Lukacher, *Daemonic Figures*, 89.

95. De Grazia, Hamlet without Hamlet, 172.

96. G. W. F. Hegel, *Elements of the Philosophy of Right*, ed. Allen W. Wood, trans. H. B. Nisbet (New York: Cambridge University Press, 1991), 164.

97. Ibid.

98. Sigmund Freud, "Negation," in *General Psychological Theory: Papers on Metapsychology*, ed. Philip Rieff (New York: Touchstone, 1991), 216.

99. An English translation—"The Tragedy of Fratricide Punished, or Prince Hamlet of Denmark"—can be found in Ernest Brennecke (in collaboration with Henry Brennecke), *Shakespeare in Germany: 1590–1700* (Chicago: University of Chicago Press, 1964), 253–290.

100. Cited in Karl von Holtei, *Beiträge zur Geschichte dramatischer Kunst und Literatur*, vol. 3 (Berlin: Haude und Spenerschen Buchhandlung, 1828), 128.

101. Jacques Derrida, *Specters of Marx: The State of the Debt, the Work of Mourning, and the New International* (New York: Routledge, 1994), 65, 168.

102. Slavoj Žižek, *Organs without Bodies: Deleuze and Other Consequences* (New York: Routledge, 2004), 13n. Cynthia Willett denies that *Hamlet* has bequeathed to modernity any properly messianic charge: "The specter of *Hamlet*—the ghost named Hamlet—forges a link between freedom and death in the modern mind. The ghost does not come forth to alert the son to the injustice of his father's death, or at least not on the modern stage." She goes on to contrast "Hamlet's ghost" with the ghost in Toni Morrison's *Beloved*, suggesting that the latter, but not the former, represents "the intimate folds of social space and the woven time of our ancestral past." Cynthia Willett, *The Soul of Justice: Social Bonds and Racial Hubris* (Ithaca: Cornell University Press, 2001), 205–206.

103. Jürgen Habermas, *The Philosophical Discourse of Modernity: Twelve Lectures*, trans. Frederick G. Lawrence (Cambridge, MA: MIT Press, 1990), 12.

104. Marx, "The Eighteenth Brumaire of Louis Bonaparte," 34. Matthias Fritsch notes that there is an implicit messianism in Marx's memorial to the victims of the 1848 massacres in Paris. Matthias Fritsch, *The Promise of Memory: History and Politics in Marx, Benjamin, and Derrida* (Albany: SUNY Press, 2005), 18.

105. Jean-Paul Sartre, *Search for a Method*, trans. Hazel E. Barnes (New York: Vintage, 1968), 45.

106. Žižek, *Tarrying with the Negative: Kant, Hegel, and the Critique of Ideology* (Durham: Duke University Press, 1993), 276n38.

107. Ibid., 285n39.

108. "All myth, lawmaking violence, which we may call 'executive,' is pernicious. Pernicious, too, is the law-preserving, 'administrative' violence that serves it. Divine violence, which is the sign and seal but never the means of sacred dispatch, may be called 'sovereign' violence." Walter Benjamin, "Critique of Violence," in *Selected Writings*, vol. 1: 1913–1926, ed. Marcus Bullock and Michael W. Jennings (Cambridge, MA: Harvard University Press, 1996), 252.

109. Slavoj Žižek, *The Parallax View* (Cambridge, MA: MIT Press, 2006), 94–95.

110. Alain Badiou, *Logics of Worlds: Being and Event II*, trans. Alberto Toscano (New York: Continuum, 2009), 88.

111. Slavoj Žižek, *Less Than Nothing: Hegel and the Shadow of Dialectical Materialism* (New York: Verso, 2012), 834.

112. Immanuel Kant, *Critique of the Power of Judgment*, ed. Paul Guyer, trans. Paul Guyer and Eric Matthews (New York: Cambridge University Press, 2000), 154.

113. Žižek, *Less Than Nothing*, 834. Cf. Kant, *Critique of the Power of Judgment*, 152, and Immanuel Kant, "The Conflict of the Faculties" in *Religion and Rational Theology*, ed. and trans. Allen W. Wood and George di Giovanni (New York: Cambridge University Press, 1996), 302.

114. Slavoj Žižek, *In Defense of Lost Causes* (New York: Verso, 2008), 409.

115. Žižek, *Less Than Nothing*, 1007.

116. Simon Critchley, "Violence, by Slavoj Zizek: A Dream of Divine Violence," *Independent*, January 11, 2008, http://www.independent.co.uk/arts-entertainment/books/reviews/violence-by-slavoj-zizek-769535.html. In the same article, Critchley calls Žižek "manic." Richard Halperin is similarly harsh toward Derrida: "Derrida-as-Hamlet has a whole row of skulls to stimulate his unfocused political urgency. … If Derrida really wants to play the Gravedigger in *Hamlet*, as he claims, it is necessary to put off his princely fastidiousness, curtail his project of endless 'filtering' and purgation, and delve in the sometimes unpleasant muck of real history." Richard Halperin, "An Impure History of Ghosts: Derrida, Marx, Shakespeare," in *Marxist Shakespeares*, 50–51. For Žižek's characterization of the "Bartleby act" as violent, see Slavoj Žižek, *Living in the End Times*, rev. ed. (New York: Verso, 2011), 401.

117. "Today, the ruling ideology endeavors to make us accept the 'impossibility' of radical change … in order to render invisible the impossible/real of the antagonism

which cuts across capitalist societies … which, however, in no way implies that this real/impossible cannot be directly dealt with and radically transformed in a 'crazy' act which changes the basic 'transcendental' coordinates of the social field." Žižek, *Living in the End Times*, 420.

CHAPTER 5

1. "For many things are thought by our intellect which do not have real being in themselves, although they may be thought in the manner of beings, as is clear from the examples brought up of blindness, a relation of reason, etc." Francisco Suárez, *On Beings of Reason (De Entibus Rationis)*, trans. John P. Doyle (Milwaukee: Marquette University Press, 1995), 63.

2. Daniel D. Novotný, *Ens Rationis from Suárez to Caramuel: A Study in Scholasticism of the Baroque Era* (New York: Fordham University Press, 2013), 108.

3. C. K. Ogden, *Bentham's Theory of Fictions* (Abington: Routledge, 1932 [transferred to digital printing 2002]), xliv. Although Bentham himself doesn't refer to Hamlet in this connection, he does appropriate one of Hamlet's lines, describing a proposed reform of language as "a consummation thus devoutly to be wished" (cxliv).

4. Eva Brann, *The Ways of Naysaying: No, Not, Nothing, and Nonbeing* (Lanham: Rowman & Littlefield, 2001), 78ff.

5. Plato, *Plato's Parmenides*, trans. Samuel Scolnicov (Berkeley: University of California Press, 2003), 54 (130c).

6. "So what subject is it, Glaucon, that draws the soul from the realm of becoming to the realm of what is? … Your reminder is exactly to the point; there's really nothing like that in music and poetry." Plato, *Republic*, trans. G. M. A. Grube, revised by C. D. C. Reeve (Indianapolis: Hackett, 1992), 193–194 (521d, 522b).

7. "Therefore *poiêsis* is more philosophic and of more stature than history. For poetry speaks rather of the general things while history speaks of the particular things." Aristotle, *On Poetics*, trans. Seth Benardete and Michael Davis (South Bend: St. Augustine's Press, 2002), 27 ($1451^b3–8$).

8. Bergson has a number of interesting things to say on this topic. First, he argues that tragedy depicts individuals, whereas comedy depicts universals. Second, he observes that because well-wrought tragic characters are individuals, they are universally regarded as true: "Nothing could be more unique than the character of Hamlet. Though he may resemble other men in some respects, it is clearly not on that account that he interests us most. But he is universally accepted and regarded as a living character. In this sense only is he universally true." Henri Bergson, *Laughter: An Essay on the Meaning of the Comic*, trans. Cloudesley Brereton and Fred Rothwell (Los Angeles: Green Integer, 1999), 145. Third, he argues that tragic poets depict individuals not by describing free-standing possible entities, but by representing their own past potentialities: "To retrace one's steps, and follow to the end the faintly distinguishable directions, appears to be the essential element in poetic imagination. Of course, Shakespeare was neither Macbeth, nor Hamlet, nor Othello; still, he *might have been* these several characters if the circumstances of the case on the one hand, and the consent of his will

on the other, had caused to break out into explosive action what was nothing more than an inner prompting" (150). Finally, Bergson refines this analysis by representing potentialities not as fully determinate possibilities but as semideterminate tendencies. After a potentiality has been actualized it seems retrospectively to have been a fully determinate possibility all along, but this is an illusion: "*Hamlet* was doubtless possible before being realized, if that means that there was no insurmountable obstacle to its realization. ... But the possible thus understood is in no degree virtual, something ideally pre-existent. ... A mind in which the *Hamlet* of Shakespeare had taken shape in the form of [the] possible would by that fact have created its reality: it would thus have been, by definition, Shakespeare himself." Henri Bergson, *The Creative Mind: An Introduction to Metaphysics* (New York: Kensington, 2002), 102.

9. Immanuel Kant, *Critique of Pure Reason*, trans. Paul Guyer and Allen W. Wood (New York: Cambridge University Press, 1998), 566–567 (A596–599/B624–627). For Suárez's influence on Kant, see Hans Seigfried, "Kant's Spanish Bank Account: *Realität* and *Wirklichkeit*," in *Interpreting Kant*, ed. Moltke S. Gram (Iowa City: University of Iowa Press, 1982), 115–132.

10. Ogden, *Bentham's Theory of Fictions*, xxxv–xxxvi, 17. "Underlying these troubles is the deadlock common to Bentham and Kant: it is possible to tell reality from fictions (in Bentham, the names of real entities from the names of fictions; in Kant, the legitimate use of transcendental categories in the constitution of reality from their illegitimate use which brings about 'transcendental illusion'); however, as soon as we renounce fiction and illusion, we lose reality itself; *the moment we subtract fictions from reality, reality itself loses its discursive-logical consistency.*" Slavoj Žižek, *Tarrying with the Negative: Kant, Hegel, and the Critique of Ideology* (Durham, NC: Duke University Press, 1993), 88. In his seminar on anxiety, Lacan argues that Hamlet's staging of "The Mousetrap" illustrates Bentham's thesis that reality (or truth) has the structure of fiction. See Jacques Lacan *Le Séminaire de Jacques Lacan, Livre X: L'Angoisse, 1962–1963* (Paris: Éditions du Seuil, 2004), 45–48. Alenka Zupančič elaborates on this theme in *The Shortest Shadow: Nietzsche's Philosophy of the Two* (Cambridge, MA: MIT Press, 2003), 13, 116–121.

11. Alexius Meinong, "The Theory of Objects," in *Realism and the Background of Phenomenology*, ed. Roderick M. Chisholm (Atascadero: Ridgeview, 1980), 76–117. Bentham anticipates Meinong: "To objects in general the system of division has never yet been applied." Ogden, *Bentham's Theory of Fictions*, 102.

12. Bertrand Russell, "Seems, Madam? Nay, It Is," in *Russell on Ethics*, ed. Charles Pigden (New York: Routledge, 1999), 80–81.

13. Ibid., 81–82. Cf. Russell's ensuing discussion of Shakespeare's Sonnet 33.

14. Ibid., 84.

15. Cf. Russell's critique of Bergson: "His imaginative picture of the world, regarded as a poetic effort, is in the main not capable of either proof or disproof. Shakespeare says life's but a walking shadow, Shelley says it is like a dome of many-coloured glass, Bergson says it is a shell which bursts into parts that are again shells. If you like Bergson's image better, it is just as legitimate." Bertrand Russell, *A History of Western Philosophy* (New York: Simon & Schuster, 1967), 722.

16. Bertrand Russell, "Disgust and Its Antidote," in *Fact and Fiction* (New York: Routledge, 2003), 29–30. Russell continues: "Lear's speeches in the scenes on the heath make the romanticism of the romantics seem thin and paltry by comparison. There is, however, a more fundamental difference: the romantics believed it all, whereas Shakespeare put it in the mouth of a man going mad. … But in *King Lear*, even in the blackest and most despairing passages, there is a redeeming sublimity. One feels in reading that, though life may be bad and the world full of unmerited suffering, yet there is in man a capacity of greatness and occasional splendour which makes ultimate and complete despair impossible. It was not in Shakespeare but in Swift that I found the expression of the ultimate and complete despair" (30–31).

17. Russell, "Seems, Madam?," 83.

18. By the time Russell was six years old, his mother, sister, father, and grandfather had died in succession. After the death of his grandfather, "he would lie awake at night wondering when his grandmother in turn was going to die." Ray Monk, *Bertrand Russell: The Spirit of Solitude, 1872–1921* (New York: Free Press, 1996), 3–4.

19. Russell, "Seems, Madam?," 82. Cf. Romeo's remark to Friar Laurence: "Hang up philosophy! / Unless philosophy can make a Juliet, / Displant a town, reverse a prince's doom, / It helps not, it prevails not" (3.3.57–60).

20. Russell, "Seems, Madam?," 83. In a letter to Alys Pearsall Smith written three years earlier (in which, after an exhilarating performance of Wagner's *Die Walküre* in Paris, he reports, "I feel like Caliban's conception of Trinculo"), Russell remarks: "I used to wonder at Keats's sonnet 'When I have fears that I may cease to be' because he puts Love and Fame together and Fame seemed such rubbish in comparison." Nicholas Griffin, ed., *The Selected Letters of Bertrand Russell: The Private Years, 1884–1914* (New York: Routledge, 2002), 121–22. Keats's sonnet concludes: "then on the shore / Of the wide world I stand alone, and think / Till love and fame to nothingness do sink." Instead of quoting Keats in "Seems, Madam?" Russell could have cited Lear's final words to Cordelia: "Thou'lt come no more, / Never, never, never, never, never" (5.3.308–309). Cf. the closing couplet to Keats's sonnet, "On Sitting Down to Read King Lear Once Again": "But, when I am consumed in the fire, / Give me new Phoenix wings to fly at my desire."

21. Bertrand Russell, "On Denoting," in *Essays in Analysis*, ed. Douglas Lackey (New York: George Braziller, 1973), 108.

22. Ibid., 110.

23. I thank Paul Livingston for helpful discussion of this point.

24. This logic of "wearing a wig" is nicely captured in Kant's joke "about the grief of a merchant who, returning from India to Europe with all his fortune in merchandise, was forced to throw it all overboard in a terrible storm, and was so upset that in the very same night his wig turned gray." Immanuel Kant, *Critique of the Power of Judgment*, trans. Paul Guyer and Eric Matthews (New York: Cambridge University Press, 2000), 210. To Hegel we may attribute the objection that Kant posits a night in which all souls wear gray wigs!

25. Russell, "On Denoting," 109.

26. The example of a father grieving for a possibly lost son is preceded by the example of a son grieving for an actually lost father ("the father of Charles II was executed"). Ibid., 106. The ensuing discussion of the opening line of Gray's "Elegy Written in a Country Churchyard"—"The curfew tolls the knell of parting day" (111–112)—sets the stage for Hamlet's (or rather "Hamlet"'s) passing appearance (117).

27. Ibid., 116.

28. Ibid., 117. "Satisfactorily" in the sense of avoiding what before had been called "intolerable."

29. Ibid.

30. Bertrand Russell, *Introduction to Mathematical Philosophy*, 2nd ed. (New York: Macmillan, 1920), 169–170. James McFarland comments: "The condition that separates Hamlet's vulnerability from Napoleon's spontaneity is the slide from the imperfect 'thought' to the perfect 'had thought.' This slide is more than a formal temporal index, but a slide that maintains reference at the cost of an ambiguous alternation between life and death. For once Napoleon has passed away, he, too, becomes as exposed as Hamlet to the abyss of forgetfulness. For Benjamin, onomastic reference is allegorical inscription, and can never lose the externality that defines it." James McFarland, *Constellation: Friedrich Nietzsche and Walter Benjamin in the Now-Time of History* (New York: Fordham University Press, 2013), 88–89. I take "onomastic reference" to mean something like rigid designation, whereby the allegorically inscribed nominatum is to be tracked not across separate possible worlds but across moments of historical time that contain irreducible potentialities. Benjamin seems to have been less interested in the naming of fictional characters than in the naming of works of art; "*Hamlet*" (i.e., the name of the play) designates a monad that transcends the order of its temporal appearings: "The so-called immortal works just flash briefly through every present time. *Hamlet* is one of the very fastest, the hardest to grasp." Walter Benjamin, "Notes (III)," in *Selected Writings*, vol. 2: 1927–1934, ed. Michael W. Jennings, Howard Eiland, and Gary Smith (Cambridge, MA: Harvard University Press, 1999), 285. Phillip Bricker, who as a proponent of modal realism would allow an infinite number of Hamletlike entities, writes, "There seems to be a fundamental rift—unbridgeable by argument—between ontologically conservative philosophers who have, what Bertrand Russell called, 'a robust sense of reality,' and ontologically liberal philosophers who respond, echoing Hamlet: 'there is more on heaven and earth than is dreamt of in your philosophy.'" Phillip Bricker, "Concrete Possible Worlds," in *Contemporary Debates in Metaphysics*, ed. Theodore Sider, John Hawthorne, and Dean W. Zimmerman (New York: Blackwell, 2008), 131. In the same collection, Jonathan Schaffer, siding with Russell, responds: "There could be more on heaven and earth than is dreamt of in the sciences," including "witches, vital forces, real simultaneity relations, and other sundries that science has learnt to discard. But I doubt it." Jonathan Schaffer, "Causation and Laws of Nature: Reductionism," in *Contemporary Debates in Metaphysics*, 92.

31. Bertrand Russell, *An Inquiry into Meaning and Truth: The William James Lectures*, rev. ed. (New York: Routledge, 1995), 294.

32. Russell, *A History of Western Philosophy*, 50.

33. Peter Hylton observes that Russell's earlier metaphysical position—according to which even nonexistent terms have being—implies that someone could be presently acquainted with a past object. Peter Hylton, *Russell, Idealism, and the Emergence of Analytic Philosophy* (New York: Oxford University Press, 1992), 365n50.

34. Russell's account of the literal *impossibility* of uttering the name of a dead person provides an interesting twist to Searle's thought experiment about a tribe in which "there is a strict taboo against speaking of the dead, so that no one's name is ever mentioned after his death." John Searle, *Intentionality: An Essay in the Philosophy of Mind* (New York: Cambridge University Press, 1983), 240. Žižek suggests that such a tribe would be psychotic. Slavoj Žižek, *The Sublime Object of Ideology* (New York: Verso, 1989), 92–94.

35. Russell, *A History of Western Philosophy*, 56; Russell's italics.

36. Bertrand Russell, *The Principles of Mathematics* (London: Allen & Unwin, 1937), 347.

37. Bertrand Russell, "A Free Man's Worship," in *Why I Am Not a Christian and Other Essays on Religion and Related Subjects* (New York: Touchstone, 1957), 114.

38. Russell, *A History of Western Philosophy*, 586.

39. Perhaps Kant would agree: "The expression 'A sea-unicorn (or narwal) is an existent animal' is not, therefore, entirely correct. The expression ought to be formulated the other way round to read 'The predicates, which I think collectively when I think of a sea-unicorn (or narwal), attach to a certain existent sea-animal.'" Immanuel Kant, "The Only Possible Argument in Support of a Demonstration of the Existence of God," in *Theoretical Philosophy 1755–1770*, ed. and trans. David Walford in collaboration with Ralf Meerbote (New York: Cambridge University Press, 1992), 118. As Brann observes, "In this removal of existence from the nature of any being Kant is so radical as to do more than foreshadow Russell." Brann, *The Ways of Naysaying*, 104.

40. See the letter to Ottoline Morrell quoted in Monk, *Bertrand Russell: The Spirit of Solitude*, 78. Cf. Bertrand Russell, *Autobiography* (New York: Routledge, 1998), 60.

41. Bertrand Russell, *Human Knowledge: Its Scope and Limits* (New York: Routledge, 2009), 74.

42. Ibid., 74–75. The same contrast is made in Russell's *My Philosophical Development* (Nottingham: Spokesman, 2007), 168.

43. Russell, *On Education Especially in Early Childhood* (New York: Routledge, 2003), 84.

44. Brann, *The Ways of Naysaying*, 96.

45. Russell, *My Philosophical Development*, 154.

46. Bertrand Russell, *An Outline of Philosophy* (New York: Routledge, 2009), 280.

47. Russell, *On Education*, 19.

48. Russell, *A History of Western Philosophy*, 1–2.

49. Russell seems to remember only the First Sailor's first line and not the extra two or three that he gets to deliver to Horatio—hardly scene-stealers themselves.

50. Bertrand Russell, "Dreams and Facts," in *Sceptical Essays* (New York: Routledge, 2004), 19–20.

51. Bertrand Russell, *Power: A New Social Analysis* (New York: Routledge, 2004), 178.

52. Cf. Hazlitt's characterization of the soul of Shakespeare: "The capacious soul of Shakspeare [sic] had an intuitive and mighty sympathy with whatever could enter into the heart of man in all possible circumstances." William Hazlitt, "Lectures on English Poets" in *Lectures on English Poets and Spirit of the Age* (New York: E. P. Dutton, 1910), 70.

53. Despite his general hostility toward religion, Russell notes that kings who believe in "Divine government of the world" are less likely to act tyrannically: "This feeling is expressed by the King in *Hamlet*, when he contrasts the inflexibility of Divine justice with the subservience of earthly judges to the royal power." Bertrand Russell, "Philosophy and Politics," in *The Basic Writings of Bertrand Russell*, ed. Robert E. Egner and Lester E. Denonn (New York: Routledge, 2009), 434.

54. Bertrand Russell, *The Problems of Philosophy* (New York: Oxford University Press, 1997), 156–158.

55. In another letter to Lady Ottoline Morrell, cited in Monk, *Bertrand Russell: The Spirit of Solitude*, 227.

56. Ibid., 227, 229.

57. Russell, *The Problems of Philosophy*, 147–148. "It was not only these rather dry, logical doctrines that made me rejoice in the new philosophy. I felt it, in fact, as a great liberation, as if I had escaped from a hot-house on to a wind-swept headland. I hated supposing that space and time were only in my mind. I liked the starry heavens even better than the moral law, and could not bear Kant's view that the one I liked best was only a subjective figment." Russell, *My Philosophical Development*, 61. Cf. 179, where pragmatism is criticized on similar grounds. Russell criticizes William James for effectively thinking that the statement "Shakespeare wrote *Hamlet*" could be true for a Stratfordian but false for a Baconian (180).

58. Quentin Meillassoux, *After Finitude: An Essay on the Necessity of Contingency*, trans. Ray Brassier (New York: Continuum, 2008), 27.

59. Russell, *The Problems of Philosophy*, 148.

60. Typically, such knowledge is by description rather than by acquaintance—Russell's way of accounting for our capacity to grasp ancestral truths.

61. Meillassoux likewise identifies the "mathematically conceivable" with the "absolutely possible," but he seems to equate absolute possibility not with "an open world of free possibilities" but with the (direct) *applicability* of mathematics to a world that isn't "correlated" with the minds of mathematical physicists. Meillassoux, *After Finitude*, 117.

62. Russell, *An Inquiry into Meaning and Truth*, 65, 88.

63. Ibid., 91–92.

64. Russell, *A History of Western Philosophy*, 173.

65. Bertrand Russell, "'Useless' Knowledge," in *In Praise of Idleness and Other Essays* (New York: Routledge, 2004), 24. Cf. Locke: "Without Liberty the Understanding would be to no purpose: And without Understanding, Liberty (if it could be) would signify nothing. … The first therefore and great use of Liberty, is to hinder blind Precipitancy; the principal exercise of Freedom is to stand still, open the eyes, look about, and take a view of the consequence of what we are going to do, as much as the weight of the matter requires." John Locke, *An Essay Concerning Human Understanding*, ed. Peter H. Nidditch (New York: Oxford University Press, 1975), 278–279.

66. Bertrand Russell, "Machines and the Emotions," in *Sceptical Essays*, 49. I have corrected the misprinted "instuition."

67. Bertrand Russell, "In Praise of Idleness," in *In Praise of Idleness and Other Essays*, 11.

68. Bertrand Russell, "Education and Discipline," in *In Praise of Idleness and Other Essays*, 144.

69. Bertrand Russell, "On Youthful Cynicism," in *In Praise of Idleness and Other Essays*, 125.

70. Bertrand Russell, "On Being Modern-Minded," in *Unpopular Essays* (New York: Routledge, 2009), 63–64. Russell makes an even more disparaging remark in *The Conquest of Happiness* (1930): "It has become the thing in America for ladies to read (or seem to read) certain books every month. … There has never been a month when 'Hamlet' or 'King Lear' has been selected by the book clubs; there has never been a month when it has been necessary to know about Dante. Consequently the reading that is done is entirely of modern books, which, of course, are seldom and never of masterpieces." Bertrand Russell, *The Conquest of Happiness* (New York: W. W. Norton, 1996), 45.

71. George Santayana, "Introduction," in *The Complete Works of William Shakespeare* vol. 30: *Hamlet*, ed. Sidney Lee (Cambridge: The University Press, 1907), ix–xxxiii. The date Russell gives corresponds to an edition in which *Hamlet* appears as volume 15.

72. Ibid., x–xi.

73. Philip Blair Rice, "The Philosopher as Poet and Critic," in *The Philosophy of George Santayana*, ed. Paul Arthur Schilpp (Evanston: Northwestern University Press, 1940), 287. A shorter version of Rice's article (which doesn't discuss Santayana's Shakespeare criticism) appeared as "George Santayana: The Philosopher as Poet," in *Kenyon Review* 2, no. 4 (autumn 1940), 460–475.

74. Cf. his remarks on Santayana in "On Catholic and Protestant Skeptics," in *Why I Am Not a Christian*, 122.

75. Bertrand Russell, "If We Are to Survive This Dark Time—" in *The Basic Writings of Bertrand Russell*, 668–669.

76. Russell, *Autobiography*, 60.

77. Willard Van Orman Quine, "On What There Is," in *From a Logical Point of View: Nine Logico-Philosophical Essays*, 2nd ed. (Cambridge, MA: Harvard University Press, 1980), 5.

78. Ibid., 7.

79. Ibid., 8.

80. Ibid., 15.

81. "A proposition about Apollo means what we get by substituting what the classical dictionary tells us is meant by Apollo, say 'the sun-god.'" Russell, "On Denoting," 117.

82. A. P. Martinich and Avrum Stroll, *Much Ado about Nonexistence: Fiction and Reference* (Lanham: Rowman & Littlefield, 2007), 1. The illustration is a reproduction of a lithograph jointly executed by Sir William Nicholson and James Pryde. Thus the cover links three pairs: Nicholson–Pryde, Martinich–Stroll, and Hamlet–Yorick.

83. Avrum Stroll, *Twentieth-Century Analytic Philosophy* (New York: Columbia University Press, 2000), 19, 25, 29, 224.

84. Christopher Hookway, *Quine* (Oxford: Blackwell, 1988), 11; James Cargile, *Paradoxex: A Study in Form and Presentation* (New York: Cambridge University Press, 1979), 186.

85. See Plantinga's analysis of the true proposition "Hamlet was unmarried" in Alvin Plantinga, *The Nature of Necessity* (New York: Oxford University Press, 1974), 153–159.

86. Saul Kripke, "Identity and Necessity," in *Metaphysics: An Anthology*, ed. Jaegwon Kim and Ernest Sosa (Malden, MA: Blackwell, 1999), 73. To show that names can succeed in referring without relying on any identifying descriptions, Keith Donnellan imagines a future in which (almost) nothing is known about Shakespeare except that he allegedly wrote the plays that we ascribe to him. If it were to turn out that the Baconian hypothesis is true, Donnellan argues, it wouldn't follow that the name "Shakespeare" would then refer in the mouths of our heirs to Bacon rather than to Shakespeare. Keith Donnellan, "Proper Names and Identifying Descriptions," in *Essays on Reference, Language, and Mind* (New York: Oxford University Press, 2012), 75–76.

87. "It is easy to see that, in virtue of the hierarchy of functions, the theory of types renders a totality of 'names' impossible. We may, in fact, distinguish names of different orders." Alfred North Whitehead and Bertrand Russell, *Principia Mathematica to* *56 (New York: Cambridge University Press, 1997), 64.

88. Cf. Žižek's discussion of a hysterical subject's response to ideological interpellation in *The Sublime Object of Ideology*, 113–114. Bradley's regress, which was geared toward denying the reality of relations, can be found in Francis Herbert Bradley, *Appearance and Reality: A Metaphysical Essay*, rev. ed. (New York: Macmillan, 1897). The denial of the reality of relations was anathema to Russell.

89. "There can be no other reason but the mere will of God, for instance, why this particular system of matter should be created in one particular place, and that in another particular place, when (all place being absolutely indifferent to all matter) it would have been exactly the same thing vice versa, supposing the two systems (or the particles) of matter to be alike." G. W. Leibniz and Samuel Clarke, *Correspondence*, ed. Roger Ariew (Indianapolis: Hackett, 2000), 11.

90. See the essays collected in *The New Theory of Reference: Kripke, Marcus, and Its Origins*, ed. Paul W. Humphreys and James H. Fetzer (Hingham, MA: Kluwer Academic, 1998). William Kneale, lobbying for the view that any name X means *the individual named "X,"* warns in passing that a logic without the concept of necessitation "is like *Hamlet* without the Prince of Denmark." William Kneale, "Modality, De Dicto and De Re," in *Logic,*

Methodology and Philosophy of Science: Proceedings of the 1960 International Congress, ed. Ernest Nagel, Patrick Suppes, and Alfred Tarski (Stanford: Stanford University Press, 1962), 628.

91. Žižek, *The Sublime Object of Ideology*, 93.

92. Examples from *The Merchant of Venice* and *Twelfth Night* can be found, respectively, in Willard Van Orman Quine, *Word and Object* (Cambridge, MA: MIT Press, 1960), 139, and Quine, *Elementary Logic*, rev. ed. (Cambridge, MA: Harvard University Press, 1980), 9–10. In reply to Erik Stenius's suggestion that he unhesitatingly settled on his conception of intensions, Quine protests: "On the contrary, my hesitation rivaled Hamlet's in its ostentation." Willard Van Orman Quine, "Replies," in *Synthese* 19, no. 1–2 (December 1968), 272.

93. To an interviewer's question, "What can a philosopher learn from a poet?" Quine replied, "I haven't read enough poetry to have really been influenced philosophically by it, or the right ones, unless one counts again 'Eureka,' what Edgar Allan Poe called a prose poem." Willard Van Orman Quine, *Quine in Dialogue*, ed. Dagfinn Føllesdal and Douglas B. Quine (Cambridge, MA: Harvard University Press, 2008), 39.

94. José Benardete, *Metaphysics: The Logical Approach* (New York: Oxford University Press, 1989), 81.

95. José A. Benardete, "Metaphysics and Poetry: The Quinean Approach," *Poetics Today* 17, no. 2 (summer 1996), 129–156.

96. G. E. Moore, *Principia Ethica*, rev. ed. (New York: Cambridge University Press, 1993), 267.

97. Ludwig Wittgenstein, *Culture and Value*, trans. Peter Winch (Chicago: University of Chicago Press, 1984), 48e.

98. Ibid., 49e.

99. Ibid., 83e–84e.

100. Ibid., 86e.

101. Ibid., 84–84e.

102. Bertrand Russell, "The Elements of Ethics," in *Philosophical Essays* (New York: Routledge, 2009), 10–11. Russell goes on to defend a version of consequentialism, observing that once general moral precepts like "thou shalt do no murder" are suitably qualified, they turn out to be as vacuous as "Hamlet's report of the ghost's message: 'There's ne'er a villain, dwelling in all Denmark, but he's an arrant knave'" (19).

103. Ludwig Wittgenstein, "Lecture on Ethics," in *Philosophical Occasions: 1912–1951*, ed. James Klagge and Alfred Nordmann (Indianapolis: Hackett, 1993), 39.

104. Ludwig Wittgenstein, *Wittgenstein's Lectures: Cambridge, 1932–1935, From the Notes of Alice Ambrose and Margaret Macdonald*, ed. Alice Ambrose (Amherst: Prometheus, 2001), 35. For a Hamletian take on the *Tractatus*, see Freddie Rokem, *Philosophers and Thespians: Thinking Performance* (Stanford: Stanford University Press, 2010), 86.

105. Bertrand Russell, *Religion and Science* (New York: Oxford University Press, 1997), chapter 9.

106. Stanley Cavell, *Disowning Knowledge in Seven Plays of Shakespeare*, updated ed. (New York: Cambridge University Press, 2003), 7. Elsewhere, Cavell discusses "Othello's (other-minds) [skeptical] relation to Desdemona as an allegory … of material-object skepticism." Stanley Cavell, *In Quest of the Ordinary: Lines of Skepticism and Romanticism* (Chicago: University of Chicago Press, 1988), 55.

107. Cavell, *Disowning Knowledge in Seven Plays of Shakespeare*, 138.

108. "I am claiming that we must understand Othello … to want to believe Iago, to be trying, against his knowledge, to believe him." Ibid., 133.

109. Russell, *The Problems of Philosophy*, 136–137.

110. Ibid., 159.

111. Ibid., 125–126.

112. Russell, *My Philosophical Development*, 182.

113. Cavell, *Disowning Knowledge in Seven Plays of Shakespeare*, 206.

114. Plato, *Phaedo*, trans. Eva Brann, Peter Kalkavage, and Eric Salem (Newburyport, MA: Focus, 1998), 80 (100c).

115. This idea was first proposed by Otto Rank in 1925. See Rank, "The Play within the Play in *Hamlet*," trans. Paul Lewison, *Journal of the Otto Rank Association* 6, no. 2 (December 1971), 5–21.

116. Cavell, *Disowning Knowledge in Seven Plays of Shakespeare*, 187.

117. Russell, *Human Knowledge: Its Scope and Limits*, 407–408. Cf. *My Philosophical Development*, 19.

118. Apart from his sustained discussion of the Hollywood comedy of marriage, Cavell makes many passing remarks about cinema, including a brief discussion of the role of "standing" in the staging of Polonius's advice to Laertes in Laurence Olivier's *Hamlet*. Stanley Cavell, *Cities of Words: Pedagogical Letters on a Register of the Moral Life* (Cambridge, MA: Harvard University Press, 2004), 50.

119. Russell, *Human Knowledge: Its Scope and Limits*, 343.

120. Bertrand Russell, *The Scientific Outlook* (New York: Routledge, 2009), 129.

121. Bertrand Russell, letter to Goldsworthy Lowes Dickinson, August 26, 1902, cited in Russell, *Autobiography*, 192. Note the allusion to *Hamlet* in his borrowing of Horatio's word "gibber."

122. Bertrand Russell, "Journal (1902–05)," in *The Collected Papers of Bertrand Russell*, vol. 12: *Contemplation and Action, 1902–14*, ed. Richard A. Rempel, Andrew Brink, and Margaret Moran (New York: Routledge, 1998), 23.

123. See Monk, *Bertrand Russell: The Spirit of Solitude*, chapter 1 ("Ghosts").

124. Cited in Monk, *Bertrand Russell: The Spirit of Solitude*, 3.

125. Ibid., 530.

126. Russell, *Autobiography*, 261, cited in Monk, *Bertrand Russell: The Spirit of Solitude*, 531.

127. Ray Monk, *Bertrand Russell: The Ghost of Madness 1921–1970* (New York: Free Press, 2001), 126.

128. Ibid., 351.

129. See the letter from Lawrence cited in Monk, *Bertrand Russell: The Ghost of Madness*, 348.

130. Ibid., 349; Monk, *Bertrand Russell: The Spirit of Solitude*, 21.

131. According to Monk, Russell "was, it sometimes seems, simply not capable of loving another human being. … He was unable to conceive of loving a person unless he could regard that person as part of himself." Monk, *Bertrand Russell: The Ghost of Madness*, xii.

132. Bertrand Russell, "The Psychoanalyst's Nightmare," in *Nightmares of Eminent Persons and Other Stories* (Nottingham: Spokesman, 2000), 21.

133. Ibid., 27, 29–30.

134. Cited in Paul Edwards, "Appendix: How Bertrand Russell Was Prevented from Teaching at the College of the City of New York," in Russell, *Why I Am Not a Christian*, 219. True to form, Russell couched his rejoinder in Shakespearean terms: "'Folly, doctorlike, controlling skill' is one of the things that made Shakespeare cry for restful death. Yet democracy, as understood by many Americans, requires that such control should exist in all state universities." Russell, "Freedom and the Colleges," 186.

135. Alexius Meinong, "On Objects of Higher Order and Their Relationship to Internal Perception," trans. Marie-Luise Schubert Kalsi, in Schubert Kalsi, *Alexius Meinong on Objects of Higher Order and Husserl's Phenomenology* (The Hague: Martinus Nijhoff, 1978), 137–208.

136. Bertrand Russell, *The Analysis of Mind* (New York: Macmillan, 1921), 18.

137. Gilbert Ryle, *The Concept of Mind* (Chicago: University of Chicago Press, 2000), 22, 328. Cf. Ryle's references to "a Hamlet of the ring" (an ineffectual boxer) and "an addict of discourse, like Hamlet" (48, 143).

138. Cited in Daniel C. Dennett, "Re-introducing *The Concept of Mind*," in Ryle, *The Concept of Mind*, xi.

139. John R. Searle, *The Mystery of Consciousness* (New York: New York Review of Books, 1997), 100. Dennett calls Freud's picture of the human mind "the Hamlet model," not because his conception of the Oedipus complex rests upon his interpretation of *Hamlet*, but because the purpose of the dreamwork according to Freud—to trick the conscious subject—closely resembles Hamlet's purpose in staging *The Mousetrap*: "We might call the Freudian model the Hamlet model, for it is reminiscent of Hamlet's devious ploy of staging 'The Mousetrap' just for Claudius" (Daniel C. Dennett, *Consciousness Explained* [New York: Back Bay Books, 1991], 14). Elsewhere Dennett lampoons questions about the location of the self by demonstrating the philosophical uselessness of calling one's brain "Yorick," reserving the name "Hamlet" for the rest of one's body. Daniel C. Dennett, *Brainstorms: Philosophical Essays on Mind and Psychology* (Cambridge, MA: MIT Press, 1981), 313.

140. Colin McGinn, *Shakespeare's Philosophy: Discovering the Meaning behind the Plays* (New York: HarperCollins, 2006), 56–57. Commenting on the "semantic opacity" of "attributions of intention," Davidson writes, "Hamlet intentionally kills the man behind the arras, but he does not intentionally kill Polonius. Yet Polonius is the man behind the arras, and so Hamlet's killing of the man behind the arras is identical with his killing of Polonius. It is a mistake to suppose there is a class of intentional actions: if we took this tack, we should be compelled to say that one and the same action was both intentional and not intentional." Donald Davidson, "Agency," in *Essays on Actions and Events* (New York: Oxford University Press, 2001), 46.

141. Alexius Meinong, *Über die Stellung der Gegenstandstheorie im System der Wissenschaften* (Leipzig: R. Voigtländer, 1907), 38.

142. Russell, "The Psychoanalyst's Nightmare," 21.

143. Gottlob Frege, "Negation," in *The Frege Reader*, ed. Michael Beaney (Malden, MA: Blackwell, 1997), 355.

144. Sigmund Freud, "Negation," in *General Psychological Theory: Papers on Metapsychology*, ed. Philip Rieff (New York: Touchstone, 1997), 217.

145. The latter quotation is cited in "The Psychoanalyst's Nightmare," 28.

146. Perhaps this was Russell's ultimate nightmare—that he was a Hegelian after all: "'When I say that Satan, Who is the non-existent, does not exist, I mention neither Satan nor the non-existent, but only the word "Satan" and the word "non-existent." Your fallacies have revealed to me a great truth. The great truth is that the word "not" is superfluous. Henceforth I will not use the word "not."' [¶] At this all the assembled metaphysicians burst into a shout of laughter." Russell, "The Metaphysician's Nightmare," in *Nightmares of Eminent Persons and Other Stories*, 35.

EPILOGUE

1. T. S. Eliot, "Hamlet and His Problems," in *The Sacred Wood and Major Early Essays* (Mineola: Dover, 1998), 58, my italics.

2. Robert Brandom, *Tales of the Mighty Dead: Historical Essays in the Metaphysics of Intentionality* (Cambridge, MA: Harvard University Press, 2002), 179.

3. Ibid., 49.

4. Ibid., 180.

5. Ibid., 196.

6. Ibid., 192.

7. Ibid., 195, my italics.

8. Ibid., 199.

9. Ibid., 183.

10. Ibid., 187.

11. Ibid., 184.

12. Ibid., 204.

13. Ibid., 205.

14. Ibid., 206.

15. Timothy Chappell, *Reading Plato's* Theaetetus (Indianapolis: Hackett, 2005), 95 (163b).

16. Brandom, *Tales of the Mighty Dead*, 210.

17. Ibid., 218.

18. "Hegel thinks of Spirit—the realm of the normative—as produced and sustained by the processes of mutual recognition, which simultaneously institute self-conscious selves and their communities." Ibid., 222.

19. Ibid., 107.

20. Eliot, "Tradition and the Individual Talent," 28; cited by Brandom in *Tales of the Mighty Dead*, 93, and by Slavoj Žižek, *Less Than Nothing: Hegel and the Shadow of Dialectical Materialism* (New York: Verso, 2012), 208–209.

21. "The principal philosopher who explicitly aimed for this sort of reflective equilibrium between his practice of interpreting philosophical texts and his theory of conceptual content is Hegel." Brandom, *Tales of the Mighty Dead*, 94.

22. Žižek, *Less Than Nothing*, 18.

23. Slavoj Žižek, *Tarrying with the Negative: Kant, Hegel, and the Critique of Ideology* (Durham, NC: Duke University Press, 1993), 22.

24. Immanuel Kant, *Critique of Pure Reason*, trans. Paul Guyer and Allen W. Wood (New York: Cambridge University Press, 1998), 553–554 (A572–573/B600–601).

25. This applies not only to what Kant calls the "principle of specification," which bids us to subdivide our concepts, but also to the "principle of aggregation," which bids us to seek higher concepts under which to subsume divergent concepts. Ibid., 603 (A666/B694).

26. My thanks to Joshua Kates for helpful discussion of this point.

27. Martin Heidegger, *Being and Time*, trans. John Macquarrie and Edward Robinson (New York: Harper & Row, 1962), 174.

28. Quentin Meillassoux argues that Kant's "correlationism" prevents him from making "ancestral statements" about past objects and events whose reality is now indicated only by fossils. Quentin Meillassoux, *After Finitude: An Essay on the Necessity of Contingency*, trans. Ray Brassier (New York: Continuum, 2008), 13–14. Žižek concedes that there is a sense in which this is correct, but he turns the argument around by observing that the true "fossil" is the human subject itself. Žižek, *Less Than Nothing*, 644–647. We could add that, for a transcendental philosopher, problematic objects belong not to the past but to the boundaries of the world. Kant's solution to the first antinomy implies that we can neither affirm nor deny the reality of something before either the big bang or whatever happens to function in our current best science as a world-inaugurating event.

29. "Therein lies Hegel's basic 'idealist' wager: every tension between notional determinations and reality can be reduced to an immanent tension of notional determinations." Žižek, *Less Than Nothing*, 807.

30. Insofar as this amounts to doing away with things in themselves, Žižek characterizes this shift as a "deontologization" rather than an "ontologization" of Kant. Ibid., 267.

31. Brandom, *Tales of the Mighty Dead*, 196.

32. Žižek, *Less Than Nothing*, 209.

33. "Officially the change of partners had never happened. Oceania was at war with Eurasia: therefore Oceania had always been at war with Eurasia." George Orwell, *1984* (New York: Signet, 1977), 34.

34. T. S. Eliot, "Tradition and the Individual Talent," in *The Sacred Wood and Major Early Essays*, 30; cited by Žižek (without the paragraph break) in *Less Than Nothing*, 209.

35. Eliot, "Tradition and the Individual Talent," 30–31. On the peculiar character of the undead for Žižek, see, e.g., *Less Than Nothing*, 788.

36. Žižek, *Less Than Nothing*, 514–515.

37. Robert B. Pippin, "Brandom's Hegel," in *European Journal of Philosophy* 13, no. 3 (December 2005), 391.

38. Žižek, *Less Than Nothing*, 552–554.

39. Slavoj Žižek, *For They Know Not What They Do: Enjoyment as a Political Factor*, 2nd ed. (New York: Verso, 2002), xiii.

40. "There is no determinate totality of contexts. For each new text makes possible new contexts. This is one reason why each generation, indeed, each reader, must reread and reinterpret potentially tradition-defining texts, and rethink the assimilations and affiliations by which they are put into the context of a tradition." Brandom, *Tales of the Mighty Dead*, 93. Brandom's only application of his interpretation of Eliot's poetics is a brief assessment of Wordsworth's *Prelude*: "That account of the roots of his self, his sensibility, and his work *is* his achieved self, sensibility, and work" (369n9).

41. Kant, *Critique of Pure Reason*, 409 (A339/B397).

42. Eliot, "Hamlet and His Problems," 55.

43. Ibid., 58–59, my italics.

44. See Žižek, *Less Than Nothing*, 477, for one of his many references to Hegel's characterization of (symbolic) Egyptian art: "The secrets of the Egyptians were secrets also for the Egyptians themselves."

45. Brandom, *Tales of the Mighty Dead*, 385n48.

46. Wilfrid Sellars, "Some Reflections on Language Games," in *In the Space of Reasons: Selected Essays of Wilfrid Sellars*, ed. Kevin Scharp and Robert B. Brandom (Cambridge, MA: Harvard University Press, 2007), 37n26.

47. Brandom, *Tales of the Mighty Dead*, 207.

48. Slavoj Žižek, *Did Somebody Say Totalitarianism? Five Interventions in the (Mis)use of a Notion* (New York: Verso, 2001), 11–12. Cf. *Less Than Nothing*, 951–952. Here we might return to Nicolas Abraham, whose "Sixth Act" effectively provides *Hamlet* with a melodramatic ending.

49. Perhaps the poisoning of Gertrude provides Hamlet with the objective correlative he had previously been missing.

INDEX

Determinate negation, 14, 141–143, 145–146, 151, 153–154
De Vere, Edward, 22
Dialetheism, 10–11, 122
Dionysus/Dionysian, 15–18, 27–28, 41, 76, 155n4
Dobson, Michael, 43, 197n60
Donne, John, 8
Donnellan, Keith, 209n86
Don Quixote, 6
Dürer, Albrecht, 97

Eliot, T. S., 10–11, 131, 142, 145, 149–154
Elizabeth I, Queen of England, 98
Emerson, Ralph Waldo, 134
Engels, Friedrich, 70
Erasmus, Desiderius, 26
Eriugena, John Scottus, 8
Essex, Earl of (Robert Devereux), 98
Euripides, 15–16, 77–78, 101, 189

Faccio, Franco, 18
Ferenczi, Sándor, 31
Fichte, Johann Gottlieb, 56–57, 64–70
Ficino, Marsilio, 25, 50
Fiction/fictionality, 2–3, 9, 12–14, 31, 51, 54, 62, 114–118, 120–122, 127–130, 135, 151, 156n9, 203n10, 205n30
Fliess, Wilhelm, 20, 22–23, 33
Focus imaginarius, 12, 50–51, 55
Forgiveness, 37–38, 89, 105, 172n132
Foucault, Michel, 6, 26–30, 34, 36–37, 90
Foxe, John, 182n94
Fraenkel, Michael, 33
Frege, Gottlob, 14, 118, 135, 139
Freiligrath, Ferdinand, 96–97, 99
Freud, Sigmund, 4–5, 10, 14, 20–23, 29–33, 35, 48, 51, 54, 72, 103, 107, 115, 135, 137–139, 153, 161n65, 163n13, 212n139
Fritsch, Matthias, 201n104
Frye, Northrop, 37
Fulda, Ludwig, 44
Furness, Horace Howard, 23

Galilei, Galileo, 5
Galilei, Vincenzo, 18
Garber, Marjorie, 179n65
Garrick, David, 2, 31
Garve, Christian, 175n17
Gasparini, Francesco, 18

Nothing, 8, 10–11, 24, 50, 52, 56–58, 60, 65–66, 70, 73, 75, 78–81, 83–84, 91, 97, 128, 159n44, 180n72
Novotný, Daniel, 114
Nozick, Robert, 156n9

Oedipus, 78–82, 84, 93, 103, 153, 166n50, 199n84
Oedipus complex, 20–22, 30–31, 81, 107, 115, 212n139
Ogden, C. K., 114
Opera, 17–18, 27, 39, 163n13, 164n19
Ophelia, 2, 10–12, 16, 25–27, 36, 60–61, 92, 97, 137, 161n65, 164n19, 175n17, 181n84, 197n62
Orestes, 99–110, 200n94
Orwell, George, 149
Ovid, 58–59

Pacini, David, 191n108
Parmenides, 7–8, 77–81, 84, 119–120
Pascal, Blaise, 83
Pascucci, Margherita, 2, 5, 9
Pepys, Samuel, 18
Pessimism, 17–18, 28, 63, 65, 67, 69–70, 74–75, 81, 123, 190n98
Phantasms, 4, 7, 9, 28, 36, 49, 157n16
Phantoms, 4, 28–29, 31–32. *See also* Ghosts
Pippin, Robert, 151
Plantinga, Alvin, 128
Plato, 6–9, 16, 24, 27, 46, 55, 76, 79–80, 87, 114, 123
Plescia, Iolanda, 182n106
Plumptre, James, 197n66
Pope, Alexander, 43
Priest, Graham, 10–11. *See also* Dialetheism
Prokofiev, Sergei, 18
Prosopopoeia, 58, 62, 150
Pseudo-Dionysius, 8
Psychoanalysis, 5, 14, 21–22, 32, 61, 91, 104, 110, 134, 136–137, 150, 153, 171n108
Purcell, Henry, 18

Quine, Willard Van Orman, 127–128, 130–132, 210n92

Racine, Jean, 44–45
Reinhardt, Karl, 77–79, 190n98
Repression, 10, 20–23, 28, 30–31, 38, 101–102, 104, 136–137, 139, 166n50
Rhu, Lawrence, 40
Rice, Philip Blair, 126
Rokem, Freddie, 210n104
Romances (Shakespearean), 37–41, 64
Rossini, Gioacchino, 17